Religion in America

ADVISORY EDITOR

Edwin S. Gaustad

*T*HE *N*EGRO'S *C*HURCH

Benjamin Elijah Mays

&

Joseph William Nicholson

ARNO PRESS & THE NEW YORK TIMES

New York 1969

Reprint edition 1969 by Arno Press, Inc.

*

Library of Congress Catalog Card No. 70-83430

*

Reprinted from a copy in
The State Historical Society of Wisconsin Library

*

Manufactured in the United States of America

Institute of Social and Religious Research

THE NEGRO'S CHURCH

Benjamin Elijah Mays

AND

Joseph William Nicholson

The Negro's Church

By

BENJAMIN ELIJAH MAYS
and
JOSEPH WILLIAM NICHOLSON

NEW YORK
INSTITUTE OF SOCIAL AND RELIGIOUS RESEARCH

PREFACE

The present study was made under the auspices of the Institute of Social and Religious Research at the request of a number of Negro leaders. It is an attempt to give an accurate description of the Negro church to-day in the United States. It is based chiefly on a first-hand study of 609 urban and 185 rural churches widely distributed in twelve cities and four country areas. The places and the churches were carefully selected in such fashion that the sample may be considered fairly representative of the Negro church both rural and urban. A detailed discussion of the criteria of selection of the churches and of the methods of gathering the data will be found in the Appendix.

The study was undertaken to fill a gap; for, surprising as it may seem, it constitutes the first comprehensive contemporary study of the Negro church. There are, however, several earlier published studies which the authors have found of much value. Among these the most noteworthy are Woodson's *History of the Negro Church* (1921) and two previous studies by the Institute of Social and Religious Research—Daniel's *Education of Negro Ministers* (1925), and Fry's *The U. S. Looks at Its Churches* (1930), which is a critical analysis of the 1926 *Federal Census of Religious Bodies.* Occasional use has also been made of various local studies, such as those dealing with Negro churches in Chicago, Cleveland, Detroit, New York, Greene and Macon Counties, Georgia; and in sections of rural Virginia.

While this study can make no claim to being either exhaustive or final, it may provide a base line for other studies of the Negro church. That the Negro church deserves much more thorough study than it has yet been given is obvious if the repeated declarations of historians and soci-

v

ologists as to the preeminent influence of the church in Negro life are accepted at face value.

In view of the recent extensive migrations of Negroes from country to city and from South to North, together with the extension of education and sophistication among the Negro population as a whole, it may be considered fortunate that this study was made while the older patterns of religious life were still to be found.

It is hoped that this volume will awaken a more active interest in the Negro church on the part of the public; that it will stimulate church leaders to improve the Negro church; and that it will be of use to social scientists and other persons interested in the church as a dominant factor in Negro development.

The authors are greatly indebted to the ministers and officials of the churches studied for an almost 100 per cent. coöperation in supplying data; to thousands of Negro college students, business and professional men, deans and presidents of theological seminaries, college registrars, and hundreds of white ministers in both the North and the South who furnished valuable information in response to questionnaires; also to officers of the juvenile courts who willingly gave the writers access to records on delinquency. Without the fine coöperation of all of these persons, the study could not have been made.

Grateful acknowledgment is also made of the indebtedness to members of the Institute Staff whose counsel was frequently sought and given during the two years of the study; to Bishop R. E. Jones who placed valuable church records at the disposal of the authors; to Messrs. Monroe N. Work, Charles S. Johnson, Jesse O. Thomas, L. K. Williams and H. M. Kingsley for helpful suggestions in the early stages of the study; to Messrs. Channing H. Tobias, W. Y. Bell, W. A. Daniel, Howard Thurman, H. W. Pope, Ralph W. Bullock and Forrester B. Washington, who read and criticized the manuscript, and to Mrs. C. M. Hill, office secretary. This book is the joint product of both authors. They each read and suggested changes in the other's work. In actual composition, however, Benjamin Mays, the director of the study, was primarily responsible for the writing of chapters iii, iv, v, x, xi, xii, xiii, xv, xvi, xvii, and Joseph Nicholson, associate director, for ii, vi, vii, viii, ix, and xiv. Chapter i was jointly written. For every statement in the book they accept full and equal responsibility.

BENJAMIN ELIJAH MAYS,
JOSEPH WILLIAM NICHOLSON.

CONTENTS

TABLES

APPENDIX TABLES

CHAPTER I

The Church in Negro Life

The settlement of the Negro in the New World brought him face to face with new conditions of life to which he was compelled to make adjustment. His status as a slave exposed him to social proscription, economic limitation, and spiritual domination, which were destined to circumscribe him for centuries thereafter.

As a slave, he had no control of his life. He was considered less than human and was bargained for and sold like any other property. His status in the New World was established as that of one whose task it was to hew wood, draw water and till the soil. He was considered incapable of mental discipline through formal training. He was denied the rights of citizenship which enable one to own property and participate in the affairs of the government. He had to worship and serve God under supervision and close scrutiny.

In this strange and somewhat hostile environment, it became necessary for the Negro to work out for himself a technique of survival. As a part of his early survival tactics, he learned to smile and dance under circumstances that would ordinarily have caused one to frown and possibly to fight. He developed a keen sense of humor, and this enabled him to release suppressed emotions in a way that did not offend, and at the same time carried him through difficult situations.

Developing a Religious Technique

Possibly the most significant technique of survival developed during the days of slavery might well be called a "religious" technique, which is represented by the Negro spirituals and by the early efforts to establish and develop the Negro church.

1

The creation of the spirituals was not an accident in Negro life. It was an imperative creation in order that the slave might adjust himself to the new conditions in the New World.

These songs are the expressions of the restrictions and dominations which their creators experienced in the world about them. They represent the soul-life of the people. They embody the joy and sorrow, the hope and despair, the pathos and aspiration of the newly transplanted people; and through them the race was able to endure suffering and survive. Clearly, the Negro spirituals are not songs of hate; they are not songs of revenge. They are songs neither of war nor of conquest. They are songs of the soil and of the soul. This idea has been well phrased by James Weldon Johnson in the last two stanzas of "O Black and Unknown Bards":

> There is a wide, wide wonder in it all,
> That from degraded rest and servile toil
> The fiery spirit of the seer should call
> These simple children of the sun and soil.
> O black slave singers, gone, forgot, unfamed,
> You—you alone, of all the long, long line
> Of those who've sung untaught, unknown, unnamed,
> Have stretched out upward, seeking the divine.
>
> You sang not deeds of heroes or of kings;
> No chant of bloody war, no exulting pean
> Of arms-won triumphs; but your humble strings
> You touched in chord with music empyrean.
> You sang far better than you knew; the songs
> That for your listeners' hungry hearts sufficed
> Still live,—but more than this to you belongs:
> You sang a race from wood and stone to Christ.[1]

---

[1] *The Book of American Negro Poetry*, edited by James Weldon Johnson (New York: Harcourt, Brace and Company). Quoted by courtesy of the publisher.

Relatively early the church, and particularly the independent Negro church, furnished the one and only organized field in which the slave's suppressed emotions could be released, and the only opportunity for him to develop his own leadership. In almost every other area, he was completely suppressed. Thus, through a slow and difficult process, often involving much suffering and persecution, the Negro, more than three-quarters of a century prior to emancipation, through initiative, zeal, and ability, began to achieve the right to be free in his church. He demonstrated his ability to preach; and this demonstration convinced both Negroes and whites that he was possessed of the Spirit of God. And it was to the advantage of the Negro that he proved his worth as a preacher; because as a result, in spite of continued restraints, prohibitions, and anti-Negro legislation, a few liberal-minded whites encouraged the Negro minister and actually helped to make it possible for him to fulfill his mission as a preacher.

Achieving Freedom in the Church

The first Negro church in America is reported to have been founded by one Mr. Palmer at Silver Bluff, South Carolina, between the years 1773-1775. A kind master, George Galphin, is said to have become a patron of this congregation, and further to have permitted David George, a slave, to be ordained for this special work, after having formerly allowed George Liele to preach to this group.[2]

The ministerial work of George Liele became of such importance that his master liberated him so that he might preach without interference. It is generally believed that he was instrumental in organizing the first Negro Baptist church in the city of Savannah in about 1779.

Andrew Bryan, though frequently persecuted, was encouraged by his master to the extent that he was allowed to erect

---

[2] Woodson, C. G., *The History of the Negro Church* (Washington, D. C.: The Associated Publishers, 1921), chapter ii.

a wooden church on the land of a Mr. Edmond Davis at Yamacraw. He so impressed the people with his gospel messages that Negroes and whites helped him to raise sufficient funds to purchase a lot upon which he erected a church. On this spot, the first African Baptist church of Savannah is known to have stood for years. Bryan purchased his freedom and continued his church work in and about Savannah.

In Virginia, between 1770 and 1800, many Negroes won fame as forceful preachers. Among them were Gowan Pamphlet, pastor of a Baptist church in Williamsburg; William Lemon, who was chosen by a white congregation to serve at the Pettsworth or Gloucester church; Josiah Bishop, who preached to a mixed audience in Portsmouth as early as 1795 and who so impressed his congregation that they gave him money with which to purchase his freedom; "Uncle Jack," who preached from plantation to plantation in Virginia, doing it so effectively that white citizens raised a fund with which they purchased his freedom; and in addition they bought him a farm where for more than forty years he continued his ministry and converted many white people; Henry Evans, a free Negro of Virginia, who preached so convincingly in Fayetteville, N. C., that the town council gave up its opposition and allowed him to erect a Methodist church there in 1790; and finally John Stewart, a free Negro of Virginia, who went to Ohio and preached with so much power that he organized white people into a church in Marietta, Ohio.

In 1780 Lemuel Haynes preached to whites in Connecticut, Vermont, and Massachusetts. John Gloucester, a pioneer Presbyterian preacher, attracted the attention of a Doctor Blackburn of Tennessee, who was converted by the preaching of this slave. Doctor Blackburn purchased Gloucester, encouraged him to study for the ministry and later granted him his freedom.

---

[3] Woodson, C. G., *Ibid.*

These illustrations, drawn from Dr. Woodson's *History of the Negro Church,* are given to show that freedom in the Negro's religious and church life had an early historical beginning, and that this fact has served to give "freedom in Negro church life" precedence over that freedom which the Negro is allowed to experience in other phases of his life. Thus quite early the Negro preacher, highly restricted in other fields, achieved freedom in the church through his own initiative and sympathetic encouragement from white people and his own flock.

This achievement was another milestone in the Negro's struggle for recognition and survival on the new continent. The freedom in his church, which the Negro merited and gained relatively early, while freedom in other realms was still denied him, has been one of the basic reasons for the rapid numerical growth of the Negro church in the United States.

Restricted Environment Increases Number of Negro Churches

Freedom in church activities won by the Negro prior to and immediately following emancipation has persisted through the years. And the proscriptions hampering him in respect to his social, economic and civic life, due to slavery, were not removed when Lincoln signed the emancipation proclamation in 1863. It was in reaction against these crippling restrictions that the freedom allowed in the church assumed larger importance and accounted in good part for the continuous development of the Negro church; especially with respect to numbers, both in the rural and the city areas. This freedom in the church opened the way in later times toward freedom in other fields; but still the Negro is freer in the church than he is in other areas of the American life. Through the years, he has received more encouragement from the ruling white majority in church organization and church building than he has received in other community or group enterprises.

Negroes Receive Special Encouragement

For the most part, the idea of a separate church has been satisfactory to white Americans and pleasing to a goodly number of Negroes. The encouragement that Negroes have received from white people to have their own churches has served to increase the number of Negro churches. The whites have stimulated Negroes to build or purchase their own churches by direct acts of discrimination against them; by financially aiding them to purchase or build churches or to start new work; by separating the Negroes under white supervision; by giving church buildings to Negroes or encouraging them to remain at old sites when the whites moved or built new churches; by willingly granting the request when Negroes desired their own church; or by friendly counsel and advice.

Examples of these types of encouragement are vividly reflected in the chapter on origins. Even Negro churches that are organizationally a part of white denominations are separately set off; and possibly the greatest systematic financial aid that Negro churches receive from white people comes from those denominational bodies that are organically and theoretically one body, embracing both whites and Negroes, but in practice separate and distinct. For the whites, who desire the separate Negro church, it solves a complex social problem; for the Negroes, who are pleased with the separate church, it furnishes an opportunity for self-expression and leadership usually denied in the white church.

The Negro has also been encouraged by white people, especially in the rural South and in small southern towns and cities, by being "let alone" provided no militant doctrine was preached and the Negro's religious emphasis was otherworldly. What the white people did not object to or prohibit in the Negro's church life, he interpreted to mean sanction or approval.

Not many years ago, the militant Negro preachers in a certain section of South Carolina were silenced by threats of violence, and in some cases actually run out of the county, because their messages were not considered the kind that would keep Negroes in their "places"; but those who preached about heaven, who told Negroes to be honest and obedient, and that by and by God would straighten things out, were helped financially in church projects. They were held up to other Negroes as embodiments of the virtues of true Negro leadership. Such Negroes could usually get a little financial aid to build new churches and renovate old ones, and they were sometimes encouraged by the whites in their efforts to split the church.

To be sure, it was not always financial aid in the building of churches or the renovation of old ones that the "safe, sane" minister received, but personal gifts such as clothes, money and public acclamation on the part of leading whites. In this study, cases were found where the site for the Negro church was given by the white landowners. Economically, it was profitable to the landowners to keep Negroes satisfied and have them honest. The Negro preacher and the Negro church were instruments to this end. And the methods most often employed were to boost and encourage the Negro preacher who taught the Negro the "right" doctrine, and to allow the Negro religious freedom in his church. In any tense situation, these Negro preachers could be relied upon to convey to their Negro congregations the advice of the leading whites of the community. Examples of this kind could be multiplied indefinitely.

Continued Restraint Causes Increase in Number of Negro Churches

The continuation in American society of artificial limits to the free functioning of the Negro in political, civic and economic life have tended both to magnify the importance of the

Negro churches and to increase their number because they alone offer him a large and unrestricted arena for his powers.

If life were normally lived in America with each man given an even chance to a livelihood, conditioned only by ability, and if the two racial groups, Negroes and whites, had similar historical backgrounds so that social caste and racial stigmatism were practically non-existent, one would naturally expect that the Negro's opportunity for leadership would be equal in all phases of social, economic and political life. It would be possible for him to have on the average, since he constitutes one-tenth of the population, a one-tenth representation in public and private concerns.

But without the need of argument, everyone knows that this is not true. Nowhere in America is the Negro's opportunity for self-expression and leadership in private and even in public affairs allowed to be equal to that of the white man's except in rare cases where the Negro breaks through and where a few fair and courageous white folk see to it that he gets a man's chance.

In political life, the Negro's opportunity is almost negligible. He has not nine nor ten senators in Washington, but none; not eighty-five congressmen, but only one. The thousands of opportunities open to whites to exercise leadership in the national congress and the forty-eight state legislatures are almost wholly denied to the Negro. Between 1925 and 1929, only twenty-seven Negroes were members of state legislatures. From 1868 to 1932 only thirty-eight Negroes served as members of Congress, and this included those who served two or more terms.[4]

Except in a few cities, the Negro has no part in the making of the laws by which his city is governed. The thousands of positions of leadership enjoyed by white Americans in city and county offices are largely denied the Negro. In the south-

[4] Work, Monroe N., *The Negro Year Book* (Tuskegee, Ala., Tuskegee Institute, 1931–32), pp. 83–4.

ern section of the United States where the Negro is largely disfranchised, he can hope only for a janitor's job around the court house or the city hall. Representation on the board of education, the park and recreational boards and the like, are almost wholly beyond the Negro's grasp. He has no voice in saying how the tax money is to be expended, though he pays his share of the taxes both directly and indirectly. Appointive positions such as those given by presidents, governors and mayors are not often given to the Negro.

The Negro's political life is still largely found in the Negro church. It is in the national, state and county Baptist conventions and associations and in the local church that Negro Baptists find political leadership. It is in the local district, state and quadrennial conferences of the Methodist churches that political leadership is displayed. The great importance attached to the political manoeuverings at a National Baptist Convention, or at a General Methodist Conference, can be explained in part by the fact that the Negro is largely cut off from leadership in the body politic. The local churches, associations, conventions and conferences become the Negro's Democratic and Republican conventions, his Legislature and his Senate and House of Representatives.

Furthermore, the Negro has usually been denied the opportunity given to other racial groups to enter and develop powers of leadership in private business concerns. Quite early, philanthropic agencies and broad-minded missionaries began to provide educational opportunities for the Negro; but it was only in rare instances that the Negro was given a chance to use his education in the big business enterprises that were open to members of other racial groups.

Thus, not finding the opportunity that is given to members of other racial groups in civic and political life, in business enterprises and social agencies, the Negro through the years has turned to the church for self-expression, recognition and leadership. It is true that within recent years a few restraints have been removed and the Negro has begun to build up for himself private concerns, thereby finding places of leadership in business, the professions, journalism and other fields; but these are comparatively recent developments, and came too late to effect a change in the number of Negro churches created in part by this desire for leadership and self-expression which was denied in other areas.

Unrestrained Freedom and Idea of a "Call"

Owing also to these restraints in the environment and the resulting strong desire for church leadership, the establishment of churches by a relatively illiterate mass has been unrestrained. There is, for example, unrestrained freedom in the Baptist church. Four laymen and three ordained ministers can start a Baptist church. In many cases, even this loose regulation is not observed. The streets are dotted with small churches, some of them store-front and house churches, organized by illiterate ministers who say they are called of God to preach.

The ideas that the church is God's house and the preacher God's prophet have made the masses tolerant toward the existence of many churches. Both the minister and the congregation have shared this belief, which made both of them "things apart." Though rapidly on the wane, especially in educated circles, the belief is still held by many people that the minister, more than the men and women of other occupations, is God's ambassador on the earth, and that he knows what he is about. The minister and the church are sacred; and even if his conduct is not exactly what it might be, he is nevertheless a man of God. Thus, he exercised and in some cases still exercises almost unlimited freedom in starting a new church.

In the majority of Negro churches there has been no standard allowing men to enter the ministry. If a man says he is called to preach, he can usually be ordained. Once ordained he must have a church; so he builds or starts a new one. The boards authorized to ordain men for the ministry have often felt constrained to license and ordain the applicant primarily because the members of the board have a conviction that the "harvest is great and the laborers are few," and that it would never do to turn down or hinder a man whom God has called to the ministry.

It is not too much to say that if the Negro had experienced a wider range of freedom in social and economic spheres, there would have been fewer Negroes "called" to preach and fewer Negro churches.

Scrambling for Positions of Leadership

Limitations and proscriptions from without have enhanced the value of positions of leadership within the church and within the race. They also tend to glorify the selfish motive. For example, almost any minister would be willing to consolidate churches if he were to be elected pastor of the new church; and often it is found that a minister divides or splits a church on leaving it when he alone could prevent the organizing of another church. His opportunity for leadership is so narrowly confined that he takes no chance of losing it. This would be true of any people, but certainly more pronounced in a group as highly restricted as the Negro is in the American commonwealth. For the same reason, it is not difficult to understand that numerous were the applicants for a social worker's position in a metropolitan southern city, a position requiring one of special training and experience; nor is it surprising that among the aspirants were porters and mail carriers, especially when considered in the light of the fact that this one position gave the Negro who held it more power and prestige than any other Negro in the community; and further that aside from the church and one other position, it was the chief avenue of leadership opened to the Negroes of that city.

Denominational Rivalry

Denominational rivalry, though not peculiar to the Negro, has also made its contribution to the multiplication of Negro churches; and it has possibly helped to swell the number of Negro church members. It frequently happens that Baptist and Methodist churches are like the Western Union and the Postal Telegraph. Where one is found the other is not far away. There is a desire on the part of denominations to swell their numbers—both with respect to churches and members. This urge to be "big" in numbers is largely responsible for padded reports in church statistics. Though there may be hardly enough members in a given community to warrant a Baptist church if a Methodist church is there, or vice versa, one frequently hears the argument that the denomination must take care of its folk. Hence hundreds of Baptist and Methodist missions are found in localities where they are absolutely not needed. There is no authority able to keep the Baptists from organizing; and as for the Methodists, the bishop often feels that if he does not allow certain ones to organize, they will join the Baptist or some other church and thus be lost to Methodism. In a small Georgia community where a Baptist and Methodist church exist with only sixty members each, including children, and where both churches were in very poor physical condition, the investigators asked one of the officials what were the possibilities of merging the two. The officer simply replied that it would take God to do that. This case could be multiplied scores of times in the sixteen centers comprising the rural and urban study.

In addition to blind loyalty to a particular denomination with respect to locating or building churches, there exists in many cases an honest conviction that *their* church is "the church" of churches. Instances like these do exist and have significance. This attitude cannot be classed as mere denominational rivalry, and it is a factor in church development.

Splits and Withdrawals

Likewise, the increase in the number of churches by division is not a distinctly Negro characteristic, and it is not entirely owing to the selfish desire of officials to hold office or "boss" something. Here again a few churches split because some people feel that a vital Christian principle is involved, and that the only way to live true to that principle is for them to withdraw. There are also friendly separations or planned divisions to meet the needs of members who live far from the mother church. In the sixteen centers covered in this study, approximately 16 per cent. of the churches are the result of divisions of some kind.

Mobility of Negro Population Factor in Church Development

The number of Negro churches has been greatly affected by the migration of the Negro population from the rural to the urban sections and from the South to the North. The influence of this upon Negro life will be more fully treated in later chapters.

Notwithstanding the fact that the oldest churches among Negroes, with the possible exception of the first Negro church, seem to have had urban origins, the largest number of Negro churches were and are still found in the rural sections of America, and principally in the rural South. This is not difficult to explain, when considered in the light of the fact that the Negro race was brought to America for farm purposes. Even today, in spite of the migratory movements, more than half of all American Negroes live in rural areas, chiefly in the South. But the fact that the Negroes are gradually becoming an urban people will certainly help to determine not only the future program of the Negro church but the number of churches both in the rural and in the urban areas. In 1900 the rural Negro population of the United States was 77 per cent. of the total Negro population; in 1910 it was approximately 72 per cent. of the total; and in 1920 the rural Negro population was slightly less than 66 per cent. of the total Negro population. It is estimated that between 1920 and 1925 the total Negro farm population of the South decreased by 789,736. Naturally this mobility and shift of the population to urban centers will tend to decrease church-membership in the rural areas and to increase the urban membership and the number of urban churches.

These economic, social, and psychological factors are responsible for the existence of the Negro church; they are responsible for its rapid numerical growth; they also go far to explain why, in proportion to population and actual church-membership, Negroes have twice as many churches as whites.

Summary of the Findings of the Study

The early history of the Negro in America clarifies in part the place of the church in his life. It indicates that the early proscriptions placed upon him by his position as a slave, together with the encouragement and freedom he enjoyed in developing his church, and his own desire for self-expression made the church of vital importance.

Prior to the emancipation of the slaves, social and psychological factors influenced the separation of both Negroes and whites in public worship. Following the emancipation, when the Negro could actually own and aggressively expand his church, the economic factor was added. Therefore, since about 1865 these economic, social, and psychological factors have permeated the structure of the Negro church. Specifically, churches originated from about five causes, namely, a growing racial consciousness, the initiative of individuals and groups, splits, migration of Negroes, and missions of other churches. While church origins due to individual initiative and missions of other churches are scattered throughout the history of the Negro church other types of origin are charactertistic of certain epochs in the history of the country. Thus

the slavery and Civil War epochs are characterized by a growing racial consciousness. Splits and church schisms charac-
terize the epoch of 1900 to 1914. The migratory movement
among Negroes contributes to the origin of many churches
and also characterizes the epoch from 1915 to the present.

The character of the memberships of urban and rural Negro
churches reveal some contrasts in the trends and development
of the churches. Not only is the average membership in the
urban church larger than in the rural church by almost 40
per cent., but the apparently steady increase in membership
is also greater than in the rural church. The total membership in the 609 urban churches studied is 357,169, and in
185 rural churches is 26,845. Over half of the urban
churches have fewer than 400 members, and less than a sixth
have more than 1,000 members. The average membership
is 586 per church. In the rural church there is an average of
145 members per church, and almost three-fourths of the 185
rural churches included in this study have fewer than 200
members.

It appears that both the urban and rural churches have
much work ahead of them in gaining a larger support from
the present membership. It was discovered that in the urban
church between 25 and 48 per cent. of the members ordinarily attend regularly, and that about 43 per cent. support
the church financially. The rural church receives proportionately better support, in that 7 per cent. more of the rural
members actually are regular contributors. But this may be
accounted for by the fact that services are less frequently held
in the rural church and by the fewer distractions in the rural
situation. Most rural centers have lost through the migratory
movement, whereas generally the urban centers have gained.

The basis for determining membership is not uniform in
either the urban or the rural churches. Three general bases
are used by both groups. In some churches every one taken

in is counted. In others, membership is determined by yearly
registration or by financial support.

The urban and rural churches likewise use similar methods
for recruiting members. With both, the professional evangelist is passing. And although his methods are often repu-
diated, many pastors make use of the same element of fear
used by him to motivate conversions and to increase church-
membership. On the other hand, a number of ministers and
churches are presenting church-membership in a different way.

An encouraging number of churches are realizing the value
of well-kept membership records. Many of these churches
employ secretaries.

The urban church in particular ranges in membership from
less than 1,000 to more than 4,000. However, from the
viewpoint of regular attendance, financial support and generally active membership the church with between 500 and
2,000 members is often doing the best work. The study
tends to show that as the membership increases above 2,000,
the per cent. of attendance, financial support and active membership gradually decrease. It is suggested that these facts
point to a need for better organization and administration of
the church program and membership and a more efficient
leadership.

In the first place, the leadership of the urban church represents a decided change in its status as compared with former
years. The younger men bring to the ministry better collegiate and theological training. They are holding, in proportion to their numbers, more of the self-supporting churches
than the untrained men. Although the total number of
theological students has decreased, the number of college-
trained men among those in the seminaries has increased. On
the other hand, there are some discouraging signs. The
number of college men contemplating the ministry is small
in comparison with the same type of men entering other
professions.

Of the present ministry, 80 per cent. are not college graduates. Less than a fourth of the 591 urban ministers have either B.D. or B.Th. degrees. In other words, the majority or fully three-fourths of the present urban ministry represent limited training in the advanced schools. In the rural church the per cent. of advanced training among 134 pastors is much less than it is among the urban ministry. Over 90 per cent. of the rural ministry have not advanced beyond the high school. The rural ministers are also generally older than the men in urban churches. The rural minister, because of his absentee relationship, is more often a preacher than he is a pastor.

The emphasis upon preaching in both rural and urban churches directs the attention to this phase of church and ministerial activity. The Negro churchgoer has been consistently reminded of the other-worldly aspect of religion and life. In the urban church, over three-fourths of the stenographically reported sermons were of the other-worldly, biblical and expository type. About one-fourth of them made direct constructive application of Christianity to life. While in the rural church, an even larger per cent. of the sermons emphasized the other-worldly and unpracticable aspects of life. If the emotional appeal made through the extremely other-worldly sermon verges on superstition, and if the highly intellectual sermon verges on simply a statement of philosophy, then somewhere about midway between these extremes the thing sought in preaching should be discovered.

Besides preaching, the rural and the urban churches conduct a number of features through their programs. These include the worship which is closely related to the preaching and follows it in general characteristics, and the organized teaching and fellowship activities.

Opportunities for intensification of the work in these program features are presented by the following: (1) The large number of workers, over 90 per cent. of 7,013, in the Sunday church school without specific preparation for their tasks present problems in leadership training and supervision. (2) The general inefficiencies of organization in the educational work of the churches challenge the church leadership to declare objectives, and to delegate organizational and activity responsibilities to avoid wastes and unnecessary duplications. (3) Fellowship activities present wholesome opportunities for greater service of the church to its membership and its community.

In addition to its own activities, coöperation between the church and other community institutions and agencies offers the church the largest opportunity for service. The church, otherwise, finds itself limited by equipment and personnel, and definitely handicapped by the lack of adequate financial support.

In both the rural and urban church, the limited economic resources demand better measures for budgeting, and for systematized financing, including the training of the membership in giving. The urban church has generally assumed larger financial responsibilities than the rural church. Over 70 per cent. of the urban churches are in debt. The margin of funds left for expansion after all yearly obligations are cared for is very small in most churches. On the other hand, ministers are not ordinarily paid large sums in salaries. The financial situation in the rural church is even worse. The economic ability of the rural church is constantly threatened by a gradually decreasing population and a people economically less stable. In the last sense, although the Negro church is in the main self-sustaining it must necessarily look forward to some very careful adjustments in its organic and financial structure to remain self-sustaining.

One method of retrenchment would involve offering the Negro churchman fewer but better churches. The streets of the towns and cities and the highways of the countryside are dotted with hundreds of churches. Many of these have nothing distinctive to offer and are jostling one another for front-rank places and public attention.

Economically the Negro is unable to adequately support so many enterprises doing essentially the same thing. This economic strength, which is apparently spread out so thinly over this wide area, may bring larger returns if it is concentrated in fewer but better churches. If concentrated, it would logically permit the acquisition of a thoroughly prepared leadership and of modern equipment and the rendering of greater service to the church-membership and community.

Church merging, which many churches are being economically forced to accept, would promote healthier church life.

CHAPTER II

Origins of the Church

The distinctive social, economic and psychological influences at work in each of five different epochs of the history of the United States affected in various ways the Negro churches that originated at the time, and are still reflected in those of them that have survived. Consequently it is of importance to point out that among the 609 urban churches and the 185 rural churches that were studied in this investigation there are representatives of each epoch.

The Slavery Epoch

The first of these epochs was between the years 1750 and 1859. During this period racial consciousness was roused by the controversy over slavery. Slavery as an institution was challenged by its adversaries. Operators of the underground railway were busily engaged transporting slaves to freedom. On the other hand, those citizens with pro-slavery sentiments were busy maintaining the institution. This controversy found its way into the churches. The reactions of the southern religious bodies were decidedly pro-slavery. The Negroes in many of the predominantly white churches voluntarily withdrew or were forced out. And likewise the whites withdrew from churches which were predominantly Negro.

Approval or disapproval of the institution of slavery was expressed, not only in the local churches, but by denominations as well. Large denominations like the Methodist and the Presbyterian found themselves divided on the issue; their divided sympathies were definitely influenced by the geographical regions in which their people lived.

The seriousness of this controversy in the church is reflected in the origins of forty-one of the 609 urban and five of the 185 rural churches of this study. Interesting and outstanding examples of Negro church origins of this early epoch are reported in the following excerpts from local church histories.

THE OLDEST CHURCH OF THIS STUDY

The oldest urban church of this study was established in Philadelphia. About the founder and the church, the autobiography of Richard Allen states, "I was born in the year 1760, February 14th, a slave to Benjamin Chew, of Philadelphia." After spending some time away from Philadelphia, Richard Allen returned and purchased his freedom. "February, 1786, I came to Philadelphia. Preaching was given out for me at five o'clock in the morning at St. George church. . . . I preached at different places in the city. . . . I soon saw a large field open in seeking and instructing my African brethren, who had been a long-forgotten people and few of them attended public worship. . . . I raised a society in 1786 for forty-two members. . . . We all belonged to St. George's church. . . . We felt ourselves much cramped; . . . We established prayer meetings and meetings of exhortation, and the Lord blessed our endeavors, and many souls were awakened; but the elder soon forbid us holding any such meetings; but we viewed the forlorn state of our colored brethren, and that they were destitute of a place of worship. They were considered a nuisance."

Forced from Knees During Prayer—A number of us usually attended St. George's church in Fourth Street; and when the colored people began to get numerous in attending the church, they moved us from the seats we usually sat on, and placed us around the wall, and on Sabbath morning we went to church and the sexton stood at the door and told us to go in the gallery. He told us to go, and we would see where to sit. We expected to take the seats over the ones we formerly occupied below, not knowing any better. We took those seats. Meeting had begun, and they were nearly done singing, and just as we got to the seats, the elder said "Let us pray." We had not been long upon our knees before I heard a considerable scuffling and low talking, I raised my head up and saw one of the trustees, H—— M——, having hold of the Rev. Absalom Jones, pulling him up off his knees, and saying, "You must get up—you must not kneel here." Mr. Jones replied, "Wait until prayer is over." Mr. H—— M—— said, "No, you must get up now or I will call for aid and force you away." Mr. Jones said, "Wait until prayer is over, and I will get up and trouble you no more." With that he beckoned to one of the other Trustees, Mr. L—— S—— to come to his assistance. He came to William White, to pull him up. By this time prayer was over, and we all went out of the church in a body, and they were no more plagued with us in the church. This raised a great excitement and inquiry among the citizens, in so much that I believe that they were ashamed of their conduct . . . we had subscribed largely towards finishing St. George's church, in building the gallery and laying the new floors, and just as the house was made comfortable, we were turned out from enjoying the comforts of worshipping therein.

The New Church—We then hired a store-room and held worship ourselves. Here we were pursued by threats of being disowned, and read publicly out of meeting if we did continue to worship in the place we had hired; but we believed the Lord would be our friend . . . Here was the beginning and rise of the first church of the denomination later known as the African Methodist Episcopal. Many of the colored people in other places were in a situation nearly like those of Philadelphia and Baltimore, which induced us, in April, 1816, to call a general meeting, by way of conference. Delegates from Baltimore and other places which met those of Philadelphia, and taking into consideration their grievances, and in order to secure the privileges, promote union and harmony among themselves, it was resolved: "That the people of Philadelphia, Baltimore, etc., etc., should become one body, under the name of African Methodist Episcopal Church." [1]

---

[1] Allen, Richard, Bishop, *The Life, Experience, and Gospel Labors* (Philadelphia, Pa., A. M. E. Book Concern), pp. 1, 19, 20, 21, 22, 32.

The first Negro Baptist church of this study was established in 1841, in Richmond, Virginia.

Until that year, the congregation was mixed. The 387 white members then retired to Broad and Twelfth Streets, and 1,708 colored members remained in the old church of worship.[2]

Many are under the impression that the old church was given to the colored members but they paid $6,500 for the building. . . . The Attorney General of the State, Hon. Sidney S. Baxter, gave his written opinion: "That it would be inexpedient to make any portion of the trustees people of color and that it might endanger the title to the property." This opinion and the refusal of the First Baptist Church (white) to transfer the property made the colored brethren warm. . . . It was transferred in 1849 to their trustees: David R. Crane, Robert H. Bosher (white), John S. Kinney, Jas. C. Ellis, and Wm. Lightfoot (colored).[3]

The second Negro Baptist church of this study in Richmond, Virginia, was established in the following way:

Of the original members of the church (2nd Baptist white), none were Negroes, owing, doubtless, to the circumstances under which the movement began. The slavery question, however, came up as early as December, 1821. It seems that shortly before that time, David Roper, the Acting Pastor, had sold a Negro and had been criticised therefor. He brought the matter before the church and asked whether, in its judgment, it was permissible for a Christian to own and sell slaves. . . . It was answered in the affirmative, but in language that makes it plain that the church could not and would not endorse promiscuous trading in Negroes. Fifty-three years later, the first Negro member was admitted. . . . Thereafter, Negroes were received freely into membership, though the minister would indicate that subsequent to the Nat. Turner insurrection the consent of the masters had

---

[2] Souvenir Program of the 50th Anniversary of Dedication of the Building (Richmond, Va., First African Baptist Church, 1928), pp. 1, 5.

[3] Johnson, W. T., *Historical Reminiscences of the First Baptist Church* (Richmond, Va., Hastings Deeds No. 82A Richmond Chancelor), pp. 9, 11. Also pp. 328 ff.

to be given before a Negro could be baptized. From the first, the colored members constituted something of a problem. In 1826, the sexton, presumably a white man, was given authority as a deacon to watch over the Negroes of the church and was encouraged to hold special meetings for them.

After the great revival of 1831, when many Negroes were received, a committee of seven of the older colored members were appointed to the task formerly assigned to the sexton. It was frankly said that the white members could not exercise intelligently the necessary church discipline. The next year an effort was made to segregate the colored members. Later, when Doctor Jett succeeded in organizing the First African Church, a committee was appointed, to act with one from the First in supervising, as required by law, the preaching at the African Church. Encouragement was also given such of the Negroes as desired to join the new congregation. Finally, it became evident, that the best results were not being accomplished and a resolution was passed not to receive other colored members except in unusual cases. Mrs. M. O. Roper's Harriett and a worthy man, Richard Balentine, were later regarded as exceptions and were admitted. After much discussion, the Negro members were finally organized as the Second African Baptist Church, and, on February 1, 1846, forty-three males and fourteen females were dismissed.

The church stood sponsor for the Second African Baptist; but apparently did not have to assume any financial liability. Annually until the close of the war between the states, a committee of the church was in general charge of the Negro congregation, attended its services, and gave counsel. When freedom came to the colored members and they threw off the tie that bound them the Second African had 1,100 members. In 1866 the committee headed by Jackson B. Wood, made a final report that contained this interesting observation: ". . . in our opinion, the organization which was formerly adopted is the very best which can possibly be carried out for the good government of the colored churches as well as for their promotion in piety." [4]

---

[4] Taken from the "Ideal" (Bound Volume) 1921–23 Volume 5 of the Second Baptist Church (white).

A separate enterprise in 1848, was begun for the thorough-going evangelization of colored people in Charleston, S. C., under the auspices of Rev. John Badger and the session of the Second Presbyterian Church. . . . The enterprise began as a branch congregation of the Second Presbyterian Church; then became a missionary church in 1857 with only 47 members. In order definitely to apportion the minister's time and the use of the church building the white members drew up the following statement.

We do hereby agree that the pastor of this church is to be selected always with a view to his suitableness for laboring most profitably among the colored people, and that for all times the services and labors of the minister shall ordinarily be so divided as to apportion the regular morning services to the whites especially, and the remaining regular service or services to the blacks especially; and we do further agree that the colored people shall always be allowed in these services designed peculiarly for their benefit the main floor of the building, excepting such seats on the right and left of the pulpit as may be appropriated to the whites.[5]

Also in Charleston, S. C., following the split of the Methodist Episcopal Church which resulted in the Methodist Episcopal Church, South, in 1844, the problems of bi-racial worship became articulate.

"This exclusion of the church from its work among colored people only increased its interest in them.[6] The "Old

---

[5] Blackburn, George A., D.D., Excerpts from the *Life and Work of John L. Giraden, D.D., LL.D.*

[6] After the split in the Methodist Episcopal Church which resulted in the organization of the Methodist Episcopal Church, South, the northern group of Methodists had no churches in the South through which it could contact Negroes. The writer being quoted here refers to the northern group as "the church" and the "old church." Churches of the Methodist Episcopal Church, South, either segregated Negroes or excluded them from worship services. The attitude of the northern group was more favorable than the southern group toward Negroes. Therefore in the face of the southern policy and the absence of any contact with Negroes because of the denominational split the northern group or "the old church" quickened its efforts to reach and christianize the Negro in the South.

Church" became their champion. During the Civil War, the proximity of the battlefield caused white people to desert their churches and flee from Charleston. Therefore, in churches where Negroes had occupied the galleries only, they occupied the body of the churches. But "When Andrew Johnson began the work of reconstruction the white pastors and congregations returned, and began to demand their churches from the colored people. They saw no necessity for the presence of the Yankee preachers in the city, and felt that white and colored members might worship according to the old regime."[7] Negroes, however did not return to worship in the galleries of the white churches. Instead they organized colored churches.

In the deep South, Negroes and whites had, as in other places, worshipped together. In the case of the First African Baptist Church of New Orleans, La., we find that they first began as a part of the white church in 1817. There were forty-eight members, including sixteen white and thirty-two Negroes. These Negroes shared the turbulent life of the white church for a number of years, and in 1827 an African church of about twenty members was organized. They had "A colored minister named Asa Goldsberry, who just before had been bound over by the authority of the city, or otherwise, to be silent six months under the penalty of a law against colored preachers." "However, during the time Elder Fletcher pastored the white Baptist church (1850) the Negro members of his church were organized into a church under the care of a white brother. This second Baptist church numbered sixty-two members and was received into the Mississippi River Association (white) in 1859 under the fostering care of the Coliseum Baptist Church (white)."[8] The second Bap-

---

[7] Centenary Souvenir: W. H. Lawrence, "A Sketch of the History of the Reorganization of the South Carolina Conference and of the Centenary Church, Charleston, S. C.," p. 1.

[8] "A Brief History and 104th Anniversary Celebration of First African Baptist Church, New Orleans, La.," pp. 23 ff.

tist church became the First African church because the church at which Asa Goldsberry was pastor did not survive.

In Philadelphia, in 1809, thirteen persons were dismissed upon their request from the First Baptist Church (white) for the purpose of forming the First African Baptist Church.[9] In the same city in 1844 a group of people sought and received the authority of the Presbytery to organize the Lombard Street Central Presbyterian Church.[10]

The five rural churches of this epoch originated in a manner similar to the forty-one urban churches. The Antioch Baptist Church is an example of these rural churches. It was organized June 5, 1818, in what is now Montgomery County, Alabama. The ground and graveyard were the gift of a Mr. Billy Wright. The church was predominantly white until about 1849 when about forty Negroes were received through baptism. In 1850 about sixteen more Negroes were baptized into the church. About this time the whites turned this church over to Negroes; but the white pastor had charge, and the property was still held by the whites. In 1854 another church called Elem, about five miles away, received forty-eight Negroes. Elem and Antioch received about 104 Negroes in four years.

In the year 1855 seven colored deacons were ordained in Antioch by the Reverend A. T. M. Handy, the white pastor. The first Negro pastor of Antioch was installed sometime in the post-Civil-War epoch, presumably about 1882.

The Civil War Epoch

The Civil War epoch, between the years 1860 and 1865, brought to a crisis the long-continued controversy, evasion and feinting over the question of slavery. From as early as 1808, the national church bodies had attempted to keep themselves

---

[9] Brooks, Chas. H., *Official History of the First African Baptist Church* (Philadelphia, 1922), pp. 11–13.

[10] Jones, Robert, *Fifty Years in the Lombard Street Central Presbyterian Church* (Philadelphia, 1894).

intact and to pass the question of slavery on to the annual
conferences by general rulings which in practice were subject
to local discretion.

Dr. Carter G. Woodson, in the *History of the Negro
Church,* states that among the rules adopted by the Methodists in 1824, one "provided that all preachers should pru-
dently enforce upon their members the necessity of teaching
their slaves to read the word of God, and allow them time to
attend the public worship of God on our regular days of
divine service."

Another rule provided that Negro preachers and official members should have all the privileges which are usual to others in the
district and quarterly conferences where the usages of the country
did not forbid it. . . .

The Presbyterians had tried to evade the Negro question but it
was again brought up in view of the cruelty practiced in the
traffic of slaves during the first decade of the nineteenth century.
The General Assembly was forced to take some action again in
1815. It then referred to its previous resolutions on the subject
and expressed regret that slavery of Africans existed, hoping too
that such measures might be taken as would secure religious
education at least to the rising generation of slaves as a preparation for their emancipation at some time in the future.[11]

These vacillations only delayed and did not help the
churches in ultimately avoiding the denominational splits
which came in 1844 for the Methodists, in 1845 for the
Baptists, and in 1861 for the Presbyterians. The church in
the South became literally a new church; and the Negro,
except for having his name on the church record, was practically shut out.

According to Woodson, the Negro in this period became
more proscribed than ever. Free Negroes were expelled from
many southern communities. Negroes were forbidden to
hold meetings except under the watchful eye of the whites.

---

[11] Pp. 124 and 125.

In slave states, the majority of Negroes became a decidedly neglected mass during the reaction, although many were nominally members of churches. When, because of the insurrectionary movement led by certain blacks like Gabriel Prosser, Denmark Vesey, and Nat. Turner, it became unpopular to teach Negroes to read and the educated white persons were not willing to supply this lack of religious workers among the blacks, there was no longer hope for ordinary religious instruction. This reaction was unusually disastrous to the Negro preacher when it was noised abroad that Nat. Turner was a minister. The rumor attached to Negro ministers throughout the South the stigma of using preaching as a means to incite their race to insurrection.[12]

These factors caused this epoch to be one of crucial importance for the development of the Negro church. Sixteen of the 609 urban, and twelve of the 185 rural churches, of this study originated during this time. The grip of these circumstances on the church was not broken until some years after the formal emancipation of the slaves.

The Post-Civil-War Epoch

The post-Civil-War and Reconstruction epoch, 1866 to 1899, gave new life to Negro enterprises. The Negro entered into as many activities as were open to him. He was particularly active in politics and educational work, but preeminently he engaged in the development of his church.

The Negro churches of this time originated especially from the initiative of individuals, groups, splits or schisms, and as missions of other churches. A study of the church origins reveals that 223 of the 609 urban and 110 of the 185 rural churches originated during this period. Of the 223 urban churches, 12 per cent. were splits; 10 per cent. were missions of other churches; and 63 per cent. were the result of the

---

[12] Woodson, C. G., *History of the Negro Church*, p. 131.

initiative of individuals and groups; and 15 per cent. were traceable to several causes. Of the 110 rural churches, 82 per cent. were the result of the initiative of individuals and groups; 2 per cent. were missions; 12 per cent. were splits; and 4 per cent. were started by the withdrawal of Negroes from white churches.

The freedom which the Negro felt in this period is best revealed by the fact that of the 333 rural and urban churches of this study which originated then, 231, or 69 per cent., came into existence through the initiative of individuals and groups. Examples of churches organized in this manner may be selected from a large number representing many localities in the United States.

In 1891 a few Baptists who lived in Nicetown (Philadelphia, Pa.) had a desire for a place of worship. After years of feeble effort this church, with the help of another church, has since grown into a self-supporting organization.[13] A group of people in Cincinnati in 1878, under the leadership of a minister, started a Sunday school which later became Calvary Methodist Episcopal Church.[14] In 1880, upon the advice of an older minister, a young minister, Matthew Anderson, took charge of Gloucester Mission in Philadelphia. This church later became the self-supporting congregation called the Berean Presbyterian Church.[15] A church was organized in Philadelphia in 1886 by a former cement worker. This man came from Washington, D. C., and began preaching to friends. The church is the outgrowth of the encouragement and help of these friends.

A church in New Orleans, originated, in 1872, because its members, formerly of another church, wanted a different

---

[13] "Souvenir Program and Brief History—Second Baptist Church," North Philadelphia, Pa., 1926.
[14] Official Anniversary Program of Calvary M. E. Church, Cincinnati, Ohio, 1927.
[15] Fiftieth Anniversary Program, Berean Presbyterian Church, Philadelphia, 1930.

type of ministry. Also in New Orleans, in 1896, a minister started a church as the result of a revival.

"In the year 1889, in Richmond, Va., for reasons presumably best known to themselves, about eighteen or twenty members of Bethel A. M. E. Church of this city withdrew from said church and sought to establish a church of their own liking and control." [16] In Chicago, in 1882, a number of members of Olivet Baptist Church withdrew by letters for the purpose of organizing a church.[17] In Baltimore, in 1874, two men with their brethren withdrew with their letters from the Union Baptist Church and organized another church.[18]

The number of churches growing out of day-schools or attempts to furnish secular education for Negroes, usually on the part of whites, are few. The most notable of these is the First Congregational Church of Atlanta. In 1867 the teachers and workers in the Storr school, a Congregational enterprise, organized the church. The school building was used as the meeting-place for a long while. "It was a church based on fellowship and love and not race or color." Individuals interested in the founding of Atlanta University were among its first members.[19]

The origin of the Ebenezer Baptist Church of Orangeburg County, South Carolina, is an example of the rural church of this period. This church withdrew from the Bull Swamp Baptist Church about 1873, according to the lone eighty-three-year-old survivor, John McCleod. Mr. McCleod's story goes that during the years when the Negroes worshipped in the white church, they sat together in the rear. Reverend William Durham, the minister, would shake hands with the

---

[16] Henry, Peter J., "Legal History of Leigh Street Memorial M. E. Church," Richmond, Va., 1931.

[17] Historical Sketch of Bethesda Baptist Church, Chicago, 1925.

[18] "Constitution and Manual of the Macedonia Baptist Church," Baltimore, 1902.

[19] Original records of the First Congregational Church (Negro), Atlanta, Ga.

Negroes and give them a hearty welcome. He liked to hear
the colored people sing, and often had them lead the singing.
For a while there were only seven Negro members. But
later, when about thirty-five new converts were baptized, a
large number of Negroes also were included. White women
were baptized first, white men second, then Negro women
and last Negro men. They were all fellowshipped into the
church. The whites first, and the Negroes last. Negroes
continued to join the church; and at a later time, about 1873,
when Reverend Durham built a new church, he suggested
that the Negroes use the old one. Many of the Negroes left
and joined the Canaan Methodist Episcopal Church (a Negro
church) which was already established. The Negroes who
remained Baptist began worshipping in a brush arbor. Their
number gradually increased to about seventy-five. They later
accepted the gift of the old white church. With the exception of this gift, the Negro church has remained practically
self-sustaining. The only relationship now existing between
Ebenezer and the Bull Swamp White Baptist is that occasionally the deacons of Ebenezer invite the white Bull Swamp
pastor to preach for them.

The New Century Epoch

In the Reconstruction epoch, 1866 to 1899, the Negro
entered vigorously upon his newly-gained freedom. During
the first years of this period, the evidence tends to show, there
was great activity in the fields of politics, education and religion. But as time passed, the vigor and consuming passion
of Negroes for independent achievement apparently lessened,
and the glamour of the earlier accomplishments waned.

The New Century epoch, 1900 to 1914, was therefore
quite ordinary. In politics and in educational pursuits the
Negro's interest was not expressed or reflected by striking
movements. There were no exciting events, no clashes of
loyalties; and as a result the history of this period is com-

paratively dull.[20] In the church likewise, there were no stir-
ring changes, although there continued a solid and steady
growth during these years.

There was no decrease in the number of churches origi-
nating (except in the rural area which declined from an
average of 3.2 churches to 1.7 churches per year) and there
was also no stimulated advance. The origins of the churches
from 1900 to 1914 show that 140 of the 609 urban and 26
of the 185 rural churches were established. Of the 140
urban churches, 7 per cent. were missions, 4 per cent. were the
result of the migration of Negroes, 14 per cent. were splits,
and 75 per cent. resulted from the initiative of individuals or
groups and other causes such as beginnings from Sunday
schools, revivals and prayer meetings. In the rural areas
during this time 62 per cent. of the 26 churches resulted from
the initiative of individuals or groups, 26 per cent. were splits,
1, or roughly 4 per cent. from Sunday schools, 4 per cent.
were missions, and 4 per cent. were withdrawals from white
churches.

The Migration Epoch

The epoch from 1915 to 1930 was characterized by the
marked migratory movement of Negroes in the United
States. It consisted of the general movement of members of
the Negro population from the rural to urban centers, and
from the urban South to the urban North. The report on
Negro Problems in Cities, T. J. Woofter, Jr., Director, and
the *Negro Year Book 1931-32,* by Monroe Work, point out
that the migratory movement brought changes in the attitude of the whites toward the Negro in the South; created
or aggravated problems of health, recreation, and housing in
the cities; and introduced new problems for skilled and un-
skilled labor in the entire country, but especially in the large
northern cities.

---

[20] Woodson, C. G., *op. cit.,* chapters ix and xi.

This period, in which the mobility of the Negro population is so sharply defined, is directly reflected in the origins and development of Negro churches, especially in the North. During this period 189 of the 609 urban and 16 of the 185 rural churches originated. The facts reveal that 54.4 per cent. of 189 urban and 63 per cent. of the 16 rural churches resulted from the initiative of individuals and groups. Church schisms or splits contributed 31 per cent. of the urban and 38 per cent. of the rural churches.

Fourteen per cent. of the urban churches were the direct result of the migration. However, a few examples may be given to show that indirectly the migratory movement also found expression in many of those church-origins labelled *initiative of individuals and groups.* In Detroit, Michigan, an unemployed Negro minister observed the large number of people who were crowding the churches in the early days of the migration, and used this fact as the basis for starting a church.

In Philadelphia a man anxious to preach started a church in a community to which Negroes had recently moved. He began preaching in a house, and later moved the church to a store-front.

The Negro denominational bodies have repeatedly taken advantage of the migration to establish churches. In Detroit, two of these denominations have divided the city into districts. A church is placed in each district by each denomination; because, as it was stated, it is necessary for the denomination to take care of its members living there.

A Colored Methodist Episcopal church was started in Philadelphia as a result of a family of Colored Methodist Episcopalians migrating to that city from the South. Likewise a family formerly of Alabama organized a church in Detroit, because they were not satisfied with worshipping in a white church. In the same city, a group of migrants from Georgia sent for their preacher and organized a church. In New

Orleans, a group of twenty people and their pastor, who had migrated from the rural districts of Louisiana to New Orleans, kept their church organization intact.

A rather unique example of the migratory movement as a source of new churches is found in the Morris Chapel Baptist Church of Philadelphia. At the time the church was organized, most of the people, twenty out of twenty-six, were from Greenwood, S. C. They had been members of the Morris Chapel Baptist Church in Greenwood. And this name was given to the new church. For the first two months the church conducted only Sunday school. After this time Reverend A. B. Jordan, a native of Greenwood, S. C., and pastor of the Greenwood Baptist Church in West Philadelphia, was invited to organize them. Later on Morris Chapel Church called Reverend Jordan as pastor.

Church Splits or Schisms

As compared with other forms of organization, splitting is a rather late practice among Negro churches. All splits or divisions do not arise from disagreements, because 10 of the 99 divisions recorded in this study were not splits in the sense of a militant breaking of relations but the result of friendly withdrawals, often accompanied by the letters of the withdrawing members.

In one church in Philadelphia, twenty men desired to dominate the membership; and, finding it impossible to do so, they withdrew and organized another church. Also in Philadelphia, a preacher was sent by the conference to another church out of the city. He preferred to remain in Philadelphia, and refused the new appointment. A number of people of his last church helped him organize a new one. Some churches have broken their denominational ties because of what they claim to be the autocracy and oppression of their denominational authorities. This type of church is found in

Chicago, Baltimore and Detroit. Excerpts from the histories of a Detroit church and a Chicago church are as follows:

The Detroit church is the outgrowth of the desire of a group of people to unite their religious and financial resources and means that they might through a centralized, inclusive effort, offer the finest privileges and the fullest possible opportunities to the whole community for the religious, social, educational and recreational good of all. . . . There is no outside governing authority and no hampering ecclesiastical affiliation. It is a church of the people, by the people, and for the people.[21]

The other church in Chicago states that it was organized "For religious liberty and freedom of action." [22] This group seeking return of a minister whom they regarded as a worthy leader, and failing to receive what they termed to be a fair hearing of their plea, and feeling at the same time that their minister had been harshly treated, drew out, as the following statement will indicate, and organized independently.

So astounding was the disappointment to the church in not having their petition granted, that many of the officers resigned, and they were followed by several hundred members of the church. The crisis had to come as the result of the reaction of the inner growth of unrest and discontent, a protest against a local dominating autocratic, ecclesiastical authority. To crystallize this reaction and protest in some permanent form, twenty men and women formed a council to take under advisement the formation of a new church. . . . After a careful analysis of the situation and the questions at issue, the final conclusion as the result of a sound and conservative judgment, they assumed the responsibility.

The Significance of These Church Origins

The data presented tend to show that churches which originated from discrimination and a growing racial consciousness

---

[21] Metropolitan Community Church, Inc., Detroit.
[22] The People's Community Church of Christ (James D. Bryant), 1927.

characterized the first two epochs from 1750 to 1865.[23] Churches which originated from the initiative of individuals or groups, that is, the desire of the Negro to manage and direct his own religious activities, are found in all the epochs, but are probably most characteristic of the third, from 1866 to 1899.[24] The number of churches resulting from schisms or splits began to grow during the new-century epoch, 1900 to 1914. Following 1915, the most noticeable factor contributing to Negro church origins appears to be the migratory movement of Negroes.[25] From the earliest epoch down to the present, there has been a scattering of churches that originated as missions of other churches; but these are not markedly more characteristic of any one period than of another.[26]

The characteristic forces underlying Negro church origins are thus seen to have been five: growing racial consciousness, individual initiative, splits and withdrawals, the migration, and missions of other churches.

The Negro church began as a means of separating an unwanted racial group from common public worship; that is, it had a social and psychological origin. It has survived because of the economic, sociological and psychological factors in the church and in its environment. The pervasive influence of these factors will be still further brought out in the successive presentation of the programs of church activity, the temperament of the membership, and the ministerial and lay leadership of the churches.

---

[23] See Appendix Table 2.
[24] See Appendix Table 3.
[25] See Appendix Tables 4, 5.
[26] See Appendix Tables 6, 8.

CHAPTER III

The Negro Ministry

The ministerial profession was the first to get a foothold in the Negro group. Not only did it have historical precedence and hold a unique place because of prominence and disinterested service, but it also had "divine sanction" from the very beginning. This combination of forces made the Negro minister supreme among Negro leaders. Unlike the Negro lawyer, business man or physician, the Negro minister did not have to achieve acceptance by the group, for he was accepted and in full authority from the start. He played a conspicuously important part in the early survival struggles of the race, and has held ever since a strategic place in Negro life. W. E. B. Dubois writes:

The preacher is the most unique personality developed by the Negro on American soil. A leader, a politician, an orator, a "boss," an intriguer, an idealist—all these he is, and ever, too, the center of a group of men, now twenty, now a thousand in number. The combination of a certain adroitness with deep-seated earnestness, of tact with consummate ability, gave him his preeminence, and helps him maintain it.[1]

Number of Negro Ministers Comparatively High

It is difficult to determine the exact number of ministers in the United States. In making use of the census material of 1910, 1920 and 1930, for this purpose, one must bear in mind that these figures are most conservative. The census enumerators classify a pastor as a clergyman only if the major part of his income is derived from the church. Ob-

---

[1] Dubois, W. E. B., *The Souls of Black Folk* (Chicago: A. C. McClurg & Co., 1903), pp. 190–191.

viously this method excludes thousands of ministers who are the pastors of churches but whose incomes are received primarily from other sources. It is believed that this method eliminates from the census data a larger percentage of Negro ministers than it does of white ministers; because there are many more very small churches, such as store-front and house churches, among Negroes than among white people.

With these facts clearly in mind, the percentage of Negro ministers may be contrasted with the percentage of Negroes in the total population. In 1910 the Negro constituted only 10.6 per cent. of the total population; but the number of Negro clergymen was 14.8 per cent. of the total number of clergymen. In 1920 the Negroes comprised 9.8 per cent. of the population, and the Negro clergymen 15.3 per cent. of the total number. The 1930 census shows that the Negroes form 9.6 per cent. of the total population, while the number of Negro clergymen is slightly less than 17 per cent. of the total number of clergymen. It is thus apparent that the ratio of Negro ministers has tended to remain appreciably higher than the ratio of the Negro element in the population.

That the number of Negro ministers is comparatively high is not surprising when the fact is considered that for decades the Negro has been highly restricted professionally, and that for quite a long while the ministry and teaching were the principal professions open to Negroes. Even today these two professions claim the larger number; and, with the exception of teaching, far more Negroes are found in the ministry than in any other profession. According to the 1930 census, there were 54,439 Negro teachers and 25,034 Negro clergymen. The same social, economic and psychological factors that have been instrumental in the organization of the many Negro churches have also been basic elements in the production of the large number of Negro ministers.

Academic Training Less Emphasized in the Negro Ministry

In spite of the age and the historic importance of the Negro ministry, and of the large number of men now in it, the academic training of the ministry has undoubtedly been less emphasized than that of other leading professions. This is certainly less true today than formerly, because the Negroes held more generally than they now do to the belief of their day that the minister was specially "called" of God, and that if God "called" him, he needed little or no academic preparation. It was believed that God would see to it that the "anointed one" was in every respect equipped for his task. Aside from this belief, there were urgent church needs to be met without delay; and further, the opportunity for academic preparation was not always available to the Negro minister.

These are the chief reasons why the academic training of Negro ministers is lower than that of white ministers.

In an analysis and interpretation of data collected by the 1926 Government Census of Religious Bodies, C. Luther Fry shows that 80 per cent. of white urban ministers and only 38 per cent. of Negro urban ministers are graduates of either college or seminary; and that 47 per cent. of white rural ministers and only 17 per cent. of rural Negro ministers are graduates of either college or seminary. Of the white ministers, 33 per cent. and of the Negro ministers, only 7.4 per cent., claimed to be graduates of both college and seminary.[2] A comparison of the Government data with the findings of this study will be made later on in the chapter.

Academic Preparation Is Not All

In studying the academic preparation of the city pastors included in this report, it should be clearly understood that the efficiency of a minister cannot be wholly determined by his academic preparation. By almost any standard of meas-

[2] Fry, C. Luther, *The U. S. Looks At Its Churches* (New York: Institute of Social and Religious Research, 1930), pp. 64–66.

urement, one would be obliged to admit that some of the most progressive and effective Negro ministers are men whose academic training has been limited. But, it is also true that any one who attempts to appraise the work of the church must consider of vital importance the question of leadership, and this must include the formal training and experience of the men who make up its ministry.

Few College and Seminary Graduates

This study includes 609 city churches and 591 city pastors. This difference of eighteen is explained by the fact that some men have charge of two churches, while in other instances the churches were temporarily without pastors. Of the 591 pastors, 118, or 20 per cent., are college graduates; 90, or 15.2 per cent., are not college graduates but have had some college training ranging from less than one to three years; 22, or 3.7 per cent., are normal-school graduates; 202, or 34.2 per cent., are high-school graduates; and 159, or 26.9 per cent., have attended or are graduates of grammar school. In other words, the data show that four out of five, or 80 per cent., are not college graduates; that 361, or 61.1 per cent., range from high-school graduates to those who have not even gone through grammar school; and that only 208, or 35.2 per cent., have had from one to four years of college training.

Of the 591 pastors, 482, or 81.6 per cent., do not have any kind of earned seminary degree; and only 79, or 13.4 per cent., are seminary graduates with B.D. degrees.

Only 55, or 9.3 per cent., of the ministers are graduates of both college and seminary, having earned the B.D. degree; only 8, or 1.3 per cent., are graduates of both college and seminary, having received the B.Th. degree; 528, or 89.4 per cent., do not have both college and seminary degrees. In fact, 427, or 72.3 per cent., do not possess a degree of any kind. (See Tables 9, 10, 11, in the Appendix.)

COMPARISON WITH GOVERNMENT DATA

The findings of this study show that 27.7 per cent. of the 591 pastors are graduates either of college or seminary or both. This is 10 per cent. less than the 38 per cent. reported in the analysis of the Government material collected in 1926.[3] In that analysis of more than 20,000 Negro ministers representing three Negro denominations, Baptist, African Methodist Episcopal, and Colored Methodist Episcopal, 26 per cent., or 5,616, were urban pastors. Of this number, 62 per cent. were reported as non-graduates as over against the 72.3 per cent. in this study.

GREATER ACCURACY OF THIS STUDY

It is the strong conviction of the authors that the findings of this study are more reliable than those of the Federal Government. This conviction is based on three factors: 1. The data of this study were collected in personal interviews, and the validity of degrees was checked in conversation. This is an advantage over the method used by the Government, in that the Government did not use the personal method but relied in the main upon collecting material through the mail. 2. The authors are familiar with virtually every Negro college or seminary of any consequence in the United States and were able to weed out those who claimed to hold degrees from colleges that do not exist, and those with degrees from high schools labeled as colleges. 3. The validity of the degrees of the pastors of this study was finally checked through the offices of the registrars of the colleges and seminaries from which the men said they were graduated. Thus 85 per cent. of the reported degrees were actually checked in this way, and only 15 per cent. were not checked because some of the institutions did not reply to the letters of inquiry. When the degrees were checked through the registrars' offices, the number of

---
[3] Fry, C. Luther, *Ibid.*

A.B. degrees fell from 155 to 118. The original number of B.D. degrees was 100; but checking with the registrars reduced the number to 79. If the colleges and seminaries representing the 15 per cent. had responded to the inquiry, the percentage of college and seminary graduates would doubtless have been reduced by more than 1 per cent. additional. This study indicates, therefore, that the Government percentages are between 11 and 12 per cent. too high.

TABLE I—AGE-DISTRIBUTION OF 118 MEN HOLDING A.B. DEGREES

Age-Groups	Total Number	Number of A.B.'s	Per Cent. of A.B.'s
20–29	21	7	33.3
30–39	108	32	29.6
40–49	220	35	15.9
50–59	160	32	20.0
60 and above	82	12	14.6
Total	591	118	

TABLE II—AGE-DISTRIBUTION OF THE 79 MEN HOLDING B.D. DEGREES

Age-Groups	Total Number	Number of B.D.'s	Per Cent. of B.D.'s
20–29	21	3	14.3
30–39	108	19	17.6
40–49	220	28	12.7
50–59	160	18	11.3
60 and above	82	11	13.4
Total	591	79	

That the Government percentages are almost certainly high is also indicated by Mark A. May in his study of white theological seminaries. He says: "Of 2,376 ministers classified by the census as college graduates, 183 named institutions not recognized as colleges, 212 merely asserted they were college graduates and 156 reported indefinitely education abroad without naming institutions. . . . Conceivably 551, or 23.2 per cent., of the total are not college graduates."

The question is often raised as to whether the younger men in the ministry are better-trained than the older men. The two tables above answer the question on the basis of the facts of this study.

The Younger Ministers Have More College Equipment

Table I makes plain that the two youngest groups, representing pastors less than forty years of age, have an appreciably higher percentage of men holding college degrees than have the three groups beyond forty. The percentage in the two groups below forty is approximately twice that of those of the groups of 40-49 and 60 and above, and half as large again as that of the group 50-59. The percentage of the men holding A.B. degrees in the first age-group, twenty to twenty-nine, is more than double that of the age-groups forty to forty-nine and sixty and above. It is more than one and one-half times the percentage of the pastors fifty to fifty-nine.

Although 20 per cent. of the pastors between the ages of fifty and fifty-nine were college graduates, as against 15.9 per cent. of the men between forty and forty-nine years of age, the men in the latter group carried a higher percentage of college degrees into the ministry when they entered than did the men in the former group. It was possible, in the case of 26 of the 32 men holding college degrees in the age-group fifty to fifty-nine, to compare their years in the ministry with their years of graduation. Of the 26, 53.8 per cent. had their college degrees when they entered the ministry. Of the 35 college graduates between forty and forty-nine, 32 gave their years in the ministry and years of graduation; 20, or 62.5 per cent., carried college degrees with them into the ministry. In the light of these facts, it is not too much to say that the younger men in the ministry under forty years of age entered the ministry with more academic and technical equipment than the older men beyond forty.

YOUNGER MEN BETTER TRAINED THEOLOGICALLY

Table II shows that the percentage of men holding B.D. degrees is highest (17.6) in the age-group thirty to thirty-nine; that it is lowest in the age-group fifty to fifty-nine.

The youngest men under thirty would naturally have a lower percentage than the men between thirty and thirty-nine, for work actually leading to a B.D. degree requires three years beyond the A.B., and the men under thirty have hardly had the time and opportunity to earn their degrees that the older men have had. Nevertheless, the percentage of B.D. men under thirty (14.3) is higher than are the percentages in the three groups forty and above. On the other hand, the pastors sixty and above have a higher percentage of men with B.D. degrees than the pastors in the two age-groups between forty and sixty.

In this connection, however, it must be pointed out that even though the pastors sixty and above have a higher percentage of men holding B.D. degrees than the men between forty and forty-nine, the actual fact is that the men in the younger groups, forty to forty-nine, carried with them into the ministry more theological equipment. For example, when the pastors sixty and above entered the ministry, 50 per cent. of them carried B.D. degrees; whereas the other 50 per cent. received their B.D. degrees from five to twenty-seven years later. In the forty to forty-nine age-group, 52 per cent. of the men had their B.D. degrees when they entered the active ministry; while the other 48 per cent. earned their degrees within fourteen years after they entered the ministry. Even though the men sixty and above carried to the ministry more than the men from fifty to fifty-nine, it is significant that the men of the youngest group, between forty and forty-nine, were better equipped theologically than those of the two groups comprising fifty years and above. The two youngest age-groups below forty have consistently a higher percentage of B.D. pastors than the three age-groups beyond forty. It is safe to conclude that in this study the younger men now in the pastorate are a little better equipped theologically than are the older men.

These facts are hopeful in that they indicate that the academic and theological status of the men in the pastorate is being gradually raised.

Among the 591 pastors, 9 have degrees other than A.B.'s, B.D.'s, S.T.B.'s, or B.Th.'s. These 9 are: 1 Ph.D., 1 S.T.D., 1 S.T.M., and 6 A.M.'s. Degrees conferred and those earned in high schools labeled as colleges were not considered. The Ph.D. is from Yale, the S.T.D. from Philadelphia Divinity School, and the S.T.M. is from Boston University. The six masters of arts degrees were conferred by Oberlin, Brown, Harvard, University of Southern California, and two were reported from foreign universities.

Tables 12 and 13 in the Appendix give the names of the colleges of the 118 men with A.B. degrees and the seminaries of the 79 pastors with B.D. degrees.

SOME COLLEGES AND SEMINARIES NOT RECOGNIZED

Many of these degrees have been conferred by colleges that would not receive "A" rating by educational boards that are authorized to grade colleges. An A.B. from many of the colleges listed above would not be accredited with more than one or two years of college work in the ranking institutions of the nation. Degrees from some of the other colleges would be ranked as equivalent only to completion of the junior college in accredited institutions. Therefore, if the A.B. degrees referred to, though validly earned, were critically appraised, the number would be considerably reduced.

A glance at the seminaries from which the B.D. degrees came also shows that a critical evaluation would greatly reduce their number.

The College Minister Gets More Than an Even Chance

It is frequently argued that the Negro congregations in the main do not wish trained leadership. It is said that the average congregation prefers a high-school or grammar-school man who is more able to give a certain type of preaching, to a more highly trained man who has had college and seminary training. This argument has made some impression upon students of Negro colleges and seminaries. Many of them believe that a college graduate does not have an even chance in the ministry with a man of less training. The findings of this study do not sustain this opinion.

Of the 591 pastors whose training is recorded, 118, or 20 per cent., have college degrees. All things being equal, it would be fair to assume that in each grouping of churches by size of membership, as in Table 14 in the Appendix, the college men would be approximately 20 per cent. of the total. This is not so. Instead of the college men having 20 per cent. of the smallest churches with memberships less than 200, they have less than their share, 12.4 per cent. Less also in the group from 200 to 400—17.0 per cent. rather than 20 per cent. From 400 and above, they have more than 20 per cent. in every instance save one, the 800 to 1,000 group. The percentage of college men serving churches with memberships between 1,000 and 1,400 doubles the 20 per cent. of college men for the entire study. In other words, there are 251 churches with congregations of 400 members and above. Of this number 67, or 26.7 per cent., have college graduates for pastors instead of 20 per cent.; or 6.7 per cent. more than their share. There are 358 churches with memberships less than 400. Of this number 51, or 14.2 per cent., are under the ministry of college men, 5.8 per cent. less than their share. Therefore the college man has more than an even chance of being called to a large church. These facts show that Negro congregations, especially the larger ones, are more in favor of trained leadership than is currently believed.

Pastors in the North Are Better Trained

Of the 591 pastors, 252 are in the North and 339 are in

the South.[4] Of the 252 northern pastors, 57, or 22.6 per
cent., are college graduates; and 41, or 16.3 per cent., are
seminary graduates. Of the 339 pastors in the South, 61, or
18.0 per cent., hold college degrees, while 38, or 11.2 per
cent., are seminary graduates.

Thus the proportion of trained or college men is 4.6 per
cent. higher in the North than in the South; and that of
seminary men is 5.1 per cent. higher.

Years in the Ministry

The number of years that 559 of the 591 pastors had spent
in the ministry was ascertained. Only two of them had spent
less than a year; 104 had been in the ministry from one to
ten years; 205 from eleven to twenty years; 141 from twenty-
one to thirty years; 91 from thirty to forty years; 11 from
forty-one to fifty years; and 5 had been in the ministry from
fifty-one to sixty years.

Previous Occupations

The occupations of the pastors before they entered the
ministry have probably a direct bearing upon the academic
training of these men. In 425 instances previous occupations
were recorded. (See Table 15 in the Appendix.)

When the occupations of many of the pastors before they
entered the ministry are considered, it is not surprising that
61.1 per cent. of the men are high-school graduates and below.
A number of the occupations do not require workers of
collegiate rank.

Degrees Are Not the Whole

As previously stated, a man's qualification for the tasks of
the ministry is not dependent solely upon the number of
years he has spent in a college or seminary. There are factors

[4] Baltimore is considered in the North along with Philadelphia, Cincinnati,
Chicago and Detroit.

that make for efficiency that cannot be measured in terms of academic degrees. The effective work that many of these relatively unschooled pastors have done and are doing is eloquent testimony to the fact that some of them have reacted more significantly to their environment, and have lived far more constructively, than a goodly number of the men who have had every school advantage. The man himself is the most important item. Furthermore, it is no fairer to assume that the unschooled man will not improve than it is to assume that the seminary or college man will improve because of his degree. But as conditions change, new elements arise and thus appraisals must be made in the light of changing circumstances.

The Changing Status of the Negro Minister

It cannot be denied that the cultural and intellectual level of the church laity is being rapidly raised, not only by the increasing number of high-school and college graduates, but through other mediums as well. It is becoming increasingly more difficult for a minister who is poorly trained to hold the attention and respect of his church and community as well today as did the minister of twenty-five years ago who had the same amount of academic training.

It is estimated that from 1820 to 1909 inclusive, a period of eighty-nine years, 3,856 Negroes were graduated from American colleges with A.B. degrees, and that the total at the end of 1925 was 10,000.[5] According to the Educational Numbers of *The Crisis*,[6] between 1926 and 1931 inclusive, a period of six years, 9,257 Negro men and women received college degrees from American institutions. In other words, approximately four times as many Negroes were graduated from college between 1909 and 1931, a period of twenty-

[5] *Negro Year Book, 1931–32*, edited by Monroe Work (Tuskegee Institute, Ala.)
[6] *The Crisis*, 69 Fifth Avenue, New York City.

two years, as in the eighty-nine years previous to 1909. In 1930 and 1931, 4,051 Negro students were graduated from college, which is more than the number graduated in the eighty-nine years between 1820 and 1909. Add to this the fact that the number of high-school graduates is rapidly increasing, that the number of professional and business men and women is constantly increasing, and that education through the radio, adult-education programs, and other channels is spreading with almost lightning speed, one can readily see that the academic and cultural level of the ministry should be raised, to state it mildly, with equal rapidity.

Ministerial Leadership Challenged

It was pointed out at the outset of this chapter that a combination of forces made the Negro minister supreme among Negro leaders. Within recent years, however, this supremacy has been, and is being, threatened. Leaders in other fields such as law, medicine, dentistry, social service, teaching, business and journalism have come on the scene in great numbers. On the whole, these men and women represent professions that require a higher academic background than the ministry requires. This inevitably affects leadership in the modern community. The Negro community does not necessarily find its leaders now only among men in the ministerial profession. A part of the unique service formerly performed only by the ministers is being rendered today by experts in these fields. Formerly, the fact that a man belonged to the ministerial profession gave him a standing in the community that no other man could command. This is no longer true. A minister is respected in the community now, not because he belongs to the ministerial group, nor because he claims to be "called" by God to preach, but because as an individual he has admirable qualities, merits recognition, and has a unique contribution to make to life. The focus of attention has shifted from the profession as such to the individual.

The Negro minister is now required to take his place along with men of other professions and win leadership by achievement, and not by virtue of his profession. Therefore the Negro ministry of tomorrow, in addition to being convinced that it is "called" of God, will be confronted with the task of making an honest, intellectual, and moral appeal to a somewhat sophisticated and critical generation. The Negro minister will be challenged to assume more and more the rôle of a true prophet—the one who interprets the will of God to men—in personal, social, economic and religious life. As some one has aptly put it: "He must not command but he must convince." With this fact clearly in mind, it is logical and timely to ask what are the prospects not only with respect to the future leadership of the 609 churches, but of the Negro church in general.

Enrollment in Negro Seminaries Decreasing

Some attention must be paid then to the collegiate status of the students now enrolled in Negro seminaries as compared with that of seminary students of seven or eight years ago.

Out of a total of 1,011 regular theological students there were in 1923-24 only thirty-eight college graduates. There are 219 high-school graduates enrolled in theological courses, of whom 171 are *bona fide* theological students; the other forty-eight are candidates for college degrees doing most of their work in college departments, but enrolled in one or more theological classes.[7]

In connection with the present study, questionnaires were sent to deans and presidents of the fifty-two departments of theology or seminaries covered in Mr. Daniel's report, in an effort to check on the academic status of the seminary men now (1931) as compared with those of 1923-24. Forty-four of the fifty-two schools included in Mr. Daniel's study re-

[7] Daniel, W. A., *The Education of Negro Ministers* (New York: Institute of Social and Religious Research), p. 51.

sponded to the inquiry. Eight did not reply. Twelve of the forty-four reported that the departments of theology had closed since 1923-24. Thirty-two responded, giving usable information. It was possible in twenty-eight of these to compare the enrollment in 1923-24 as reported by Mr. Daniel with the enrollments of 1930-31 as recorded by the schools in response to the inquiry.

In 1923-24, the twenty-eight schools under discussion had an aggregate enrollment of 667. In 1930-31, the same twenty-eight seminaries or departments of theology reported an enrollment of 657. This shows a decrease of ten. Although this decrease is very slight, it takes on significance when the twelve schools that have closed their theological departments since 1923-24, and the eight that made no response to the inquiry, are considered. Ten of the twelve that are now closed had a total enrollment of 187 in 1923-24. The eight that did not respond had an enrollment of 114 in 1923-24. Thus, the number of students, 301, enrolled in these eighteen schools, and especially the 187 that were enrolled in the ten that are closed, must be accounted for in newly established seminaries, in northern white seminaries, in the eight that did not respond to the inquiry, or in the probability that a decreasing number of men are entering the seminaries.

That new seminaries have been organized that would account for the enrollment of the 187 just referred to is very doubtful. It is more than probable that if any new seminaries had been organized within recent years, the fact would be generally known. The tendency has been in the direction of closing Negro schools and seminaries rather than in that of founding new ones. Nor can this number be accounted for in northern white seminaries. Eleven of the leading white seminaries report sixty-nine as the total enrollment of Negro students in 1931-32. They are Boston University School of

Theology, Boston University School of Religion, University of Chicago Divinity School, Colgate-Rochester, Drew, Garrett, Hartford, Oberlin, Princeton, Union and Yale. One of the seminaries failed to comment on the question as to the number of Negro students enrolled five or ten years ago. Three said that they make no racial distinction in keeping a record of students. The seven that do keep a distinct racial record had 34 Negro students five years ago and 39 ten years ago. If the enrollment of the seven, five and ten years ago, should be taken as a clue to the number enrolled in the other four, then the enrollment of the eleven five years ago was 53 and ten years ago it was 61. The present enrollment of 69 in the eleven white seminaries is only a slight increase over the enrollments of five and ten years ago, before the ten Negro seminaries were closed.

It is furthermore highly improbable that the 187 can be accounted for by enrollment in the eight schools that did not comply with the request for information; otherwise the enrollment of the eight would show a far greater increase than the twenty-eight that did comply. This is hardly possible since, as to size, these eight are negligible. The evidence, therefore, appears to be conclusive that there is a considerable decrease in the number of men entering the seminaries now as compared with a decade ago.

Number of College Men in the Seminaries Is Increasing

In 1923-24, Mr. Daniel found 38 college graduates among 1,011 regular theological students, and 219 high-school graduates enrolled in theological courses. Although there is an obvious decrease in enrollments there is a marked increase in the number of college men in the seminaries. An analysis of the academic standing of the 731 students now enrolled in thirty-two theological schools shows the following results:

TABLE III—ACADEMIC TRAINING OF 731 THEOLOGICAL STUDENTS

Academic Background	Number	Per Cent.
Completed 4 Years College	85	11.6
Some College (1 to 3 years)	144	19.7
High School Graduates	258	35.3
Less than High School	222	30.4
Special and Ungraded	22	3.0
Total	731	100.0

Only 38, or 3.75 per cent., of the 1,011 students enrolled in Negro seminaries in 1923-24 were college graduates; as compared with 85, or 11.6 per cent. of the 731 enrolled in thirty-two seminaries in 1930-31—a percentage increase of more than 100.

Challenge to Seminaries

As encouraging as these figures are, the progress in raising the academic requirement for seminary men is still disturbingly slow. Exactly 88.4 per cent. of the men enrolled in these seminaries are not college graduates. As high as 68.7 per cent. of them are of high-school-graduate status or below. Of the 731, 33.4 per cent. have not graduated from high school. One's respect for the medical, dental or legal departments of Howard, MeHarry or Harvard would decrease considerably if 68.7 per cent. of the students in those departments were only of high-school calibre and below, and if 33.4 per cent. of them did not even possess a high-school diploma.

Few College Men Looking Toward the Ministry

In reflecting the probable future leadership of the Negro church, it is also necessary to get an estimate as to the number and percentage of college students who are looking forward to ministerial careers. A study of the occupational outlook of 1,714 Negro men who are college students was completed in August, 1930. Of the 1,416 of these who had made definite choices of occupations, 69, or 4.87 per cent., went on record as having chosen the ministry. This is in striking contrast with the number contemplating other professions; for example 350, or 24.72 per cent., chose medicine; 301, or 21.26 per cent., chose teaching; 100, or 7.06 per cent., dentistry; and 96, or 6.78 per cent., expressed the desire to study law.[8]

Another check was made in connection with this study. In the student section of the Negro church study, a question on vocational choices was answered in two-thirds, or 2,099, of the 2,935 student questionnaires that were filled out. Approximately 1,000 of the 2,099 were schedules filled out by men, less than 4 per cent. of whom indicated a desire to enter the ministry. This confirms or checks the 4.87 per cent. discovered in the occupational choice study just referred to.

If these studies in any way give adequate clues as to the attitude of Negro college students toward the ministry, then it must be admitted that Negro churches in the main will be controlled for some time yet by men who have not had collegiate training.

Approximately 2,000 Negroes are being graduated annually from American colleges. It is safe to assume that 1,000 of these are men. Judging on the basis of the percentages just mentioned, fewer than fifty college graduates enter the ministry annually and many of this number will not be actively engaged in the pastorate because an increasing number of young college and seminary men ordained as ministers engage in work outside the church. On the other hand, this situation is probably balanced by the fact that a goodly number of men decide to enter the ministry after their graduation from college.

The Outstanding Findings

This phase of the study shows:

1. That 80 per cent. of the urban pastors of this report are not college trained; that 86.6 per cent. do not have B.D.

---

[8] Mays, B. E., "After College What—For Negroes?" (*The Crisis*, December, 1930.)

degrees; that 81.6 per cent. have neither B.D. nor B.Th. degrees; and that 72.3 per cent. have neither college nor seminary degrees.

2. That, on the whole, the younger men are better-trained academically than the older men; and that they carry more academic equipment into the ministry than the men of former years.

3. That the 118 college men in this study get more than an even chance to become pastors of large churches.

4. That the northern pastors are better-trained than those in the South.

5. That the number of college men in the Negro seminaries is increasing; but the total number of students in Negro seminaries has decreased within the last eight years.

6. That the number of college students contemplating the ministry is small in comparison with the number that is entering some other profession; and, because of this fact, Negro churches for the most part, will have relatively poorly trained pastors.

Hopeful Signs

Despite the decreased number of men in the seminaries, and the small number of college men who are looking forward to entering the ministry, there is evidence that the number of college men is increasing in the seminaries and that the younger men are better-trained than the older men. This is a hopeful sign and bodes well for the future. It shows that the academic quality of leadership is being gradually raised.

It is the belief of the writers that, despite the present trend, a larger number of trained men will enter the Negro ministry in the future. This belief is based on three factors: Negro colleges that have almost neglected their departments of religion are already beginning to see the error of allowing this department to lag behind other departments; so college and university officials here and there are building departments of theology that will be the peers of other departments. In the second place, when the occupations open to Negroes are properly analyzed and presented to young students, it is believed that they will see that the opportunities for development in the ministry and pastorate are at least as great as they are in other fields. They will probably see that the sacrifices to be made are no greater than those that must be made in any other profession. This study shows that the current belief that the chances of trained Negroes in the church are slim is erroneous, and that the college-trained man really has more than an equal opportunity in church leadership. Finally, the salaries of the ministers included in this study, as meagre as they are, no doubt indicate that the average minister fares just as well economically as the average man of any other profession.

Significant as this study of the academic background of 591 pastors has proved to be, the following chapter, dealing with the message of the Negro minister, is no less essential to an adequate understanding of the Negro ministry today.

CHAPTER IV

The Message of the Minister

The Negro church is one of the greatest, perhaps the greatest, channel through which the masses of the Negro race receive adult education. It would be safe to say that a vast number of Negroes do not avail themselves of the opportunity to improve themselves mentally through reading and organized study. Many cannot, owing to a lack of economic and educational facilities. They are also cut off from cultural contacts such as attendance at grand operas and first-class theatres, either because of economic inability or social restrictions. For many of these people the church is the chief place where they are stimulated morally and intellectually. It becomes then the center of religious, moral, and intellectual teaching for that part of the Negro population that is cut off from cultural and moral contact in other areas. Furthermore a goodly number of Negroes believe what their pastor tells them. He still exercises a dominant influence in the lives of many.

It is of vital importance, then, that some idea be given of what the church people are being taught from the pulpit. In addition, therefore, to securing information concerning the academic background of the pastors and their years of experience, the authors studied the thought-content of sermons. To this end, stenographic reports were made of one hundred sermons, most of them those by pastors of the largest churches in the twelve cities included in the study.

Definition of Terms

Although the sermons are discussed here under many subtopics, they are roughly divided into three classes: those that touch life situations, sermons that are doctrinal or theological, and those that are predominantly other-worldly. An other-worldly sermon is, in the opinion of the writers, one that is concerned so predominantly with the hereafter that the practical aspects of the life on earth are secondary or submerged, or one in which fear or reward, not in this life but in the world to come, is the dominant note. It is a sermon that places more emphasis on the mysterious, the magical, and heaven than it does on daily living and those things with which the people are familiar. A sermon that touches life situations is one that attempts to relate religion to everyday life. It is a sermon in which neither fear, reward in heaven, nor being good for the sake of inducing God to bestow special favors is the prevailing note. The doctrinal or theological sermon is a treatise or exposition about God, Jesus, the Sacraments or some abstract virtue. These are loose divisions and some overlapping is inevitable.

Of the one hundred sermons, twenty-six touched concrete life situations or were what may be called practical; and in a few instances they had social implications such as the relating of religion to the economic, racial and international aspects of life; fifty-four were predominantly other-worldly; the other twenty were highly doctrinal or theological.

Touching Life Situations

The twenty-six sermons that touch upon life situations are roughly divided into three types: those that deal primarily with the personal aspects of religion; those that deal with social and economic problems; and sermons that are highly flavored with racial emphases. Examples of these are given:

PERSONAL EDIFICATION

The following words have been selected for the text: "Who Shall Roll Us Away the Stone from the Door of the Sepulchre?"
The text is a serious and perplexing question asked by some

friends of Jesus who were on their way to the sepulchre. The large sealed stone in the entrance to the tomb offered a real problem to those despairing pilgrims of the way. The situation is thought provoking. Not only, who will roll away the stone from that tomb, that massive piece of granite, but who will roll away the stone of despair from their discouraged souls? The question merits wider application; consequently we find ourselves face to face on this Easter morning with the problem of sealed lives, both individual and social.

Many are the human souls in this world with the capacity for the expression of the abundant life, if only the stone of remorse could be rolled away from the doorway to their hearts. Others there are whose lives would be gems of abiding influence if the stone of conceit could be rolled away. Whole communities could be electrified, changed, transformed, if stones of shallowness, indifference, indolence, could be rolled back, so that the entombed life might come forth with glorified power and revolutionize the social order. This rolling back of human repressions is absolutely essential to the peace and happiness of the world.

A wailing, whining, complaining disposition may overthrow the finest possibilities. How many souls are driven to their graves by those thoughtless, ever diligent messengers of woe, who never have enough sense to apply genius to drive away the stones of winter in a friendly sort of way. The truism is obvious. Summer can never come, my friends, until the signs of winter have been driven away. For sunshine to come into your soul or into mine we must have an opening to receive its warm and happy rays.

Then again, preoccupied souls lose sight of the big things in life; overlook the value of coöperation; refuse to dim their light in the way of friendliness and contact. We retard substantial progress. We give ourselves to the task of building more barns, which are transitory things. We do these things instead of building our character—that immortal, everlasting thing. This leads us naturally to a question. Who shall roll us away the stone from the door of the sepulchre? Or better still: who shall roll away the sealed stone of remorse, conceit, shallowness, indifference, from human hearts? There is only one answer. The power of God through the spirit of the risen Christ. If in the human heart there is a capacity imprisoned, that human heart through the spirit of the risen Christ can be released to a broader life.

Who shall roll away the stones which seal the possibilities of social progress within the sepulchre of inertia and retrogression? There is only one answer. You and I liberated from the tomb of fruitless decay. A spiritual earthquake in our lives, as it were, can do the job. Liberated personality is God's most successful force, by which whole communities may be elevated from spiritual lethargy and transformed into resplendent life. It must be through liberated personality, manifest in the spirit, in the will within, and the soul of God in us as we deal with our fellow men.

EXAMPLES OF SERMONS DEALING WITH WORLD PROBLEMS

Peace and War Text found in Jeremiah the 8th chapter.

We have had war and rumors of war and this old world is rocking with the effects of the world war of 1917 and 1918 and it will take one hundred years or more before everything will be back at the normal state again. Our children and great-grandchildren will pay the debt of men's folly in 1918. This cry of peace is continually raised when there is no peace. No time was there when more thought was given to peace than the period just before the world war. The peace doctrine was discussed and just at that very moment the world was preparing to enter the great war. Jeremiah stood up before Israel and cried about peace. You need to have your minds disillusioned as to peace actually existing in the world today, for you have been fooled. You might ask the question, What is going to bring about peace? We have been going about it in the wrong way, trying to deal with the matter slightly and this is what the prophet tried to emphasize. The fact was that they had been trying to heal by applying ointment when what was really needed was an operation. The daughters of my people cry peace, peace, when there is no peace. The cry of peace was being raised when the true prophet raised his eyes to the north, heard the rumbling and saw the people coming down to destroy Israel. Jeremiah had his ear turned to the north and heard the rumbling and could see the crowds that were ready to break in on them, and the host that would come and carry the people into captivity. There is no peace, you have just anointed yourselves, haven't gone about it in the right way. But there were two or three things that were existing in the life of the people and Jeremiah looked into these things and said, "You must get rid of these things before you can have peace."

One of these things was religious corruption. Idols were worshipped and altars to the idol god Baal were built, who was the god of harvest, the god of crops. But God said, "Thou shalt have no other God before me." They cried, peace, peace, but Jeremiah said there is no peace. In order to have peace, we must return to God. We must go back to God. We must get away from the point that Baal is our god. Only through the true and living God and Him only can peace be established. Get the things cleared up, for you can cry peace all you want, but there is no peace. You are just fooling yourselves. The prophet emphasized that they could not find peace by alliance with allied powers. At this time Palestine was looking to foreign powers for help, but it is not by might or power but through God that you will find peace. There is no peace to be had by allying yourself with foreign powers. At the same time that the cry of peace had been going forth, preparation for war had been going on.

So it was in 1914. Just before the outbreak of the world war people cried, "peace, peace." The peace sentiment was never stronger than before the outbreak of the world war, yet as soon as war broke out, the nations proved that they had been preparing for war all the time while they were crying peace. You know peace is a thing that is costly. It cost something to have peace and the reason the world does not have it this morning is the fact that the world is so selfishly constructed that it is not willing to pay the price. It is of great value and the world is not willing to pay the price. You won't have peace, my friends, unless you can get at the root of the evils. Human society is suffering from certain diseases and the only thing that will get them out is an operation, not the applying of a little salve.

Some of the prices that must be paid before peace can be established in the world: A peace psychology must supplant the war mind, the fighting mind. Men like to fight, they are trained to fight. We have got to get away from the worshipping of war heroes. In many cities there are avenues where monuments are standing and men who fought at various times are being kept before the public as great heroes. We should prepare for peace as earnestly as we do for war. We will have to educate for peace, preach it in the pulpit, have it in the text books and give it out in the press. We should take the R. O. T. C. out of our schools. The government wherever possible has put the R. O. T. C. in our schools and colleges.

We must get away from the hero worship of the great warriors. In history we read of Napoleon who is spoken of as the lord of conquests. Much attention is given to his conquests and the shedding of blood as a result of these conquests. But, my friends, you cannot have a beautiful world if you are going to glorify war. In the city of X—— there is an avenue known as Monument Avenue, up and down which are statues erected to men; many of whom were just outright devils, many of whom were against the Union; yet the world bows down to them in worship. Men go week after week and pay homage to these men. The world would be better off if these statues were torn down and junked. The idea of putting all of that money in the glorifying of war heroes, when it could be used in educational institutions! We have got to do something else. We must stop being fools over big parades such as flag day. We have too much false patriotism in our American life of today; not that I do not believe in the American flag and the principles for which it stands, but I think we have taken patriotism a little too far. Just before the great world war Frenchmen and Germans were friends and then over night the war came on and waved a magic wand which changed friends into enemies. But they were not really enemies, they were made to believe that they were enemies. A good illustration of this is the book *All Quiet on the Western Front.* This illustration brings this to my mind. Just before the armistice was signed, which told that hostilities had ceased, they were lying on their sides ready to kill; but at the very moment the armistice was signed, men of all nationalities exchanged cigarettes and candies or whatever they had. In truth they were never enemies.

There is no such thing as an enemy; but in war, people who profit by war, teach us that we have enemies.

The final price must be paid. We must have faith in the potentiality of good will. There are many wonderful machines which are invented and with just a click of a button, one machine can do the work of a thousand people. I do not wonder why some men bow down to science in its wonderful discoveries, but wonderful as science is, it cannot turn out a machine that can turn out one ounce of good will. God works through the incarnation of Jesus Christ, in that Christ died for us. Let not your heart be troubled. Your heart must not be troubled if you would have peace in the world. You must pay the price. If any one this morning wants to unite with the church, let him come now.

"Thy Kingdom Come."—Its Social and Economic Implications

Habitually and obviously without thought, we pray "Thy Kingdom come." But in reality, we do not want the Kingdom to come. If I understand what is meant by the Kingdom, it means the existence of that state of society in which human values are the supreme values. It means the creation of a world in which every individual born into it would be given an opportunity to grow physically, to develop mentally and progress spiritually without the imposition of artificial obstructions from without. Everything in the environment would be conducive to developing to the nth degree the individual's innate powers. At the center of our social, religious, political and economic life would be not a selfish profit motive, not a prostituted conception of nationalism, not a distorted notion of race superiority; but at the center of our lives would be the sacredness of human personality; and whatever we did, the chief aim would be to protect life and improve it. If this is the meaning of the Kingdom, then frankly, we must admit that we do not want it.

Let us see for a moment, what would happen if such a Kingdom as this should come to the world. As an individual, I would not wish any good thing for myself that I would not wish for every other man on God's earth. And if the thing I want, though beneficial to me, would be damaging to my neighbor of whatever color or class, I would not want that thing. I would not and I could not pile up my millions if I had to do it at the expense of long hours and low wages on the part of those who produce the wealth.

Our government with such a Kingdom as this could not spend 78 per cent. of its national income on past and future wars. The nations of the world would not spend their billions in preparation for human slaughter. It would not be a question of the reduction of armaments but the abolition of armaments. We talk about disarmament; but really there is only one way to disarm and that is to disarm. If I possessed twelve pistols, I would be potentially dangerous; if I had only one pistol, I would still be potentially dangerous. The way to disarm, is to disarm. As long as nations prepare for war, they are going to fight war. Girl babies do not hate dolls as a result of giving them dolls to play with. Our young men will never hate war as long as we make gods out of war heroes and as long as our government gives students war implements to play with.

If this kind of Kingdom should come to the world, there would not be a mad rush to control and dominate the economic resources of the earth; but a passion to share all the goods of God's world with all of God's people. There would be no need of armies and navies, aeroplanes and submarines for war purposes, and no need of poisoning gases, battleships and machine guns. The nations of the earth would trust each other. And until they do trust each other, the world will continue to be a burning volcano capable of eruption at any moment.

If this kind of a Kingdom should come to the earth, no race would want to keep another race down. Our military forces would not be in Nicaragua; they would not be in Haiti. We would gladly help the Philippines to independence and without condescension and without patronage. India would be free and Africa would not be exploited. All forms of segregation and discrimination such as those that exist in the United States in the expenditures of public funds, in travel, in politics and those that operate against us in social and economic areas would all disappear if the Kingdom of God should come. The fact is, America does not want these discriminations to disappear. America does not want the Kingdom of God. We talk about it; we preach about it; and we pray about it. But we do not do anything to make it a reality in our lives. There are many things to doubt in this world; but there can be no doubt about this: The world will accept the Kingdom of Love and survive; or continue to repudiate it and cease to be. There is no other choice.

The first step, however, toward ushering in this Kingdom is a personal one. You and I must see to it that the Kingdom for which we pray is given a chance to function in our own lives. I must see to it that my own heart is free of selfishness, void of hatred and prejudice, and clear of all those things that retard the coming of the Kingdom of God. If I am not willing to give it a chance in my own life, certainly I have no right to advocate it. When we as individuals assume the responsibility of creating the Kingdom in our own hearts, we will be well on the way towards creating a world fellowship.

SERMONS WITH SPECIAL RACIAL EMPHASES

Teaching Negroes Group Self-Respect

My text consists of one thought for today. It is found in Numbers 11:5.

Moses was feeding the children of Israel with quail on toast. They wanted fish, onions, leek and garlic. He was taking them to a land flowing with milk and honey. It is said that when the cows came in from the pastures at night that milk would be dripping from their bags; and the bees made their hives in the rocks all over Palestine. That is why it was called the land flowing with milk and honey. It was also a land of corn and wine; but they wanted to be back in Egypt, where there were fish, cucumbers, melons, onions, leek and garlic. They were rebellious against their leadership; therefore, Moses had a hard time leading them from the common things of life. That seems queer to us. If they had asked us to vote, we would have voted one hundred per cent. for the land of milk and honey, wouldn't we? The other side would not have gotten a ballot. I am not so sure of that!

I went into a shop to get my shoes shined and there was a man sitting next to me on the stand. A man who said he had a pretty

good job and he seemed to be in good circumstances. In talking
he said he did not like the city. When asked why, he remarked
that he never got a good hunting game here . . .! They never
take me where the game is good. I am going back to Mr. Jim
(white folk). Nobody bothers Mr. Jim's niggers—white folks
don't bother Mr. Jim's niggers! There he was wishing himself
back in Egypt eating onions and garlic—back in slavery under
the white man. We have a lot of folks serving as slaves and don't
want to be anything else but slaves; live in a hut, sleep on a straw
bed, have three meals a day of cornbread and side meat, rather
than shoulder the responsibilities of freedom. He was bound by
the lure of the flesh pots of Egypt. We ought to try and find
some way to help such people. We must vote for the land of
milk and honey instead of Egypt's flesh pots.

As I preach from Sunday to Sunday I never fail to emphasize
to our people to respect each other in business. We have been
taught to disrespect members of our race. When I was pastoring
in a certain city a supposedly very fashionable, intelligent lady of
the church came there one Sunday morning and listened to my
sermon—went home without commenting upon the same. That
afternoon Mr. X, the white minister, said the same thing over
the radio in one of his talks—That night she got up and related
what a wonderful preacher I was. She did not value my sermon
until she tuned in and heard a white pastor say some of the same
things her pastor had said earlier in the day; then she came back
to church and recognized her pastor as being great. She could
not recognize his greatness until the white man had said the same
things. We must be able to recognize the greatness among our
own people.

I spend a dollar with somebody's colored business nearly every
day. It may so happen that same person may marry my daughter
or my son. Sort of, "Bread cast upon the water may return after
many days." A loaf of bread bought from a man of your own
race with courtesy is just as good as any white man's bread; yet,
we like to buy from the disrespectful white man, who calls us
Jim or Sallie or anything he thinks or cares to call us. Let us
spend our money where we can receive courtesy, and by so doing
it will cause us to flee from Egypt's flesh pots. We cannot render

the best services until we come away from the flesh pots. We cannot enslave ourselves to other people. We have got to have an economic foundation to build upon.

Teaching Negroes to Be Thrifty and Courageous

The church must concern itself more with the world in which we live; must teach Negroes how to live in a scientific way; how to live in their homes, how to buy their own homes; teach them to stop buying fine automobiles when they don't own their own homes. This Avenue is much more important right now than the golden streets of heaven, of which we know nothing. Preach that kind of religion, teach the people how to spend their money with Negroes instead of other people—not selfishly, but if we do not patronize Negroes, other racial groups will not.

While Jesus was praying, his disciples were asleep. If we look at the church today, we find it, seemingly, fast asleep. Every time you take up a paper, somebody is being lynched. It seems as if the American people have gone to sleep on the question. If every minister from the lake to the gulf would denounce this crime, it seems to me that there would be a stop somewhere. But the ministers are cowards and are afraid to speak out.

Teaching Negroes to Be Mentally and Morally Free

There are people who love the easier ways of life so well that they ignore their positions of public trust for personal benefits. Our racial group is heavily burdened with those who have become mental slaves to ideals which for the moment allow them to be warmed by the smiles of their oppressors. If you are not made to feel sick every time you get on a Jim Crow street car—there must be something wrong with you. If you cannot see the folly in paying your good money to be jim-crowed in theatres, you have lost your sense of proportion and values. But worse than these; I understand that here in your city, you have white principals in your colored public schools. I understand that each time some colored citizens petition for colored principals that certain colored teachers counter-petition for the white principals to remain. Of course, they do remain!

It is a sad and pitiful thing in the schools where black boys and girls are being taught and trained for future leadership that the same persons who train them should shut doors in their faces: But the trouble lies in this fact: These teachers are afraid of their jobs. They prefer to betray Negro public trust to losing their jobs. They would rather bask in the warmth of white favor and poor paying jobs than to be men and women, confident in their ability and rights. Their bodies may be emancipated but their brains and souls are yet enslaved.

Teaching Negroes to Be Satisfied with Their Race and Stop Imitating Others

"Princes shall come out of Egypt; Ethiopia shall soon stretch out her hands unto God."

It would do you good to know something about the background of the Ethiopian people so that you would stop trying to get away from your race. Nothing disgusts me more than those who want to be taken for members of any other race than their own. We will never amount to anything as long as we let our young people know that we think it is wrong to be anything but what we are. I love my race, thank God. I want to live in the midst of my race because this race of ours will never rise any higher than the lowest man in it. I don't care how many lawyers and doctors we have, when it comes to a scale of measure, we are measured by the lowest class in the race, politically and socially.

We must stop imitating the worse in other races. A white woman comes on the stage with no clothes on and after that every woman who comes to church has got no clothes on. That's not funny at all! It is a sin before God. God wants the Negro women to lift up a standard that other women may know that they are walking before God, not the most loose women but the strongest and the most godly; not the most immoral, but the most moral. We must respect and protect our women. They have had and still have much to contend with. Place another woman in the position of our mothers when they were slaves. I tell you that they would not have come out half as well as the Negro women did. And the Negro women would be much better off if some of the Negro men would stop betraying them.

They have always tried to kill us out. Every time I read about the death rate of the Negro being so high I wonder. My God from high heaven! If we hadn't been a chosen race of the Almighty God, we would have been gone long ago. Out on X——— Avenue where Negroes live, they won't put in sewers and give them the same protection as in white neighborhoods that are further out. They call out race riots and shoot us, yet they expect us to be as good in every respect as they are. It makes me angry; on the other hand, it makes me have confidence in God. God is on our side.

Other-Worldly Sermons

Of the one hundred sermons, fifty-four did not deal very specifically with life situations; but were highly other-worldly, or at least ended with a distinctly other-world emphasis.

IMAGINATIVE AND DRAMATIC

Let us start at the left hand side of the middle cross. We see the three crosses. The first is of the dying thief. He represents rebellion and stubbornness. When you have a stubborn disposition you are carrying a crushed cross. Stubbornness is worse than idolatry. Idolatry cannot be worse than when a Christian is so stubborn that he takes the wrong attitude toward the church, God and his fellow men. This first cross represents those scoffers who are always running down the church. It represents the Negro who will run down his own race, just in order to be able to be noticed by some of the opposite race. Some husbands will join the crowd talking about their wives or some wives will join the crowd in talking about their husbands, the ones who are making their daily bread. This first cross is the cross of stubbornness and rebellion.

The world wants you to come down from your high place. I love my enemies, but I won't join them in pulling down anyone. I wouldn't even do this for my friends.

Let us walk to the second cross. A man whose brow is bleeding, whose side is pierced; but at the same time is not criticizing. I can hear him praying, "Father, forgive them for they know not what they do." I see written above the cross in Hebrew, Greek, and Latin, "King Jesus of Nazareth, King of the Jews." He is the Lord of Lords. He is the Son of God. He is the Babe of Bethlehem and a rock in a weary land. I hear him cry, "O Father, why hast thou forsaken me?" He cries that he is thirsty, they give him vinegar to drink. He is treading the winepress alone, hanging there on the cross swaying between heaven and earth. No wonder the earth began to tremble, the heavens became dark. Here he is dying on the cross and the hills begin to jump. All these represent Jesus dying for man. He can open doors no man can shut, and can save a dying soul.

(Congregation very much worked up.)

I pass to the third cross, another thief is hanging on this one. The difference between the two is that this thief has made a change. He hears his partner cursing and swearing. He calls across to him, "Oh partner, don't you know that you should not do that? We are all dying on the cross: he is dying unjustly, we are dying justly for we have done many crimes." Peter and all His apostles fled away, calling him everything but a child of God. This thief was the only one convinced that this was the Son of God. He had the courage to stand up for him. My friends, you should have the courage to stand up for someone when everyone else is trying to pull him down; to stand by some woman when all her so-called friends are against her. This thief rose above the Apostles. When he finished speaking I know he must have had a vision. (Pastor very emotional, walking up and down platform, clapping hands.)

He saw the crown of thorns become a crown of pearls. The nails in his hands became bracelets. The loin cloth became a girdle. He became so inspired that he said, "Lord, Lord, when you are ready for me, take me in." Jesus looked with bloody face and said, "You have been my friend, on this day I take you home." Jesus died before the other two. Just before he died he drew on all his strength and said, "Wait, I want to take my friend home, he is not dead. I will wait until he finishes dying." They all heard this, heaven and hell heard him. From his broken body and his crucifixion we get water for baptism and blood for redemption. The other thief died. He joined Jesus in his chariot. They rode on, higher and higher they went. The thief asked, "Is this Heaven?" Jesus answered, "No." As they went higher he again asked if he reached heaven, Jesus said, "No, drive on, this is not heaven." Bye and bye he was able to reach the pearly gates. Jesus said, "I will give him a crown." I will tell you about him later.

The three crosses are before you today. Are you willing to suffer for Jesus? Do you love him enough to stand by him when the world is against him? Are you repenting of your sins today? Oh, friends, take the cross of stubbornness out of your life.

A PLAY ON WORDS

Brothers and sisters, friends and fellow ministers, we are assembled here at this late hour to speak to you out of this glorious Book which we accept as the Word of God. I hope nobody here is in a bigger hurry than I am. The church has the key to heaven. God does not give it to the preacher. When you want to go into the house you must have a key. So a child of God must have the key to enter the Kingdom of God. So much of this burglary; it is a case of the men having the key. Seldom do they break in, but they use a key that fits the door. The Lord told Peter "Upon this rock I build my church"—truth—an unchanging truth. Sometimes when I was in the country I would want to steal a little rest; but I was always afraid of lizards. You know the kind I mean, some green just like a leaf and when they jump on a rail they will turn brown or turn whatever color the thing they rest upon is. I was afraid of those things and I am afraid of people that change like that. God can't depend on them if men can't depend on them. Nobody in this town is more afraid of a dog than I am or more afraid of a man who is sometimes on his feet and sometimes on his hands. I am going to talk about the "CRYING ROCK." We spoke last Sunday about Jesus Christ, the Golden Rule, and the Sunday before that we discussed Jesus as being the friend of sinners. Zacchæus was a little man, small of stature, but he wanted to see Jesus. He climbed into a tree so that he might see him as he passed by and when Jesus passed he told Zacchæus to come down and Zacchæus asked for forgiveness if he had done wrong to any man. I tell you that if these should hold their peace the stones would immediately cry out. These are the words of the text.

It looks like you might see him coming up to Jerusalem, no previous preparation having been made, only prepared hearts. That is one thing I like. He wants a prepared heart. He has said, "Give me your heart." I saw them making preparation for Jesus as they brought the colt for there was a crowd who had made preparation for Jesus, made preparation in their hearts. So much form, so much indulgence, so much selfishness and leaving off Jesus. I see them pulling off their coats and putting them down before him. They tell me the people climbed in palm trees to see the triumphant entry and they tell me those palm trees grew forty feet in the air. I don't know how they got up there and got the palm leaves; but they were there waving the branches of the palm tree. Sometimes when I see myself born down in Georgia where there are so many hardships, I can tell that my dungeon shook and my chains fell off. I don't know how Jesus saved me; but I am saved. I don't know how they got up in those palm trees, but they got up there and got palm leaves and waved them in the wind. They said we have no cornets, no instruments to make music. They said that this is the day that music should animate the souls of men. There is nothing we can do but use our voices. What will we sing? Nobody knew what they ought to sing. Jesus said this is the day of my inauguration and they began singing "Hosanna." We see those men who were the main officers, who controlled the city, staring, but Jesus Christ said I am going to let them know that my message is a brotherly message. "I am the Lord of Lords, the King of Glory, my dominion being an everlasting dominion, heaven and earth may pass away but my dominion will last forever." They said make them hold their peace. But he said, "This is the day that I must be presented, this is the day that I shall take the reins of time. Yes, if these will hold their peace, even the rocks will cry out." The world has been trying to get you to hold your peace; but you cannot get a child of God to hold his peace. I don't know what God meant when he said the rocks will cry, but I think he meant if he should make them hold their peace, then the rocks would cry out and proclaim him Lord. To let you know that I am king of kings, the rocks will cry out. Look like you might see those ignorant people who did not believe. And you can see them this morning who do not believe. But those who believed, their dungeons shook and their chains fell off.

The rocks would cry out, a crying rock, a crying rock. He was not talking to any special group of people. We have some people in the church, some big people, the 400, they look to the ignorant people to praise God. That is foolish. Nobody else can praise God for you. Every man and woman that have been born again will praise God for themselves.

If they would hold their peace, even the rocks would cry out. I have had people to join the church and say that they had religion for forty years. I don't see how they could hold it. It is a fire in the soul and gets in the heart; it keeps on burning and gets in the bones; it gets between the marrow and will just keep on burning and will burn until somebody will know that you have been born again. So if these people hold their peace, the rocks will cry out. I can leave down here in Y—— city and take a trip to heaven right now. Seems like to me the day is a fine time to praise God, no use putting off until the evening of life. We went through one of the hardest winters we have had in our lives. God wouldn't let them put us out of doors and we were fed at soup houses. God took care of us. Don't you think he won't keep preparing. Oh, yes, Brother Z—— wants to be prepared. Somebody said hush. Somebody in the church saying hush. They will continue to say hush. What are you going to do about it, church? Are you going to let them make you hush? They are trying to tell us how long to hold our services, but nobody can tell me how long to hold the service of God. If you don't come to church until 12 o'clock, I am going to wait for you and then have the service of God. Are you going to let them make you hush? I said that if they would hold their peace, the rocks would cry out. If the church don't praise God naturally nature will praise God anyhow. I wonder if you are in the crowd, I mean the crowd who was talking about Jesus in Judah. I am talking about Jesus in heaven. I am talking about Jerusalem. I can see it. I wonder if any of you can see it. Heaven prepared for me. Oh, I wonder if you have got your tickets? I want to see if we can get up in Jerusalem. Over yonder I see Jesus riding on a colt and the people praising him. But after a while the people began singing "Hosanna," and the other people said make them hush. But Jesus said, "I cannot make them hush, for if they hush, the stones will cry out. He turned water into wine, but he said, that if they hush, the stones will cry out. Oh, it looks like you might see a happy crowd. Talk with me. They were crying, "Hosanna." You must be born again. He has got up on the Mountain and he looked at Jerusalem and he said the kings and prophets will be in Jerusalem; but Jerusalem is lost if it does not repent of its sin. "Oh, Jerusalem, how long will it take to get you under my wings? I longed to shelter you, I longed to protect you, I longed to take care of you and then I called you and you wouldn't come." I am sorry for Jerusalem, and He was so anxious that the tears ran down His cheeks.

You can't help but cry. Oh, Sinner, my God is bothered about you. You ran away. My God, my God, and they try to make us hold our peace by limiting my preaching. No man can limit me to preach God's word. God called me to preach and it would be woe unto me if I did not preach. When I come up to the judgment I want my God to say "Well done, well done." When I lay down to die and when I shall go back to Him, I shall not be afraid. When I shall look over that mystic river and see my Saviour on the shore I want to wait until I hear his voice and see the print of the nails in his hands, I am going to shout and sing and pray until I get to glory. When the war is over, when the war is over, I shall stack up my hymn book and Bible. In the morning, in the morning, when the war is over, and when the saints go marching in, I mean to be in that number. O, church, do you remember when your dungeon shook and your chains fell off?

AN EASY ROAD TO HEAVEN

God said, "Give them something to eat." "We haven't anything but there is a lad with two fish and five loaves of bread." He said "Have them sit in groups of fifty and bring the fish and loaves to me." And when they had sat down in groups of fifty, he looked up to heaven and blessed the bread and fish and gave it to the disciples. In a desert with 5,000 men and children with two fish and five loaves, after they had had all they wanted to eat, the disciples took up twelve baskets full. This aroused curiosity. Nothing but Christ out in the desert. Friends, friends, it makes no difference where you are, whether out there in a desert, just as he fed the multitude, he will feed you. The people hurried back to the city to tell that Christ had fed the multitude, never had they seen anything like it before. O, church out in the desert, men criticizing the church, some of the members saying the church can't go. Christ whispers in a small voice "Give them something to eat." How can I feed the church? "Feed them on my word." "You remember out in a desert land I fed 5,000; my word is sufficient today to feed a multitude." The church today is in a desert. The heads of the church sometimes almost give up in despair, and someone in the crowd sees the little Bible and reads and reads until he sees where it says, "I am bread in a weary land and water in a dry land." A long time ago I can remember how I went off by myself on bended knees with hands tied with sin but after a while I got in touch with him who died on Calvary. He gave me bread to eat and water to drink and drove away my doubts and fears. I prayed a little longer until I got a faith that said, Oh, for a faith that will not shrink. One day, one day, about this old church some pilgrims in the desert were asking for bread. Someone came up and said I know where you can get bread, get on bended knees. The soldier after praying went on his way rejoicing telling the news, saying "I have been redeemed." Do you know the day you met Jesus Christ? One morning on my knees I put away doubts and fears. I am glad that I can serve a God like that.

Oh, church in the desert, get on bended knees and call my God that rules in Zion and tell him to come down. They want him to come down and feed the multitude. Must I be carried to the skies on flowery beds of ease, etc.? After while, when life is ended, one morning the Saviour will come out and tell the host that has been fed, to come up higher. Sometimes there were tears in your eyes, sometimes you were hungry, sometimes the way was dark; but you stayed on bended knees and you came on anyhow. The Master told me to feed them. Don't send them away. If you send them away you will lose the church. Feed them, feed the bread of heaven. When all of us will have passed away, a few more rounds on the firing line, we will get a message from God to feed the people. Often I get insults from those I am feeding, sometimes I don't have a friend, but I am to feed the folks. Feed them a few days and the Master will come ahd say "Lay down thy weary soul, don't fight any more."

Christ will wipe the tears from our eyes. He will say, "You fed my people in a desert, come on up and rest from your labors." Are you going up in that morning? Bye and bye, the battle of life will be over. You must feed the folk, feed Christ folk the bread of life. I am going to stay in the battle field. Stay in the battle field until Jesus comes. Don't send them away. Bring in Christ who died on Calvary, bring Him in and present Him to the folk. The blood of Jesus Christ is sufficient to feed. Feed the folk, give them to eat. Will you help me sing this song "When the Battle is Over We Will Wear the Crown."

SHOUTING THE PEOPLE

We invite your attention to the 13th chapter of Exodus and the 15th verse for our text "And it came to pass, when Pharaoh would hardly let us go, that the Lord slew all the first born in the land of Egypt," etc. The subject of our message is "You cannot pass." Ever since the slaying of Abel by his brother Cain, men have had enmity for each other and it has moved on from Cain to nations and has caused them to war against each other. The chief desire of men is to overcome each other and make him his servant (repeated). That is true, that is true. That is the reason that our fathers were in slavery, because white men wanted to overcome the Negro and make him his servant.

This hatred among men moved on from Cain and got into the nations of the world. Men want to overcome one another, but God intervenes with mercy. But it is not the will of God that man should be ruled with an iron hand. Thus, he helps man to overcome. It is not the desire of God that any man or any nation should be overcome by another nation and that man or nations should rule with an iron hand. We realize today that God is over all nations and we remember that God Almighty made a promise to Israel (repeated) back there when Abraham offered up his sacrifice to God. He said all the families of the earth will be blessed but you notice that man tries to overcome his brother and make him his servant. That spirit came up from the days of Cain. The twelve sons of Jacob had enmities. Because Joseph was well loved by his father, the other brothers wanted to get rid of him; but you know God Almighty has always kept his promise to his children and will protect them. I tell you what worries me is to hear a man get down on his knees and tell God what he intends to do. God stands by his promises. I'll tell you another thing about God. God always takes care of the church. The church is always above the man. But I tell you what I believe in, I believe that the church of God will roll on when that man is on his way to hell. When Joseph was well favored by his father, his brothers plotted against him. Those brothers sold him into captivity, but God took care of Joseph just as he takes care of his church.

Regardless of where we may be, God almighty is able to take care of us. The Egyptians made the Israelites their servants and made them labor under hard task masters, and today the same thing that caused Israel to live under a hard task master is causing you to live also under a hard task master. And this is sin. But I will tell you that God almighty always had a man to stand by his cause.

Another thing I like about my God. Every way you turn and cry, you know God will hear that cry. I will tell you what my Father will do for you if you have faith in him. He will make a friend for you right in your enemy's house. This Negro race up from the beginning was oppressed and burdened down, but God almighty gave the Negro a friend right in the white man's house. God is waiting for the Negro race to get to the place where they can stand prosperity. God is waiting until we can stand to have something. God is waiting for us to equal up to any nation, so that he can bless us as he has blessed them. The trouble with the average nation, they don't acknowledge God. Men say they go to church. They get in their cars and go all day Sunday, but if God Almighty had kept them poor, they would have been in church that Sunday morning.

So my brothers and sisters God Almighty always has somebody

to lead his people upward. He had Moses who, when he grew to manhood, was standing looking upon the Egyptians and he saw a fight between an Egyptian and a Hebrew and he slew the Egyptian and buried him in the sand. The next day he saw two Hebrews talking. He thought that they were discussing the crime, but they were there to make peace. Like some church members now. You go to make peace and they say you are tearing them down. They said you want to slay us as you did the Egyptian yesterday. The wicked flees when no man pursues him. Moses said I had better go from here. We see Moses going out from the presence of Pharaoh. God found him. He said he wanted to have a talk with him. Abraham had experience on the mountain. Jesus Christ had experience on the Mountain of Transfiguration, and every man must have experience on the mountain top. You know Moses saw a bush on fire yet the bush was not consumed. I tell you, church, I have studied science, but no scientist can tell what kind of fire that was.

But I decided within myself that it was the holy fire. The holy fire that will not consume the body. Moses stood there and saw a strange sight, a burning bush but a bush not consumed by the fire. Something said to Moses "Pull off your shoes for the ground that you stand on is holy ground." Oh, church, that is the reason I am so careful of God's presence. For you are standing on holy ground. A man should have a holy heart to stand in this place. When Moses moved his shoes from his feet, he felt the presence of the Almighty God. I like one thing about my God. He is a universal God. I cannot stay in any city on earth that my God is not there too. If you take a plane and go across the Atlantic ocean, go on down into Australia, go on into Jerusalem, you will find the same God down there too. Africa is a heathen land, but you will find my God is there too. The civilized world is trying to teach this heathen about our God. You will find Jesus there too. You will find Jesus everywhere.

I can hear Moses talking with his God and God speaking out of the burning bush. Hear him telling Moses to go back down and tell old Pharaoh to let my people go. He said, "Who am I to go to that great king and tell him to let my people go? Pharaoh will ask me who I am, what must I tell him?" God

said, "Go tell Pharaoh I am the God of all, I am the God that
was long before the angels sang their songs. I am the God that
stepped out on the planets one morning. I am the God that fed
the thousands. I am the God that planted my feet on the milky
way. I am the God that caught the wheels of glory and placed
it out by Jupiter. I am the God that stepped out upon the earth.
I am the God of glory that sits on high. Go tell Pharaoh that I
sent you. I am the God that planted my footsteps in the sea. I
am the God that walked the water. I am the God that even the
hosts in heaven shall bow to and the cherubim shall bow, crying
holy, holy, Lord of Hosts."

Go tell Pharaoh to let my people go. Moses said, "Those
people down there can do anything, but I am in your hand."
God said here is a rod and I will put power in that rod. I tell
you, church, it takes a strong Christian to go as Moses did. If
you get the love of God in your heart you will go and tell the
world about their sins. When Moses arrived and told Pharaoh
what God had told him his heart kept getting harder and harder.
It is like plenty of sinners in this city. They hear plenty of
sermons but they let the devil make their hearts harder and
harder. But then God decided to let Pharaoh know who he was
and he told Moses: "I am going to pass over Egypt tonight. Yes,
kill a lamb and paint the door post of the houses over their
homes." God sent out the death angel, sent him out from glory
to slay the first-born in every home even to the first-born of
Pharaoh. In the morning Pharaoh sent for Moses and told him
to tell those people that they could go.

I can see mothers and fathers crying about the loss of their
children. But God will take care of his children. We say God
will feed us when we are hungry. Moses with the help of God
almighty led the children of Israel into the wilderness and then
Pharaoh's heart got hard and he decided to pursue the children
and bring them back into bondage. He had his chariots to go
down and try to overtake the children of Israel to bring them
back. But God led the children across the banks of the Red Sea
and parted the water and they crossed over safely to the other
side. Moses looked and saw Pharaoh and his chariots coming
down the dusty road, and the children of Israel began complain-

ing, but God said, "Stand where you are. You need fear no evil, God is with you and all power is in his hand."

Oh, Glory! The waves rolled back on both sides and the children of Israel walked across and as they journeyed they sang "Glory to His name." (Shouting) Glory to God. God said, "Go on down, Pharaoh cannot pass." I don't care where you are my God will find you sure enough. I don't know where I will be next year but I know I will be standing in line marching somewhere. He will fight your battle for you. You should serve the same God that brought the children of Israel out of bondage for he will take care of you. The same God that drowned Pharaoh is the same God today. After a while, bye and bye, when the war is over. The church will be there. I will be there. Will you be there church? I imagine when the war is over that Gabriel will step out with one foot planted on the land and the other planted on the sea and time will be no more. I want to know what the trumpet of God will say. That morning when the trumpet of God will sound, we shall wrap our armour around us. There will be a great army that morning. I imagine King Jesus will be there in his chariot. (Reporter records, "I cannot understand a word—so much shouting.")

As they go on their march, the people will ask what place is this? The children of God will cry "What place is this?" But they will say "Heaven is farther still, farther still to go," and the church will march on. The people will cry again "What place is this?" But the answer comes "Heaven is farther still." Still another time "Angel of God, what place is this?" But the march still goes on. Then those in heaven will look down and see that it is the church people who are God's people that are on board and they will ask, "Who are those coming up from the lower world?" Jesus will say, "These are they who carried their burdens in the heat of the day." In that morning there will be angelic host marching around and I am going to be there that morning. (Shouting.)

Song—"Tell the Story How We Overcome."

Doctrinal and Theological

Twenty of the 100 sermons are slightly other-worldly but

not distinctly so. They are neither this-worldly nor other-worldly and warrant a classification somewhere between the two. This classification includes the theological, doctrinal, or cultural sermon. It is an exposition about God, Jesus, the sacraments, or some abstract virtue. One example follows:

Text—*"This Do in Remembrance of Me."*

There are two sacraments only—The Lord's Supper and Baptism. The Church of Rome has five more which make seven. We find in the original language the word translated Sacramentum which in our version is a mystery. It reveals secrets. . . .

The sacrament of the Lord's Supper in common with the sacrament of Baptism is an action and has all the sanctification of an oath. Taking it, the communicant swears that he will keep his part of the Covenant and, listen friends, God will keep his part and if the Covenant is broken, it is not on the part of God. It is on our part, and if we fail to keep the covenant, it is not God's fault. This use, therefore, has no relation to any covenant engagement with God and man. . . .

The Sacrament or Lord's Supper is first the badge of Christianity. Unworthy persons often wear the badge but the badge does not make the man. It increases the hypocrite's condemnation. You know slanderers wear this badge. A man who will take of this sacrament and go off and slander his brother or sister is not helping his brother but is hurting himself. Every Christian ought to wear the badge. It is essential. If he is not fit or not worthy to wear this badge, he ought to leave the church. It is a confession and what is that confession—I belong to Christ. It is more than a badge. It is a sign of grace and good will of God to us. It is a sign of his works in redeeming us, of the obligation of the soul and of the beauty of love. There are so-called Christians in the church who dislike each other and who say I do not like to commune with him, I do not like to eat with him. As we come this morning and partake of this sacrament, remember, it is love and fellowship not only with our sister and brother, but with Jesus Christ.

It is more than a badge of protection. It is a sign. Hear me this morning, Christian brothers and sisters, every time you partake of this sacrament, it is a sign to the world that you have left the world and come on the Lord's side and the world expects to find in you that outstanding principle. And if they do not find it, they will be able to hate you. A hypocrite has a hard time. A good Christian has nothing to fear. Walk straight and upright. A hypocrite gets it hard. The way of the transgressor is hard.

It is more than a badge—it is a profession, and a sign in the age. It is a seal to the covenant of redemption whereby He engages himself to keep his part of the covenant and all of his promises. God has never made a promise that he has not kept. Not only is it a badge but it is a seal of the covenant whereby every one of us engages ourselves to keep our part of it. It is a covenant or transaction to be kept by Christians. The failure of one of us to keep our part of the covenant releases the other. If we fail to keep the covenant, we release God of keeping his part of the contract. One breaking the contract releases the other. The contract is between God and the individual. If the individual keeps his part of the contract, remember, God is going to keep his part of the contract. Not one bit of it will God break. When we fail to keep it, we release God.

Suppose God were left upon the broad principle of justice. Where would we be if God would act upon the broad principles of justice? . . .

In prayer there is a union of spirit and of soul with God in Christian service.

Sacrament—it is a pledge. As often as we eat and drink, this covenant is renewed in remembrance of the Lord's death until He comes again. We can see this morning why so many fall by the wayside. They fail to eat and drink of Jesus' blood. "If you fail to eat and drink of my body, you have no life in you." Look over your history this morning. Look over your record this morning and see how many have died—not in physical death but in spiritual death. Men and women who once had the power of an engine but they got slack and absented themselves from the Lord's table and this morning they are spiritually dead.

It is a memorandum, seal and pledge—This do in remembrance of Me. The passover was a type of remembrance. This do in remembrance of Me. I am going to finish my task. I am going to complete my work, and I want you to do this in remembrance of Me as I have given my blood for you. This do in remembrance of Me.

Terms Frequently Not Defined

In the 100 sermons, the word "sin" or "sinner" is used 68 times; but in no case is either word defined. Ten per cent. of the hundred sermons advised people to "trust God" or "wait on Jesus" without explaining what it means to "trust God." The meaning of religion is often vague; especially is this true of other-worldly sermons. Examples follow.

We can rejoice, if we know our sins have been forgiven—if we know Jesus has taken our sins upon himself. Oh, how glorious is that feeling. It is a glorious feeling to be relieved of our sins.

In almost each instance, sin is taken for granted and the pastor talks about it in vague, abstract terms. Sin is given as the cause of the depression without defining it and without showing casual relations.

"TRUST GOD AND ALL IS WELL"

Do not worry about those who leave you. God will bring you out all right. We find that David had to go away. But when the army came we find David up yonder on the hill waiting and trusting in God. It pays to serve Jesus. It pays every day, it pays every step of the way. The trouble with most of us is, we try to hide ourselves from Jesus. But it pays to serve Him. It comes hard sometimes, but just trust on. You may not have bread to eat, but my God has a plenty. . . . Serve God, trust Him, do right and He will fight your battles for you.

The greater the trust, the greater the preserving power of God. The children of Israel knew that God preserved the lives of those who put their trust in Him. They found the bank of the water and crossed in time to be saved from the enemy. He will destroy your prosecutor. Put your trust in God through Jesus. He will save you in the fiery furnace, in the lion's den. Put your trust in the Lord, because those who trust Him always make it. . . . But if you don't trust Him there is no progress. Enemies won't interfere with you because of your trusting God. If disease constantly harass you, and you wish to get rid of it, and it still hangs on, you are not making God your trust; if enemies harass you, you are not making God your trust, because when you are trusting God, He will give you words that will have driving power and you will be able to drive the man or woman away who is harassing you.

In many of the sermons there is a strong disposition to identify the church with religion; also to identify churchgoing and paying dues with being religious. God and Jesus are interchangeably used; and the gospel of faith is more pronounced than the gospel of works.

A Lack of Logic

In more than half of the sermons there is a lack of sequence and continuity; especially is this true in the other-worldly type of sermons. It is hardly possible that fifty-four sermons, with fifty-four different texts, could all logically end on the idea of heaven.

Period of Depression Makes Little Impression

This study was made in the very midst of that economic period, commonly referred to as the period of "Depression." The 100 sermons were collected between September, 1930, and November, 1931. Only six, or 6 per cent., of the sermons make any direct reference to the depression; and most of these are incidental statements and are negatively proclaimed. It might be implied that the 26 per cent. of this-worldly sermons deal with the depression indirectly. The two statements below are typical of the way reference is made to the depression.

Today I was coming to church, I stopped at the bootblack stand to get a shine. As the boy was shining my shoes, someone asked what was the cause of the depression. That ignorant boot-black answered "God is mad with the people." That is just about the keynote of it all at that.

I read in the *Literary Digest* that one of the causes of this period of depression was that folk were so busy buying luxuries that they couldn't buy necessities.

The God-Idea as Reflected in the Sermons

A man's conception of God may go a long way toward determining his conduct. The nation that believes that God is a God of war would hardly have any hesitancy in making all kinds of preparation for war, and may give little thought to the question of right. People who believe that God is a God of revenge would probably feel that it is quite all right to avenge the one who has wronged them. In like manner, those who actually believe in the kind of God that Jesus believed in would endeavor to regulate their conduct in the light of the God-idea as set forth by Jesus. But it is quite likely that those who believe that God will take care of them, that He will fight their battles if they will only pray, attend church, and pay their dues might take a do-nothing, "laissez-faire" attitude toward life and simply fold their hands at a time when real action is required.

GOD IS LOVE, MERCIFUL, AND FORGIVING

There are certain qualities that God has. Jesus said "God is Love." Therefore we say anyone who has love is like God, since love is an attribute of God. We call a loving person a godly person.

God is truth. It is a quality of God and anybody who is truthful in life is like unto God.

The godly characteristics—those characteristics that make up God—are truth, love, mercy, and justice. Paul calls them the godly qualities of godliness.

We do not know His fatherhood; we do not know of His tender mercy; we do not know His righteousness; we do not know His meekness and humility; we do not know His forgiveness; we do not know those qualities of God, except that we have seen them and do see them in Jesus Christ, and when we take Jesus Christ out, there is not much left of God. God in order to let us see Him as he is had to show Himself in the form of Jesus Christ and we can look at Jesus Christ and know what God is like. We can see Jesus forgiving the sinner. We can see Jesus humbling himself before his persecutors and we know the spirit of God is in him. We can see the meekness of Jesus. We can see how Jesus loved mankind in whatever walk of life. Therefore, we see how God loves all mankind.

GOD IS REVENGEFUL

The Lord spoke to Manasseh and the people and he tried to warn them of doing those things which created evil in the heart of God. But they would not heed God. We have so many folks today to whom God is speaking, trying to get them to repent, to listen, but they are stubborn. The Christian world is not in harmony with God and God is pleading for them to come back to Him, but the folks won't hear God. So God causes calamity to come unto them.

You are too busy with things of the world to stop and confer with God. You are compassed about with things of the world and saying that it is impossible for you to find time to work for God. God will lay such persons on the bed of affliction—too busy to serve Him.

A GOD OF DETERMINATION, CRUELTY AND ARBITRARINESS

The elect are God's children chosen before the world was. God foresaw that they would accept Jesus Christ by grace—God had his attitude toward Jacob and Esau before either was born as He knew what they would be.

TRUSTING GOD A PANACEA FOR ALL ILLS

If you know how to stay in touch with God, you can win any battle. David stayed in touch with God and he won his battle. I think sometimes we can be wonderful if we know how to stay in touch with God on our knees. I fear prayer has no charm for us. Mothers and fathers haven't got time to pray and yet they expect God to help them. Go back to the knee way. The hard times that are coming, the misunderstanding, they come because of a lack of prayer. Go back to prayer and God will fight your battle!

If a man's ways please God, he can be awake at the hour of midnight with a smile on his face and solve the problems and he will defeat those who try to retard his progress. He simply kneels down and tells God about his problems and God will solve it.

GOD THOUGH OMNIPOTENT EXPECTS US TO DO SOMETHING

There is one song I love and some Christians hide behind it. "Jesus paid it all." That does not mean that there is nothing for us to do because Jesus paid it all. It simply means that Jesus paid all that He was obligated to pay, but not that which we are obligated to pay. Jesus has not done our part and there is a part for you and a part for me to do. And God is not going to send His son down here to do our part. All of us have work to do. This church may not be what God wants it to be. And if He wanted to He could blow his breath and get rid of the trash and rubbish that is in the visible church, but He wants us to do that. That is our work.

GOD IS CREDITOR

We are indebted to God for creation. You may describe creation from the evolutionary point of view but we are indebted to God for creating us; not only that, but we are indebted to God for saving us, when we were lost in sin, before Moses cried from the bulrushes; and in due time Jesus came bearing the cross and brought salvation into the world. We are indebted to God for giving his son, also for the day and night, for permitting us to rise and face a new day each morning. There is nothing that we can do without God, not even eat without the assistance of God. We see by this time that we have quite a large account for which we are indebted. The next question is how much do we owe? If you will look about you, you will see that we have different talents. God wants us to use these to benefit humanity. Some of us have one talent and some of us have many talents. I want you to put them into use to benefit humanity. How are we to pay God? Let us consecrate to God our minds, thoughts, strength, and our time. These are the things God has given us with which we can pay Him back.

THE PURSUING GOD

The subject is "The Pursuing God." Jesus showed us this by using the parable of the ninety and nine. This shows us that we do not only pursue God, but that God is forever pursuing us. What a comfort it is this morning to know that God is ever seeking us. Satan may put blockades in the way but God goes in seeking to find what our cup of bitterness is.

Whenever you are scorned, rebuked, don't be discouraged, God is seeking you. Man seeking God is the romance of religion. We humble ourselves and kneel at the altar of God. This has been the story throughout the ages, but do we ever stress the fact that God is forever looking for us?

Let us talk over the various styles in which God pursues man. Let us review the story of Elijah. Elijah followed God because he realized that God was always with him, always seeking him. When he realized that his enemies were upon him he knew that those against him were not stronger than those that were for him. So I say again that the history of the race will be "God's pursuit of man."

God followed Abraham and had him to tell Sarah not to worry for deliverance would surely come. God goes out into the fields with David. God finds Job in the ash heap and there He speaks to Job telling Him to follow him.

We could go on enumerating thousands of ways in which God has pursued man if we only had the time. I do not need to tell you that it is never too late to know the good graces of God.

There is only one person who can give us the satisfaction that a Christian worker should have and that person is God.

I will cite a little incident that happened one evening while I was on my way home from work. This happened before I was in the ministerial work. I was walking down X street when a light snow was falling. I could see by the tracks in the snow that only two people had preceded me since the snowfall. When I looked ahead of me I saw two men running, one looked as if he was pursuing the other. I quickened my steps trying to see just what was the matter. Finally one of the men turned into the ——— Hotel, the other right behind him. When I reached the hotel I heard the first man tell the clerk that someone had been following him. The other man held up a wallet and asked him if it was his. The other man said, "Yes, there is ten thousand dollars in that wallet which I was going to deposit in the bank in the morning."

This shows us that many times we run from God while he is trying to pursue us. God calls to you today and wants you only to respond to that call. He is imploring you to listen to His call. If you will only heed His call you will be safe for all eternity.

GOD OF SPECIAL FAVORS

I knew a family during the world war that had four sons. They had a faithful father and a praying mother. After these boys had sailed and were fighting in the war, this mother came to my house and said to my mother, "The Lord told me that none of my sons will perish in Flanders' field." She said this in the heat of the war. She said the Lord said none of them would perish. When the war was over those boys came back and threw their arms around her and said, "Mother, we have come home." The Lord saved them, they did not perish.

OTHER CONCEPTS

Other concepts such as "God sees all that you do and hears all you say," "God is near and accessible at all times," "God is the maker of the world," "He is a universal God," are concepts that are quite prevalent.

Reverting to Type

One may possibly think that the highly other-worldly sermons, those that seem to be designed to make the people shout, are sermons preached by men whose academic standing is very meager. This is not necessarily the case. One of the four other-worldly sermons used as types is that of a college man. Easily 10 per cent. of the 54 distinctly other-worldly, shouting sermons are those preached by college graduates. To the contrary, among the 26 per cent. of this-worldly sermons are to be found those that were delivered by men who are not college-trained. It is frequently impossible to distinguish the college man's sermon from that of one who has had only high-school or less than high-school training. And this would seem to be because there is a precedent for that sort of preaching; and because of the persistence of the idea prevalent among many young men in the ministry and some of those anticipating the ministry, that one must give the people what they want; meaning, that the minister must appeal more to the emotions than to the intellect. This idea prevails in spite of living evidence to show that many of the most outstanding Negro churches are ministered to by men who do not strive to "shout" the people, and who do not specialize in other-worldly, highly emotional sermons.

It is a conviction of the writers that preachers often underestimate the intelligence of their audience and fail to give men and women of little formal training credit for being able to appreciate and follow a logical, constructive discourse. It is a further conviction that ministers frequently try to hide their own nakedness, their lack of preparation, when they resort to a type of preaching that seems to be designed to "shout" the people.

During the course of the study, the authors discussed the practice of "heavenly" preaching and excessive emotionalism in preaching, with a number of ministers. Almost invariably they condemned it and apologized for it. Many who condemned it were found doing it; and this may raise the question of the sincerity of the men who resort to that type of preaching.

The Passing of Excessive Emotionalism in Preaching

One of the strongest proofs, however, that the other-worldly, highly emotional type of preaching is passing is found in the difficulty the minister often experiences in getting the people to shout and say "Amen."

The shouting, highly emotional, sermon cannot survive
except in an atmosphere where the response is spontaneous
and warm; and two years' observation during the period of
this study would lead one to believe that the "shouting"
sermon is rapidly on the wane. A minister has to work too
hard to get a verbal response or shout. It was really pathetic
to watch a college graduate try to shout his audience during
three distinct intervals in his sermon by picturing a graphic
scene in heaven where his hearers would meet again their
beloved dead. There were two or three "amens"; but for the
most part the audience appeared indifferent, and each time
the minister had to retreat.

Reflecting the Experience of the Race

In slightly more than 65 per cent. of the this-worldly, and
in many of the other-worldly sermons, one is able to glimpse
the present social and economic problems that confront the
Negro. There is definiteness in many of them as to what a
minority group should do to make better adjustment to a
social and economic order constructed primarily to meet the
needs of the ruling majority.

The other-worldly sermons also reflect the experience of
the race. Other-worldliness is an element in the Christian
tradition. As the Christian teachings are accepted rather literally, it is not surprising that a high percentage of the 100
sermons are flavored with the idea of eternal salvation to be
experienced outside the processes of history. Church history
shows that to a large degree other-worldliness has at some
time characterized Catholicism, both Greek and Roman, and
practically all forms of Protestantism. It first arose in Jewish
history at a time when Israel had been subject for generations
to domination by one or another of the imperial powers.
When the Jewish people, after prolonged suffering and persecution, accepted the idea that they could never hope to gain
lasting political supremacy in this world, the belief in an age

to come in which justice would hold complete sway came more conspicuously to the front.

The other-worldly idea therefore finds fertile soil among the people who fare worst in this world; and it grows dimmer and dimmer as they get a strong social, economic and political foothold. It is pointed out in *Middletown* that "it is in matters of belief that the churches apparently retain their most complete dominance over the lives of their members in certain groups of the working class, who on the one hand, have less opportunity for other approaches to problems than the business class, and, on the other, have fewer enjoyments in this life and more urgent needs," that "it will be made up to us in Heaven." [1]

With the Negro, it could hardly have been otherwise. His 244 years of slavery, and the continuous proscriptions inflicted upon him since his emancipation, have been all conducive to developing an other-worldly view in which the righteousness of God would be vindicated and this suffering people delivered. Seeing little or no hope in this world, the Negro has done what other people have done, he has projected his hopes in a heaven above.

There are no available historical data on this subject with which the findings of this study can be compared. One can surmise, though, from experience and observation, that the emphasis on the other world among Negroes is becoming less and less pronounced. The educational and cultural levels of the Negro are being rapidly raised; he is getting a firmer economic hold; and there is some reason to believe that the restrictions in the environment are being slightly relinquished. Future studies bearing on this point will probably show an increasing number of Negro ministers who seek primarily to relate religion to life in this world.

---

[1] Lynd, Robt. S., and Helen Morrell, *Middletown* (New York: Harcourt, Brace & Company, 1929), p. 405.

CHAPTER V

Membership in Urban Churches

The membership of the Negro urban church was specially studied because much regarding its composition, size and distinctive characteristics has remained unknown despite its great and ever-increasing importance. Many factors contribute to the desirability of a study of the membership in the urban church: the gradual exodus of the Negro since 1900, and especially since 1910, from the rural to urban centers; the increase in the number of urban churches and members, especially in northern cities, caused primarily by the migration; the significance of the store-front church in the North relative to problems of social and religious adjustment; the large membership size of the urban church when compared with the rural church; and finally the concentration of wealth in metropolitan areas. These factors will be discussed in turn in an analysis of the membership of the 609 urban churches of this study.

Economic and Social Causes of the Migration

In the period from 1910 to 1920, there was an economic upheaval that greatly affected the mobility of the Negro population. The World War put a stop to the influx of immigrants from Europe into the industrial centers of the North; and this created a demand for Negro labor. It is estimated that the number of foreign immigrants decreased from 1,218,480 in 1914 to 326,700 in 1915. Almost simultaneously in 1915 and 1916, there was a collapse of the one-crop system of the South, caused primarily by boll-weevil ravages; and this was aggravated by unusual floods in the principal cotton states during 1915.

Life on the farm became very unstable and precarious for the Negro. The old practice of mortgaging the crop before it was produced suddenly broke down. Hundreds and thousands of landlords dismissed their tenants and closed their commissaries by which thousands of Negroes lived. Banks and merchants could no longer afford to extend credit, since cotton could no longer be relied upon for security. In this situation, northern industries, since the number of foreign immigrants had decreased owing to the war, began to bid for Negro labor, offering attractive wages.[1]

Although this upheaval, resulting in the migrations, was largely economic in character, the movement of Negroes to urban centers was greatly accelerated by the inadequacies of the rural school system in the South; the disfranchisement of Negroes in almost the whole of the South; the inhuman and brutal treatment of Negroes in the courts; the inferior accommodation on railroads; lynchings; and the fear of the mob.[2] From 1889 to 1914, there were 2,256 Negroes lynched, principally in the South.[3]

Numerical Result of the Migration

The drift of the Negro population from rural to urban centers from 1900 to 1920 caused the Negro city population to increase 1,557,465, while that of rural areas increased only 71,572. The cityward movement took place slowly from 1900 to 1910; but rapidly from 1910 to 1920 and from 1920 to 1930. T. J. Woofter explains in *The Economic Status of the Negro*:

The movement from 1900 to 1910 merely drained off some of the natural increase of the southern rural districts, leaving a slight increase in Negro rural population. But from 1910 to 1920

---

[1] Scott, Emmett J., *Negro Migration During the War* (New York: Oxford University Press—American Branch), pp. 14 ff.

[2] *The Negro in Chicago* (University of Chicago Press, 1922), ch. iii.

[3] National Association for the Advancement of Colored People, 69 Fifth Avenue, New York.

and 1920 to 1930 the movement was so rapid that the cities not only absorbed all the natural increase of the country districts, but actually depleted the rural population by about one-half million in twenty years.[4]

In other words, from 1910 to 1920, the Negro city population increased 874,676; from 1920 to 1930, more than a million Negroes moved from the southern rural district—650,000 to southern cities and 450,000 to northern cities.[5]

The Effect of the Migration upon the Church

This shift of the Negro population has led to a rapid increase in the number of urban churches and an increase in membership, especially in northern centers. According to the *Federal Census of Religious Bodies,* there were in 1916 a total of 127 Negro Baptist churches in Chicago, Detroit, Cincinnati, Philadelphia and Baltimore. In 1926, the *Federal Census of Religious Bodies* reported 319 Negro Baptist churches in these five cities, an increase of 151 per cent. The reported membership of the 127 churches in 1916 was 59,863; the membership of the 319 in 1926 was reported to be 178,637, an approximate increase of 200 per cent. The number of African Methodist Episcopal churches increased in these five cities from 37 in 1916 to 83 in 1926, an increase of 124 per cent.; the membership increased from 18,973 to 35,183, an increase of 85 per cent.

The increase in the South during the same period was much less marked. Charleston, Birmingham, Memphis, New Orleans and Richmond had a total of 278 Negro Baptist churches in 1916; the number had increased to 304 in 1926, an increase of 9 per cent. The Baptist membership increased during the same decade from 76,049 to 100,808, an increase of slightly less than 33 per cent. The number of African Methodist Episcopal churches in six southern cities, including

---

[4] Woofter, T. J., *The Economic Status of the Negro* (Institute for Research and Social Science, University of North Carolina), pp. 24–25.

[5] *Ibid,* pp. 24–25.

Atlanta, was 68 in 1916 and 81 in 1926; and the membership was 20,273 in 1916 and 22,678 in 1926. This gave an increase of 19 per cent. in the number of churches, and slightly less than 12 per cent. in membership. Proportionate increases are revealed in other Negro denominations, especially the Methodist Episcopal, the Colored Methodist Episcopal, and the African Methodist Episcopal Zion.

THE INCREASE WAS PROBABLY GREATER

Since the number of Negro churches located during this study by a street to street canvass is so much greater than the number given in the *Federal Census of Religious Bodies* for 1926, it is safe to conclude that the census reports are probably too conservative; and that many churches, recorded in this study, were not reported to the Government in 1926. It is the belief of the authors, therefore, that the increase in the number of churches and that of membership in these cities between 1916 and 1926 was appreciably greater than that revealed by the *Federal Census of Religious Bodies*. The Negro urban church has, therefore, been placed in a position to become an important factor in the adjustment of the rural Negro to the social, civic, religious and economic conditions of the city, all of which differ widely from those in rural areas.

THE PROBLEM OF ADJUSTMENT AND THE STORE-FRONT CHURCH

How well the urban church was prepared to assimilate the rural Negro into its membership and to assist him to become adjusted to city church life, one can hardly say with certainty. There was some adjustment in program, as chapter vii will show. Church-membership increased as this chapter and chapter x reveal. But that the rural and small-town Negro sought to adjust himself religiously in the city, and especially in the North, is readily seen by the following examples, which make it plain that many migrants did not feel at home in the city church, and possibly that the city church was not prepared for the emergency caused by the migration:

I. A man in Detroit, deacon in a store-front church, told one of the workers that he could not pray in a big church. Further inquiry into the meaning of this statement revealed that the deacon really meant that he could not pray in the big Detroit church as he was accustomed to praying in the rural church of the South. His long, loud prayer would not be in place in the semi-sophisticated Detroit church. He therefore organized a church of his own.

II. In Detroit, a pastor of a house church told one of the writers how he happened to organize a church. He stated that he talked with a large number of southern people who desired a church similar in worship to the churches in the rural South. As a minister, this man felt obliged to start a church for these people.

He expressed the conviction that many Negroes in Detroit, formerly faithful church people in the South, had suffered moral and religious shipwreck because they could not make the necessary adjustment and the resident Christians did not always have the requisite sympathy, imagination, and resourcefulness to make them feel at home and to introduce them gradually to new ways of life and thought. An hour's interview with this pastor disclosed the fact that for forty years he had been a leader in the rural South—pastor, moderator of conventions and associations, and a big man in his lodge; now, he was suddenly thrust into an environment in which leadership in church and other areas was so completely monopolized that he could hardly hope to be the leader he once was. It is not to be wondered at that this man organized a church in his house. These psychological factors are not only basic elements in discussing the effect of migration on the increase in the number of urban churches, but basic also in a consideration of the increase of church-membership in urban areas. Many members of store-front and house churches would forsake the church altogether if the big churches were the only reliance.

URBAN CHURCH-MEMBERSHIP RELATIVELY HIGH

A study of the membership of urban churches is also important because even though the cities have slightly less than 24 per cent. of the churches, they have slightly more than 43 per cent. of the reported membership. Since the large and more significant Negro churches are concentrated in cities, the best-trained Negro ministers are also found there. This drift of the Negro population from the rural to the urban areas has also been accompanied by a larger concentration of Negro wealth and finance in metropolitan centers. According to the *Federal Census of Religious Bodies,* the expenditures of Negro urban churches in 1926 were slightly more than 61 per cent. of the expenditures for all Negro churches, although the urban churches comprise only 23.9 per cent. of the entire number of Negro churches. Thus the Negro urban church is becoming increasingly more important in Negro life.

On the basis of 10,158 Negro urban churches with an estimated membership of 2,238,871, there is an urban Negro church for each 220 members. If these figures of the Federal census are correct, the 609 churches of this study constitute approximately 6 per cent. of the total number of Negro urban churches, and their membership is slightly less than 16 per cent. of the total urban membership.

An Analysis of Church-Membership in 609 Urban Churches

THE PROBLEM

The membership here given of the 609 churches, even though pains were taken by the investigators to check the reported membership wherever feasible, can be only an estimate of the actual membership. The difficulty springs from the lack of an adequate method of recording the membership in many of the churches. It is shown elsewhere in this volume that a goodly number of the churches do not have paid secretaries, and that churches that do have them usually pay such meager salaries that they cannot demand either full time or efficiency.

"Nobody knows," said one minister, "how many folk are in a Baptist church. Reverend A. counts about one hundred members that I count." A Methodist minister said:

Some ministers pad their reports in order to impress the conference and the bishop that they are doing a great work; while others minimize the number of their members for the purpose of reducing financial assessments. A goodly number of the ministers consider it a reflection to report to the conference fewer members than their predecessors did even though they may actually find a smaller number than the previous pastors reported. There are still others who are accurate in their records.

Another minister expressed it this way:

It is difficult to keep up with the people who join the church. Quite a few of them are renters and roomers. They move frequently, leaving no addresses. Many of them leave the city without notice, or join other churches in the city on Christian experience, in which cases they never get their letters of dismissal.

OCCUPATIONS OF MEMBERS

The pastors and officers of 575, or 94.4 per cent., of the churches are of the opinion that the overwhelming majority of their members are either domestic servants or laborers, or a combination of the two, and that only 2.4 per cent. have memberships in which skilled tradesmen, business and professional people are in the majority.

WOMEN MORE HIGHLY CHURCHED THAN MEN

Relative to the number of members as to sex, no statistical data were obtained on the 609 churches. Observation with respect to attendance shows that women are usually in the majority, often approximating a two-to-one ratio. It is the opinion of pastors that there are more women members than men, and that women do more of the church work. A study covering a larger scope than this one in regard to the sex of members, shows that women are more highly churched than men.

The number of colored women 13 years of age and over included on the rolls of Negro churches represents 73 per cent. of the total number living in the United States, while for white women this ratio is 62 per cent. Interestingly enough, Negro men not only make a far lower showing than colored women, but even lower than the white men. Only 46 per cent. of all adult Negro men are in church, compared with 49 per cent. among the white men. These findings tend to explode the idea that the church has a peculiar hold upon Negro temperament. Certainly, if interest in organized religion was primarily the result of a racial attitude of mind, this factor should influence Negro men as well as women.[6]

METHODS OF RECRUITING MEMBERS

The methods of recruiting members have changed somewhat in recent years. Five hundred and sixty-one churches had one or two revivals the year previous to the interviews, or something equivalent to a revival such as a period of prayer or Lenten observance, as a means of reviving the church and recruiting members. In addition, each service is considered evangelical or revivalistic in all of the churches, in the sense that an invitation is extended to those in the audience who may care to join. The invitation is democratic—in only one case would one have reason to believe that a few members actually planned to have it otherwise. In this instance, some of the members did not want the pastor to open the doors of the church; but instead to let the members of the church

---

[6] Fry, C. Luther, *The U. S. Looks At Its Churches* (New York: Institute of Social and Religious Research, 1930), p. 11.

recommend the people they desired to have as members. In three or four churches, the spirit seemed current that "ours are aristocratic churches and are not for the common herd." It is the opinion, however, of some of the laymen of these churches, and the pastor of one of them, that this exclusiveness is not good for these churches and that they are slowly dying. The pastor just referred to said: "This church is too hidebound to grow. It is bound by tradition and an aristocracy that means nothing."

THE PROFESSIONAL EVANGELIST PASSING

Of the 561 pastors who ran revivals the year previous to the field work of the study, 341 stated whether it was an evangelist, the pastor, or a visiting pastor who conducted the revival. Seventy per cent. of them either conducted their own revival or invited other pastors, leaving 30 per cent. who used only evangelists, or a combination of pastor and evangelist.

This high percentage is not significant in itself; but the reasons the pastors gave for not using a professional evangelist are significant. A few expressions follow:

I prefer another pastor. He understands the needs of the church and is more concerned with permanent results.

An evangelist draws more people, but his results are less effective.

Professional evangelists excite the people, and it is hard to straighten them out after they go. They commercialize their messages. The people have more confidence in pastors.

The evangelist over-persuades. He wants numbers.

It takes three years to straighten the people out after the evangelist has gone.

If you get a sensationalist, the effect is short-lived and the people are worse off after the revival than before it.

It is my experience that people who join the church under the excitement of evangelists, who exploit the emotions, do not make very faithful members, although there are notable exceptions.

These expressions, and the percentage of men who prefer other pastors to professional evangelists in membership recruiting, seem to say that the life of the sensational evangelist is short-lived and that a different type of revival is being demanded. Among those who had no revival last year, a good many expressed the view that each Sunday is evangelical and a revival of the old type is not desired.

AN APPEAL TO FEAR

The statements quoted above would lead one to infer that the pastor's basis of appeal in recruiting members differs widely from that of the professional evangelist. It is to be noted, however, that the method employed by the pastor is not wholly different. It is rather commonly found that in the minister's appeal the element of fear is played up; and quite often it is the only ideal held up to the individual as the reason why he should join the church. The pastors and the evangelists frequently exploit the emotions by proclaiming the obvious, such as:

Before next week this time some one in this audience may be called to meet his God.

You had better cast your lot with God's people. You do not know what is going to happen to you. You may be killed on your way home. (This is sometimes followed by the tragic story of a John Doe who was killed recently or died suddenly.)

You should prepare to meet your mother in heaven.

Even when the appeal connects with a higher type of ethical or moral living for a more constructive and fruitful life in this world, to gain heaven or shun hell is often the ultimate reward for that quality of life. The pastor's appeal is not as spectacular as that of the evangelist, but in essence it is the same. It is not this way in every case; but it is to be feared that it is more often this way than otherwise—the men who do it differently are the exceptions and they are rare. Frequently no reason at all is given for inviting one to join the church.

THE LACK OF A UNIFORM BASIS OF MEMBERSHIP

There is no uniformity among the churches for determining the basis of membership. This is often true of churches of the same denomination; it is wholly true of churches of different denominations. Some churches actually consider as members all the people they have taken in over a period of years, including the dead, the backsliders, and the non-resident people whose names are enrolled elsewhere. Many churches decide the membership on the basis of registration, excluding people who do not register.

There are other churches that make finance the basis of membership and count as members only those who are in good financial standing, thus barring membership to sporadic workers and givers. Clearly the basis of membership in many of the churches is not very well defined.

EFFORTS AT ACCURACY

To the contrary, however, honest and courageous efforts are being made by an appreciable number of ministers to keep adequate accounts of their memberships. One pastor reported a membership of approximately 500; but hastened to add that the investigator should see the secretary who knew exactly how many members there were. The secretary not only had the names and addresses of the 520 members, but she makes a thorough check monthly of the entire membership. A pastor who said his membership was 600 advised the worker to check through the office of the secretary. The secretary had on record 625 members.

A progressive young minister was elected to the pastorate of an important church which for years had boasted of a membership of several thousands. Before the arrival of the new pastor, a roll had been given containing 1,462 names. The new pastor requested that he be given six months to comb the roll and locate the members of his church. At the end of the stated time, he sent to the office a roll of 687 members. Another minister was called to the pastorate of a church that reported 1,200 members. After making a thorough investigation, he found 400 people. In the interview, he gave 400 and not 1,200.

For the most part, the memberships reported by pastors, membership clerks, and secretaries were accepted by the workers. With the coöperation of ministers and secretaries, however, further checks were made in 106 churches, in which cases duplicates of church rolls were given; or the rolls were made accessible to the workers; or the number that had registered during the first six or eight months of the year was given. The result of this checking is referred to in another section of this chapter. Though accepting in the main the memberships as reported, this analysis should prove more accurate than those church reports collected through the mail where no method of checking is employed. In this study, the interviews were personal, and direct checks were made in the 106 cases.

TABLE IV—MEMBERSHIP SIZE OF 609 CHURCHES

	Number of Churches	Per Cent.
Less than 200	217	35.6
200– 400	141	23.2
400– 600	74	12.1
600– 800	47	7.7
800–1,000	34	5.6
1,000–1,200	18	3.0
1,200–1,400	13	2.1
1,400–1,600	18	3.0
1,600 and above	47	7.7
Total	609	100.0

More than half of the churches, 358, or 58.8 per cent., have fewer than 400 members; whereas 96, or 15.8 per cent., of the 609 churches report memberships of 1,000 and above.

TABLE V—NUMBER OF CHURCHES STUDIED AND THEIR MEMBER-
SHIP IN 12 CITIES

City	Number of Churches Studied	Combined Membership	Average Number per Church
Atlanta	49	30,428	621.0
Baltimore	50	32,124	642.5
Birmingham	55	30,770	559.5
Charleston	50	14,336	286.7
Chicago	56	56,189	1003.4
Cincinnati	51	20,414	400.3
Detroit	44	30,671	697.1
Houston	50	19,513	390.3
Memphis	51	22,374	438.7
New Orleans	51	11,769	230.8
Philadelphia	50	59,469	1189.4
Richmond	52	29,112	559.8
Total	609	357,169	586.5

A total of 609 churches with a combined membership of
357,169 makes an average of 586.5 members per church.
The average number of members per church as revealed by
the present study is believed to be more than average for
Negro churches generally. A closer approximation to the
average membership is the 220 members per church which is
reported in the *Federal Census of Religious Bodies*. This
preference for the census figures is supported by the fact that
in each of the twelve cities included in this study, the very
small churches are far more numerous than the large or the
very large ones, and this means that of the fifty churches,
more or less, studied in each of the twelve cities, proportionately more of the large churches were studied than of the
small or very small ones. A few churches reporting exceptionally large memberships would probably make the sample
somewhat weighty at the upper end. For example, Philadelphia reports a church that claims 12,000 members. It would
take 120 small churches with 100 members each to equal that
one church. The general membership of the 609 churches,
though representative of the 609, could hardly be accepted
as representative of the average membership per church on
the basis of the total number of churches in the twelve cities.

A more representative case is presented in chapter xi where the total number of churches is set over against the estimated number of adults who are church-members. The four cities that have the highest averages per church, Philadelphia, Detroit, Baltimore, and Chicago, as will be seen in chapter xi, are the cities that are less churched than the other eight cities included in the study. The average per church would naturally be greater in those cities that have relatively fewer churches.

MORE MEMBERS PER CHURCH IN THE NORTH THAN IN THE SOUTH

Of the 609 churches, 251, or 41.2 per cent., are northern churches with a combined membership of 198,867, or an average of 792.3 members per church. The remaining 58.8 per cent., or 358 churches, are in the South and have a combined membership of 158,302, or an average of 442.2 members per church.

When one considers the periods of the migratory movements from the South to the North since 1915, it is not surprising that the 251 churches in the North report more members than the 358 churches in the South. Census data from the Department of Commerce show that the Negro population in Chicago increased from 109,458 in 1920 to 233,903 in 1930; in Detroit from 40,838 in 1920 to 120,066 in 1930; in Philadelphia from 134,229 in 1920 to 219,599 in 1930.

In no instance, in the southern cities studied, was the percentage of increase as great as the places just indicated. In fact, the total increase in the Negro population from 1920 to 1930 in six of the seven southern cities included in the study, Atlanta, Birmingham, Memphis, New Orleans, Houston and Richmond, was from 383,138 to 531,659; an actual increase of 148,521, or 38.8 per cent. The increase during the same decade for Chicago, Detroit, Philadelphia, Cincinnati and Baltimore was from 422,926 in 1920 to 763,492 in 1930; an actual increase of 340,566, or 80 per cent. The Negro population in Charleston, S. C., along with that for the entire city was less in 1930 than it was in 1920. Interviews with ministers and church officials support the contention that as a result of migration, Negro churches in the North almost grew over night from memberships of a few hundreds to thousands. While the southern city church may have relatively held its own owing to natural growth and the migration of rural people to southern cities, the northern church, especially in great migration centers like Chicago, Detroit and Philadelphia, grew by leaps and bounds.

THE ACTUAL MEMBERSHIP IN 106 CHURCHES

"Actual" as used here refers to the membership in 106 churches based on the number obtained from church rolls and data received from registration clerks as to the number registered during the first six or eight months of the year. It is used to distinguish it from "reported" membership, which is the number given the investigator at the time of the interview. The "actual" membership is used to check the "reported" membership.

REPORTED MEMBERSHIP HIGHLY INFLATED

The reported membership in 106 churches is 136,260. The actual membership of the same 106 churches is 83,241, or 61 per cent. of the reported membership. In some churches, the actual membership coincided with the reported membership. In a few, the actual membership was more than had been reported. But in the majority of cases, the actual membership was discovered to be considerably less than that reported, as revealed by the 39 per cent. discrepancy in comparing the reported with the actual membership in the 106 churches.

It is more than probable that a thorough check on the churches that have accurate rolls, and the results of campaigns to discover actual members on the part of churches without adequate records, would show a much wider discrepancy between the number of reported and of actual members than the 39 per cent. to which reference has already been made. For example, one church reported a membership of 3,000. The church roll contained exactly 1,549. It was an old church roll which carried the names of the dead, names of those no one could locate, and the names of many who were known to have lived in other cities for years. Even church rolls are not necessarily adequate checks as to actual membership. It is the opinion of the writers that on the basis of the 106 churches checked, and the experience gained in the study, it would be a rather conservative act if the total reported membership were reduced 39 per cent. This discrepancy of 39 per cent. between the actual and reported membership leads one to infer strongly that a thorough check of the church statistics accepted by the Federal Government in compiling the material for the religious census would reveal similar discrepancies, and that the reports as now given are highly padded.

THE FINANCIAL LOAD IS CARRIED BY LESS THAN HALF OF THE MEMBERSHIP

Of the 586.5 members, which is the average per church in the 609 churches, the average number of regular contributors is 256.7 persons, or 43.8 per cent. of the reported membership. On this basis, the financial load of the churches is carried, in the main, by less than half of the membership; or 56.2 per cent. of the membership cannot be relied upon for any dependable financial help.

MORNING AND EVENING ATTENDANCE RELATIVELY SMALL

The reported membership is 357,169. The combined average attendance at the regular eleven o'clock service of the 609 churches is 151,745, giving an average attendance of 249.2 persons per church, or 42.5 per cent. of the total membership.

The per cent. of average attendance, 42.5, compares favorably with the per cent. of regular contributors, 43.8. On the average, 57.5 per cent. of church-members, or more, are not present at services on Sunday morning. The evening services do not compare favorably with the morning services. In a few isolated cases, the evening congregations are larger than those of the morning, or are equal to them; but these instances are rare. The average evening attendance per church is 130.4, slightly more than half of that reported for the morning services. There is no way to check the number of visitors who worship in these churches. It is obvious, however, that if an investigation could be made at this point, it would show that the average attendance on the part of the membership would be considerably reduced. It must also be stated that the average Sunday membership attendance at church cannot be appraised by attendance at any one service. Many people go to church only once on a Sunday; and it may be to attend Sunday school, eleven o'clock service, young people's society or evening worship.

ATTENDANCE AT PRAYER MEETING NEGLIGIBLE

Three hundred and eighty-eight churches gave 15,156 as the attendance at the mid-week services or prayer meetings. On this basis, the average attendance per church at prayer meetings is 39; or 6.7 per cent. of 226,748, the combined membership of the 388 churches.

PROBABLE IMPLICATIONS

The very small attendance at the night services and prayer meetings when compared with the total membership and the attendance at the eleven o'clock services, can be explained in part by the fact that nothing very attractive goes on at these services. Ordinarily the minister preaches his best and most effective sermon in the morning. He is not only physically less fit at night, but he is mentally less prepared. As for the prayer meetings, they are usually of the traditional kind: songs, long prayers, lectures and testimonies. They do not appeal to the older members, to say nothing of youth. A few pastors who have made special efforts to make the evening service of equal quality with that of the morning service, and who have put themselves whole-heartedly into the prayer meetings, testify that the night services and prayer meetings can be made effective and constructive.

THE EXCESSIVELY LARGE CHURCH

If a church of 500 members reports that 250, or 50 per cent., of its members are regular donors, does it of necessity follow that a church of 1,000 members would have 500, or 50 per cent., of its members regular contributors? Would the percentage be the same if there were 3,000 members?

When the 609 churches are divided into groups according to size of membership, it is discovered that the percentage of contributors is a rather constant quantity up to a membership of 2,000—that is, the percentage of donors is almost uniformly 49 per cent. in the four groups, less than 500, from 500 to 1,000, from 1,000 to 1,500, and from 1,500 to 2,000. But from 2,000 upward there is a decided decrease in the percentage of contributors as related to the membership. Table 16 in the Appendix illustrates the point under discussion on the basis of a grouping of 1,000.

Stated another way, in churches with fewer than 2,000 members, the percentage of contributors is 49.6; whereas in churches with enrollments of 2,000 and above, the percentage of members who give is 33.0, a decline of 16.6 per cent. Table 16 in the Appendix also shows a similar decline in the percentage of average attendance in churches with memberships beyond 2,000; it shows that in the churches with memberships less than 2,000 the percentage of average attendance is 48.5; in churches of 2,000 members and above, it is 31.4 per cent., or a decrease of 17.1 per cent.

ORGANIZATIONAL AND EDUCATIONAL IMPLICATIONS OF THE LARGE
CHURCH

In essence, this decline in the percentage of regular contributors and average attendance beyond 2,000 members
means that the larger the church the more organizing genius
is required to make it function proportionately and effectively. Educationally, it signifies that the larger the church
the more impersonal the institution becomes, in that it is
increasingly more difficult for the pastor and his staff to
administer to the individual needs of all or most of the members. These findings may not be arguments against exces-
sively large churches, but they certainly are arguments in
favor of better-organized churches; especially when the memberships are very large. If close personal relationship on the
part of the pastors and members is a desirable thing, then
from the point of view of educational procedure, the exces-
sively large church may not be an asset.

THE MEMBERSHIP PROBABLY INCREASING

No adequate and reliable answer can be given to the question as to whether the membership of the 609 churches is
increasing. Most of them show increases. The number of
members taken in during the year is usually reported as being
in excess of the number lost. But the churches are more likely
to keep a better record of the number of people added to the
church than of the number of people lost to the church. The
former is easier. Furthermore, the authors were not able to
get enough uniform data on membership increases or decreases during the last decade to enable them to speak with
authority on this point.

It must suffice to rely upon a previous study, which in
regard to membership covers a wider scope than the present
one. In analyzing the *Federal Census of Religious Bodies*
for 1926, Dr. Fry states:

The relative number of Negroes in church has increased appreciably since 1906, while the proportion for the whites has changed but little. In 1906, only 39.1 per cent. of all Negro men were on the rolls of a church compared with 45.5 per cent. now; for Negro women these proportions are 64.4 and 73.1 respectively.[7]

Dr. Fry points out, however, that most of these increases occurred during the decade 1906 to 1916. Nevertheless, it is safe to conclude that the membership in the 609 churches studied here is increasing.

There are three outstanding revelations in this chapter which should challenge the attention of church people:

1. That more than half of the reported membership in these churches is relatively idle, leaving the work of the church to be carried on by less than half of the members.

2. That the reported membership is highly inflated, as is proved in the case of 106 churches, and that if it were reduced by 39 per cent., the reduction would probably be conservative.

3. That there is a limit in the number of church-members beyond which the percentage of average attendance, and that of regular contributors, decrease appreciably; and that, for the most part, the big church with membership beyond 2,000 is not an asset unless there is exceptional genius in organization and church management.

---

[7] Fry, C. Luther, *op. cit.*, p. 50.

CHAPTER VI

Church Buildings

In addition to getting an acceptable minister, and a large membership, there is little doubt that most churches consider an adequate church building a necessity. The emphasis placed upon the building supports the belief that it is one of the chief concerns of the church. If one were to question why massive stone or brick buildings or even humble store-fronts should be of such importance, the answer may be revealed in the evidence that the building not only symbolizes the church but often assumes the potency of the higher thing it is supposed to symbolize. Sentiment serves to enforce the authority of the church through its building. This authority is demonstrated in several ways. A church without a building seldom receives recognition as a church. In preceding chapters it was brought out that after the Negro church movement was started the pride of ownership, self-direction and management was largely expressed by the possession of places of worship. No other single objective in the history of the Negro group has commanded the degree of financial support from members and even non-members like that of church buildings. Not even educational institutions, fraternal orders, business and the like.

For example, later, in chapter x, it is shown that although the economic status of many congregations is unstable and generally weak, they continue to make large commitments for property. Expenditures for interest and reduction of the church debt, together with the relatively small payments for upkeep and maintenance, so deplete the funds of many churches that they can do very little more than buy a building. And in spite of all other demands the congregations continue to support these buildings. Since the hold of the building is so strong and commands such sacrifices, an examination of this phase of present church equipment is important.

Today the buildings are of three kinds, namely: conventional church buildings; residences; and storerooms, usually called "store-fronts," formerly occupied by groceries, drugstores and other small business enterprises.

The residence and store-front churches are primarily emergency quarters for churches that look forward to owning conventional church buildings later on. These emergency quarters at times acquire aspects of permanency, especially when a church's occupancy lasts ten or fifteen years, as has happened in many instances in New Orleans, Richmond, Chicago and Detroit.

A residence or a storeroom usually has for the congregation that long occupies it all of the attributes of a conventional church building, and it is seldom used for any other than church purposes.

The major first impressions regarding the buildings of the 609 urban churches of this study may be gained from these facts; that 561, or 92.1 per cent., of them are of the conventional type; 35, or 5.8 per cent., are store-fronts; and 13, or 2.1 per cent., are residences.

The conventional church buildings make, of course, the most impressive appearance. The majority, 344, or 61 per cent., are of brick and stone construction; while 217, or 39 per cent., are frame and stucco buildings.

It should not be assumed, however, that all of the brick and stone buildings are good, and that all of the frame and stucco are poor, in appearance. Such an assumption would not hold true with these buildings, because the general upkeep, age, and state of completion are important in judging the condition of each building.

Study of the 609 buildings shows that 16 of them are in very good condition, well built, painted, clean, and in good repair. A shade of difference in upkeep distinguishes 171 buildings as good, while the largest number, 240, are in fair condition.

The buildings that are definitely poor because they are in need of repair, paint, and general renovation comprise 182, or something over one-fourth, of the 609 churches.

Building Sites

The church sites are usually in Negro districts or neighborhoods. There are relatively few down-town churches for Negroes. The great majority, in so far as their building sites are concerned, are neighborhood churches. The Negro church, like other racial churches, usually follows the neighborhood expansion. And the number of churches found in white or partly white neighborhoods is very small. Of the 609 urban churches of this study 308, or one-half, are located in what appear to be permanent Negro neighborhoods; 137, about one-fourth, in localities in which the Negro residents are increasing; and 108 in localities where the Negro population is decreasing; while 33 are on the border of Negro neighborhoods. At least 78.3 per cent. of the churches are well located. The remaining 21.7 per cent. are in white neighborhoods, business sections, or depopulated Negro neighborhoods.

Building Interiors

The secondary impressions of the churches come from the interior of these same buildings. The auditorium, which in some churches is entered immediately from the street, sets the standard for the building in virtually all churches and is the main room. It is customarily the largest room in the building; and in 140, or about a quarter of the 609 urban churches, it is the only room.

In addition to the 609 auditoriums, there are 2,241 rooms in the 469 churches that have more than an auditorium. These rooms are distributed according to use: 469 basements, 158 offices, 331 pastor's study rooms, 281 classrooms, and

1,002 auxiliary and service rooms. The actual distribution of the 2,850 rooms per church, including all of the auditoriums, may be found in the Appendix.[1] The aggregate seating capacity of the church auditoriums is 322,400. Of the 609 churches, 93 will seat fewer than 200 persons, 188 will seat between 200 and 400 persons, 118 will seat up to 600, and the seating in 210 of the churches ranges from 600 upward to 2,000 and over with 2,500 as the outside limit.[2]

Additional Buildings and Ground

Buildings and grounds in addition to the main church building and its site are not common among Negro churches. Thirty-four of the 609 churches have an additional building. These buildings are used for educational purposes by ten of the churches, and as orphans', old folks' and girls' homes by twenty-four churches. The thirty-four buildings do not include the parsonages or rent-houses and other property owned by the churches.

There are sixty-two churches that own vacant ground, and four of these use this property for recreational purposes.

The general appearance of the church buildings, and the fact that over three-quarters of them are well located in or near Negro neighborhoods, have much to do with attracting and holding members. New people coming into the community, and old residents without other influences such as denominational affiliations or friendships, often gravitate toward the churches with the larger and better buildings. On the basis of these facts alone, the leaders in a number of churches have assumed that a big church building is a prerequisite for a powerful church.

If the building is adequate in size, arrangement, and location, the program is greatly helped. If, however, the building

[1] See Appendix Table 17.
[2] See Appendix Table 19.

is inadequate in these respects, the program must often be one-sided and ineffective.

The determining principle in erecting or purchasing any new church building is that the plan should be suggested by the kind of program that the members and the community need and can maintain. This leads naturally to a consideration of the program of the Negro church.

CHAPTER VII

The Program of the Church

Although the programs of the Negro churches are occasionally marked by distinctive features, they have from the beginning followed in general the pattern set up by the white churches. This fact is not surprising when it is recalled that the public services, preaching, prayer services, Sunday schools, and auxiliary organizations that characterized the early white church were the heritage of the Negro church.

The Influence of the Past

From this early time, the program of the Negro church has included those things common to most churches of the working classes and people of ordinary means. However, in more recent years, especially since the cityward movement of Negroes, there have been definite demands upon the churches for a richer program. The increase in the number of churches and in their memberships, particularly in the North, together with the growth of Negro urban populations both North and South, have made such activities as the Sunday church school, the young people's work, the worship services, and the fellowship and community activities vitally more important. The nature of these activities, including their strong and weak features, will be discussed.

Representative Programs

The reactions of the church to the new stimuli toward modified programs presented by the migration have been various. Many churches, both North and South, have retained unchanged the traditional program inherited from the parent church, except for the addition of one or two general social

119

features. A growing number, however, have definitely expanded the traditional program; or have added specialized non-religious activities, particularly of the social and community-serving type.

THE ADDITION OF NON-RELIGIOUS FEATURES

The "B" church, which shows the addition of social activities, is located in Chicago, has a membership of 529, and a yearly current expense budget of approximately $7,117. Besides the traditional activities, the church conducts Boy Scout activities, basket-ball teams for both sexes, and a vacation church school. The church building is equipped with a small gymnasium, lockers and showers. The minister, who holds both A.B. and B.Th. degrees, has had eight years' pastoral experience and has been at this church six months. He receives a salary of $3,000, while the part-time religious education and recreational director receives $600 yearly. Churches similar to this one generally do not have any paid worker other than the pastor, as is indicated in the next description.

Church "C," in Baltimore, has a membership of 1,000, pays its pastor $2,000 yearly, and has no other professional employee. The minister holds three degrees: A.B., S.T.B., and B.D. He has had sixteen years' experience as a pastor and has been at this church five months. The yearly budget is $4,230 for current expenses. In addition to the traditional activities, the church has volley-ball and basket-ball teams.

INTENSIVE PROGRAMS OF NON-RELIGIOUS FEATURES

Churches "D" and "E" are examples of those that are attempting especially to emphasize non-religious activities, particularly those intending to serve social and community needs.

The "D" church is located in a northern city and has a membership of approximately 1,300. Out of its yearly current expense budget of $14,825, it pays its pastor $2,800 and its social-work secretary $1,200 yearly. The pastor, who has had some college and seminary work, has spent two of his twenty-eight years in the ministry at this church, which owns and operates a community house equipped with offices, parlorrooms, clubrooms, dormitory quarters for young women, cafeteria, laundry, a gymnasium and a roof-garden. The church program consists of the traditional activities. The Sunday church school meets in an assembly room and three or four classrooms in the church building, and its program is decidedly traditional. In addition to its traditional activities, the church conducts a vacation church school, athletic teams, basket-ball, volley-ball, tennis and gymnastic work, Boy Scouts, Camp Fire Girls, Boy Rangers groups, and the community house referred to. Also included are handicraft, dramatic, and art classes. A number of other activities were listed in the "paper" program of the church, but were not being actually carried on at the time of the investigation.

The "E" church is located in a southern city. It has a membership of 215. The pastor holds A.B. and B.D. degrees. Six months of his ten years' pastoral experience had been at the church. In addition to the pastor, who receives $2,000 yearly, the church, with outside financial help, employs a general worker at $720, a social worker at $1,080, a nursery matron at $360 yearly, and six other people. The total current expense budget for the year is about $7,085. The church has a community house in addition to its church building. Its program includes the traditional church activities, an employment agency, a day-nursery, a clinic, and a kindergarten. Although this church is located in a community in which the facilities for Negro welfare are quite limited, it is finding it necessary to curtail some of its activities because of a lack of finances. It happens that a clear illustration is furnished here of one of the dangers attending when a church performs the special or technical social-welfare activities. The emphasis on these activities has served in a great measure to subordinate the regular church activities; and in the minds of the persons in charge, the church work seems to be secondary. When a comprehensive list of the activities taken from all the churches is examined, it appears that about ten activities and organizations are generally used. Those used by 100 per cent. of the churches are: preaching, union services and interchurch coöperation, missionary societies, and various forms of club work. Approximately all of the churches have a Sunday church school, give relief to the poor, and conduct revival meetings. About three-fourths or more have choirs, young people's work, and prayer meetings. Table VI shows a summary of forty activities included in the programs of the urban churches studied.

TABLE VI—ORGANIZATIONS AND ACTIVITIES OF 609 URBAN
CHURCHES, BY PER CENT. OF FREQUENCY

Number of Churches	Organizations and Activities	Per Cent. Frequency
609	Preaching	100.0
609	Union services and interchurch coöperation	100.0
609	Missionary societies	100.0
609	Clubs (Soc., Ed., Fin.)	100.0
608	Sunday church school	99.8
590	Poor relief	96.9
561	Revivals	92.1
503	Choirs	82.6
398	Young people's work	65.4
388	Prayer meetings	63.7
191	Recreational work	31.4
77	Pastors' aid boards	12.6
30	Gymnasium classes	4.9
22	Church papers	3.6
21	Extension work in missions	3.4
18	Feeding the unemployed	3.0
13	Junior churches	2.1
10	Daily vacation Bible school	1.6
6	Benevolent societies	1.0
5	Clinic (free)	0.8
5	Motion pictures	0.8
5	Coöperate-Y.W. and Y.M.C.A.	0.8
5	Girl Scouts	0.8
5	Boy Scouts	0.8
4	Kindergarten	0.7
3	Nurseries (day)	0.5

TABLE VI—ORGANIZATIONS AND ACTIVITIES OF 609 URBAN
CHURCHES, BY PER CENT. OF FREQUENCY—*Continued*

Number of Churches	Organizations and Activities	Per Cent. Frequency
2	Auto buses	0.3
2	Employment agency	0.3
2	Visiting nurse	0.3
2	Music classes	0.3
2	Brotherhood	0.3
2	Branch library of city	0.3
2	Homes for girls and old people	0.3
2	Public forums	0.3
2	Mid-week adult Bible class	0.3
1	Orphans' home	0.2
1	Health classes	0.2
1	Dramatic club	0.2
1	Lectures	0.2
1	Mission-study class	0.2

The Educational Activities

In the educational activities of the churches, the Sunday church schools are the most emphasized. Table VI shows that there are 608 Sunday church schools, 398 young people's groups, ten daily vacation church schools, and two formal week-day educational groups in the 609 urban churches.

THE SUNDAY CHURCH SCHOOL

The Sunday church school, although the most emphasized of the organized teaching activities, continues to follow historical and conservative methods. However, the methods of organization, pupil administration and accounting, the administration of the teaching staff, and the planning of the curriculum are becoming increasingly important. The gradual extension of education among Negroes has led to an increased demand for a type of religious training and experience that will help them make successful adjustments in life. The future work of the schools will depend largely upon the methods used to satisfy this demand. At present these schools do not vary widely in their methods.

THE ONE-DEPARTMENT SCHOOL PREDOMINATES

The one-department school, composed of all age-groups, administered by one general superintendent and set of officers, and generally using uniform lesson material, is most common in Negro churches. Its officers include a superintendent and an assistant, a secretary, and a treasurer. About 549, or 90.3 per cent. of the 608 schools, have one department only. In the remaining 59, or less than 10 per cent., there are forty-five schools with two departments, ten with three departments, one with four, and three with five. No school of the 608 is fully departmentalized.

In most of the churches the organization of the Sunday church school is definitely affected by the number and regularity of attendance, the available prepared leadership, and the available building equipment.

HOUSING THE SUNDAY CHURCH SCHOOL

Many churches find it difficult to departmentalize their Sunday church schools because of the limited space afforded by their buildings. In chapter vi it was shown that 140 of the 609 churches have one room only. One of these churches has no school. Thus 139 of the schools are narrowly proscribed by the inadequacy of the buildings. An additional eighty-four buildings have two rooms, making 224 churches with building space of two rooms or less. To overcome the difficulties of too little space, it is possible for Sunday church schools in these churches to rearrange their schedules and have sessions for different age-groups at different times. This method is working successfully in a few Negro churches; for example, the very young may come at 9:30 A. M., and older groups at 1:00 P. M.

Ten churches were found, however, with educational buildings; and 384 have available rooms ranging in number from three to twenty or more per church. The following are concrete illustrations of certain types of Sunday church school housing equipment and use.

Church "X," in a southern city, shows the possibilities of success arising from better use of building space. When first studied, this church held its entire school in the auditorium. The enrollment was approximately twenty people. The church building has three rooms suitable for the Sunday church school: the auditorium, capacity 500; a choir-room, capacity 30; and the pastor's study, which will accommodate 15 comfortably. Six months later, after this church began work on a suggested plan for using all of its available space, including the separation of classes in rooms where possible, its enrollment had increased from 20 to 55. This school, when last observed, planned to divide its session into two, a morning session for young children and a later one for seniors, young people and adults. If this plan is carried out, it will permit more intensive work with the particular age-groups present in each section. While these facts are encouraging, it must be understood that better use of building space will not result in success for every school, although almost any situation may be helped by this procedure.

Surely better use of present buildings is for many churches the one way out; because financially they are unable to enlarge their present plants or build new ones. Chapter x shows that the amount of present debts, overhead obligations, and current expense and upkeep leaves, for most churches, nothing whatever for expansion purposes. In other words, expansion of present equipment would mean an overloading of an already heavy financial burden.

On the other hand, there are many churches with an adequate number of rooms that are not being used.

Church "Y," in a northern city, is an example. Church "Y" has a Sunday church school of 200 members. There are nine classes. The building contains seven rooms besides the auditorium and pastor's study. Of these, only four are in actual use by the Sunday church school, although all are suitable, light and large.

Training in giving in the Sunday church schools has resulted in making this activity's offerings one largely of pennies. Since there are virtually no established, business-like methods of financing, the money for the schools is received through class collections, rallies, and special appeals; and by other methods designed simply to collect as much as possible. It is disbursed for the local church treasury, honorariums, literature, missions, conventions, entertainments and equipment.

The aggregate collected by the Sunday church schools during the fiscal year 1930, was $154,563. This amount is 5 per cent. as large as the total reported by the churches. Table 20 in the Appendix shows the finances of churches and Sunday church schools according to memberships.

The administration of the finances of the church and of the Sunday church school is entirely separate in three-fourths of the churches.

SCHOOL ENROLLMENT RELATIVELY SMALLER IN LARGE CHURCHES

The membership of most of the Sunday church schools is less than half the church-membership.

The aggregate enrollment in the schools is 109,865, while the aggregate church-membership is 357,169. Fully 75 per cent. of those who attend the schools are children. The Sunday church school enrollment is 40.7 per cent. of the membership in churches with fewer than 1,000 members; 31.3 per cent. in churches with between 1,000 and 2,000 members; 20.0 per cent. in churches with between 2,000 and 3,000 members; 15.5 per cent. in churches with between 3,000 and 4,000; and 18.0 per cent. in churches with 4,000 members or more.

It is revealed that as the church-membership increases the

percentage of Sunday church school enrollment decreases. The larger the membership of the church, the less likely is it to have a school enrollment comparable with its size. The ability or capacity of the school to interest and hold the attention and support of its members as the number of members increases, presents a challenge to the church school.

AVERAGE ATTENDANCE REFLECTS TEACHING AND PUPIL-ADMINISTRATION

While the total enrollment of the Sunday church schools is 109,865, the average attendance is only 65,211, or 59.4 per cent. of that enrollment. The large number of absentees (about 44,654) presents a problem, in that schools must discover some way of reducing this number. It reflects upon the program, the teaching, and the administrative work of the schools. In churches with large memberships, not only is the Sunday church school enrollment proportionately less than in smaller churches, but the average attendance is also less. The average attendance in the school where the church-membership is less than 1,000, is 61.9 per cent. of the school enrollment; while the average church attendance is 48.4 per cent. of the total church-membership. In Sunday church schools where the church-membership exceeds 4,000, the average school attendance is only 49.5 per cent. of the enrollment, and the average church attendance is 25.7 per cent. of the total church-membership.

RECORDS AND REPORTS

Records as measurements of achievement are limited. The most commonly recorded data are membership, attendance, and finance figures. As a result, these records, of which 604, or 99.3 per cent. are in permanent book form, are of very little value in measuring the work of the schools in the achievement of objectives other than those indicated by membership and finances. If, however, items concerning the objectives and policies adopted by the official actions of the school were recorded, together with facts about growth and use of equipment, teachers' reports, methods of work, social activities, church-membership of pupils, other signs of religious growth, and the like, a better check on the achievements of the school would be possible.

LEADERSHIP OF THE SUNDAY CHURCH SCHOOL

The leadership of the Sunday church school logically begins with the pastor of the church. In most churches, however, the details of the teaching and supervisory work are made the responsibility of voluntary lay leaders. The study reveals that three churches had employed directors of religious education.

Educational Preparation for Leadership—The roster of workers in the church schools consists of directors of Christian education, general and departmental superintendents, secretaries, treasurers, teachers, and assistants. There are 7,013 persons identified with the leadership of the 608 Sunday church schools. Study of their training shows that 46 per cent. were grade-school, 41 per cent. high-school, 4 per cent. normal-school, and 9 per cent. college people.

Experience—Ministers everywhere report that they have a difficult task getting persons professionally or technically trained to accept work in activities like the Sunday church school. Study of the general and professional experience shows that of the 7,013 workers in the 608 schools studied, 5 per cent. were public-school teachers; 3 per cent. were physicians, lawyers, business men, mail carriers, Y. M. C. A. secretaries, chemists, nurses, social workers and morticians; and 92 per cent. housewives, common laborers, domestics, and public-school students.

Selection of Workers—Considerable care often governs the selection of workers for the Sunday church schools. Unlike the public school, in which the standards of teacher-preparation are established and where a taxpaying public demands that the teacher meet them, the church does not generally hold its workers engaged in organized teaching activities to any prescribed standard. Usually likeableness, "being a good Christian," and availability, are the factors. The very limited training of the great majority of those available for the work makes the problem of selecting workers most difficult. There appears to be a consensus of opinion that no applicant for work, regardless of training, should be denied the opportunity.

The responsibility for selecting the teachers rests with the pastor in 17.4 per cent. of the churches studied; in 13.8 per cent. of them with the Sunday church school superintendent; in 17.6 per cent. with both pastor and superintendent; and in 51.2 per cent. the teachers are selected by the teachers, the school, or the church's official board. The responsibility placed upon the teachers of the school suggests that the methods of selection are inadequate.

Supervision of Teaching—The responsibility for supervising the instruction and work of the Sunday church school is also shifted about considerably. Supervision, as the term seems to be defined by use in the churches, includes checking on the presence or absence of workers, and supplying substitutes for absentees and visiting classes; but does not include other more technical work of the supervisor, such as demonstration-teaching and the training of teachers.

The 608 churches demonstrate that no accepted methods are in use. In a fourth of them the pastor is the supervisor; in nearly a third, the supervision is the superintendent's responsibility; in a fifth of them, it is that of both pastor and superintendent; in 1 per cent., the supervision is by directors of religious education or public-school teachers; and in 25.8 per cent. of the churches, there are no supervisory officials.

Workers' Conferences—The custom of holding workers' conferences or teachers' meetings is continued by a number of these Sunday church schools. The meetings are used for instructing teachers in the lessons of the Sunday session; for business meetings; and for social contact among the teachers. About 75 per cent. of the churches hold these meetings regularly. The other 25 per cent. follow a haphazard schedule in which meetings are held irregularly. In 98 per cent. of the churches, the entire staff of workers meet together; and in the remaining 2 per cent., there are departmental meetings. The section on organization shows that 549, or 90 per cent., of the churches have one-department schools. It is therefore reasonable that the teachers in the single-department schools should share a single teachers' meeting.

It might be supposed that the duties of the teachers' and workers' conferences would include appointment of substitute teachers, planning programs, checking on school or class projects, and apportioning the work of the school in the active program of the whole church. Actually, however, this is not always the case as the methods of handling substitute teachers will illustrate; 556 of the 608 Sunday church schools have substitute teachers; and if they are to teach, 99 per cent. of these are not notified at the teachers' meeting, but on Sunday morning. The observations of the authors suggest that much unfairness may result to both the substitute teachers and the pupils by this method. Under the present system of organization and administration, the substitute teachers have nothing to do as long as the regular teachers are present. They are not ordinarily required to sit with the class or to assist the regular teacher. As a result, they do not regularly prepare to teach like the teacher with regular responsibilities. They are, therefore, likely to be unprepared when notified on Sunday morning.

Leadership Training—Community schools in leadership training are being held in many of the larger cities. In some cities these schools are conducted by the denominational boards or by the combined effort of two local churches. In other cities schools conducted on a large plan are supported by several denominations. Schools of the latter type are usually promoted by the Council of Churches, or a City Council of Christian Education. During the last decade these schools have developed to the point where they now boast of hundreds of credits issued and a large number of full graduates. The records of the crediting agencies, the local councils, the denominational headquarters, or the International Council give only denominational representations, not data for the individual churches. But in Chicago, over a five-year period, these schools have issued 656 credits to Negroes; in the year 1930–1931, 215 credits were issued in Philadelphia; and in Detroit, over a brief period of years, 376 persons have earned 498 credits. One is therefore led to believe that persons from these churches shared in this leadership-training work.

Curriculum—The main element of the curriculum of most of the Sunday church schools is the lesson sheet or pamphlet containing biblical material.

The lesson material used by the Sunday church schools consists mainly of that supplied by denominational publishing houses and commercial publishers. Usually the schools supply each pupil with a lesson pamphlet which must be left at the church. A majority of the schools use the improved uniform lessons. Excepting in the classes for very young children, where cards are given, all persons in the schools study virtually the same lesson material. Of the 608 schools, 94.8 per cent. use Improved Uniform Lessons, and 5.2 per cent. use either group, or strictly graded, material.

Extra-biblical material is not generally used. Little or no account is taken of the teaching values available in history, biography, stories, pictures, nature, animal life, seasons, and plant life. Some exceptionally good teachers in the churches studied find use for these features.

Service and Study Projects—Activities growing out of consideration of the needs of others, and the planning and carrying through of means to meet these needs through offerings, gifts and personal service or contacts, occur in the study and project phase of the curriculum. These include all of the learning activities, such as dramatization, investigation, and excursions to sections of the city inhabited by foreign-language groups, to the countryside, to botanical gardens and parks for nature study, to juvenile courts for observation purposes, and to other places of particular interest. In using these features and activities it is hoped that actual life-situations are brought closer to the learning processes, and that the relationship between the ideals and life will be revealed.

In this field, the schools report practically no activity. Except for the help given the local church in a financial way, and mission work, there were no other activities. Two churches reported that members of the school were receiving wholesome training in contributing to foreign missions. Besides giving, they were learning to give out of an appreciation for the value of the work to which they contributed by studying the history and life of the people to whom their money went and the part the mission station played in the lives of these people.

The Teaching Work—The program and the organization and administrative activities all come to fruition as the Christian personality of the individual for whom they exist develops. The individual is brought into direct contact with these features through the teaching work or situations of the school. The teaching situation in these schools consists chiefly of class work and worship services. The question and answer, and the lecture methods are the most popular types of teaching in the churches studied.

Pupil Participation—Pupil participation in the work of the schools is best illustrated by the class sessions. The extent to which pupils actually enter into the activities depends very much upon the teacher or the leader of the class. The teacher's ability to motivate pupil activity will of course be limited by his or her own natural ability and training. The teachers get their pupils to enter into class activities and to use the teachings in actual living in much the same manner. Various kinds of persuasion are used, including appeals to pupil self-respect, racial differences, fear, and rewards. Observation of a large number of teaching situations suggests that fear is most used to motivate activity. Quite often pupils are urged to accept lessons uncritically because religion is interpreted as submission, and a rather credulous acceptance of biblical statement even in spite of the fact that it may contradict present experience. In some cases the class period shows a lack of balance both in the points of the lesson emphasized and in the methods used.

To obtain a clear understanding of pupil participation, a large number of class sessions were stenographically reported. Samples of these reports show that in some classes only a few pupils participate, while in others more pupils enter into the work.

```
        SAMPLE I—A YOUNG MEN'S CLASS
  1  2  3  4  5  6  7  8  9  10  11  12  13  14
  x  x  x  x  x  x  x  x  x   x   x   x   x   x
     —                           —               —
     —
     —
     —
     —
     —
     —
  x = pupil
  — = pupil response
```

There were fourteen persons in this class. The number of underlines indicates the number of times the particular individual spoke, answered, or asked questions.

In this case, the teacher began the class period by admitting that he had not studied the lesson. Pupil number two obviously consumed much of the thirty-minute period, during which he responded or spoke nine times. As the reader will note, only two other members of the class (Numbers 10 and 14) participated in the discussion of the lesson.

SAMPLE II—A MIXED ADULT BIBLE CLASS

```
1  2  3  4  5  6  7  8  9
x  x  x  x  x  x  x  x  x
─           ─
   ─
```

x = pupil
— = pupil response

This class of nine persons was taught by the pastor of the church. Both the question and answer and the lecture methods were used. However, in his enthusiasm for the Bible, the teacher both asked and answered his own questions. Since the members were not very assertive, and the teacher was confident of his position, there was little or no exchange of opinion during the forty-minute class period.

SAMPLE III—MEN'S ADULT BIBLE CLASS

```
 1  2  3  4  5  6  7  8  9 10 11 12 13 14
 x  x  x  x  x  x  x  x  x  x  x  x  x  x
 ─     ─     ─     ─  ─     ─        ─  ─
 ─     ─     ─     ─     ─  ─           ─
                      ─
15 16 17 18 19 20 21 22 23 24 25 26 27 28
 x  x  x  x  x  x  x  x  x  x  x  x  x  x
    ─     ─           ─     ─           ─
    ─     ─           ─     ─           ─
```

x = pupil
— = pupil response

In this class session both pupils and teacher were interested in the practical values of the lesson. A general discussion, indicated by the participation "dashes" under thirteen of the twenty-eight people, occupied the first few minutes of the class period. Following this, the class was divided into six small groups for further discussion of the lesson.

It is reasonable to assume that class situations in which both teacher and pupils enter freely into the work produce the best results. The results are observable in the knowledge acquired, the church-membership maintained by the individual participants, and other signs of religious growth.

Young People's Work

The young people's organizations are usually designated by such names as the Young People's Union, the Epworth League, and the Christian Endeavor. The young people's work receives less emphasis than that of the Sunday church school. There are 398 churches reporting young people's work, as against 608 of the 609 reporting Sunday church schools. A number of churches studied reported having young people's groups in previous years; but for one reason or another these organizations did not last.

ORGANIZATION

The young people's work is usually organized to provide for both general and special groups for study and discussion purposes. These forms of organization permit the use of a variety of programs, which include study of denominational lesson material, discussions, special speakers and musicals.

The officers of the young people's group ordinarily consist of a president, several vice-presidents, a secretary, and a treasurer. Additional officers are found in varying local situations. Meetings are customarily held on Sunday evenings preceding the evening preaching and worship service.

PURPOSE

The purposes of the young people's groups vary from the study of the Bible, to social gatherings. In one organization the purpose may be both social and Bible teaching. In another it may be discussion of "timely themes"; while another has as its purpose giving young people "something to do."

There seems to be no generally accepted function for young people's work. The purposes it will serve are determined almost entirely by the local church. If a clew to its purpose is sought in the denominational literature it uses, two things are usually apparent: (1) There is a strong effort to "pep up" the young people's work with attractive quota-

tions and selected readings. (2) There is a definite parallel-
ing of the Sunday church school literature.

MEMBERSHIP

The number of members in the young people's organizations is not at all certain. The records, where they do exist,
take very little account of actual membership and attendance.
Not only is this true, but the organizations have a fluctuat-
ing attendance. There may be a crowd of people on one
Sunday and very few the next. The attendance group is
made up of visitors or "floaters." These people go from
church to church and are usually attracted by the nature of
the particular or special programs offered. Consequently a
large sustained enrollment and attendance over a period as
long as a year is the exception rather than the rule. The 398
churches reporting young people's work have an aggregate
membership of approximately 18,050.

LEADERSHIP

Leadership of the young people's work is almost entirely
in the hands of laymen. In many churches the same leaders
and workers serve in both the Sunday church school and the
young people's work. While this activity is called *young
people's work*, ordinarily no real age-restrictions are enforced.
A very large number of young people's groups are managed
by older people; and they plan their programs almost entirely in terms of adult experience.

THE WEEK-DAY AND VACATION ACTIVITIES

In the churches studied there are fewer week-day than vacation activities.

Two churches made reports of week-day teaching activities.
In each, these activities were conducted in conjunction with
the mid-week prayer service. One of them will illustrate not
only what is being done but also the possibilities of this kind

of work. Approximately 400 people attend the mid-week Bible class and prayer service. The pastor, who is the leader and teacher, makes his talks and his replies to questions deal with actual life-problems, although each lesson is based on a biblical passage. The meeting lasts about one and a half hours, and a part of this time is used for devotions and prayer. There is evidence of the genuine interest of the people in that they are prompt in attendance, in that they participate freely in the meetings, and in that their statements and questions are apparently backed by some thought.

During the summer-vacation months, the churches are more active in week-day activities than at other seasons. In 1930, ten of the 609 reporting had daily vacation Bible schools. A general description of these shows that they were organized mainly to give the children something to do from four to six weeks during the summer. Most of them had one teacher, and seldom were there more than two. These teachers drilled the pupils on Bible passages, taught some handwork, and supervised their play for about four hours a day five or six days a week.

The teachers were each paid a small salary. The church building, and probably a near-by playground, served as the base of operations. The average budget for these schools, with their limited equipment, was about forty-five dollars. This money was contributed mainly by the local churches where the schools were held. According to the verbal reports of some of the pastors, some of these schools had previously been conducted as subsidized activities of the city Federation of Churches, or of some white church-group. But at the time of the study, for some reason not revealed, this support had been withdrawn and the schools were being continued under the support of the churches of which they were a part.

Although the organized teaching activities command a great part of the attention and energy of the churches, other major features must also have places in the program.

CHAPTER VIII

Worship Activities

The activities of worship are probably the ones most emphasized in the church. Worship in the form of spirituals and hymns, which have always been prominent in the Negro services, preceded the use of the formal service. But a brief review of the history of the churches of this study will show that, since the early days, changes in the manner and spirit of worship have been influenced by changes in the social conditions of the Negro.

During the days of slavery, and in the early days of the organized Negro church, worship was largely begun as an unconscious imitation of the white church; but it soon developed characteristics of its own. The spirituals, which gave free expression to the ravaged feelings and aspirations of the Negro in bondage, expressed his fear, his hope of deliverance, and less often his joy.

Like the minstrel in medieval Europe, the Negro transmitted history, group contributions and feelings in song. Because of his illiteracy, he depended upon memory. While the spirituals were almost entirely original with him, he readily adopted many of the songs used in the white revival meeting which he attended.

Changes in Manner of Worship

The form and manner of worship has gradually changed in the church. The growing intelligence of the people has encouraged efforts to improve the services of worship. Illiteracy has gradually decreased among Negroes from 70 per cent. in 1880 to 22.9 per cent. in 1920, and to 16.3 per cent. in 1930. This gradual extension of the ability to read and write has

138

permitted the churches to make their services appeal to the intellect as well as to the emotions. More sermons attempt to be thought provoking. The spirituals, along with other published songs and hymns, are still widely used; but no longer is there absolute dependence upon memory. The music in most urban churches is now led by choirs, and accompanied by instruments, including organs and orchestral pieces.

The services of the urban churches studied consist of the Sunday church school, the junior church service and the regular public worship services. Following is an account of each of these activities.

Worship in the Sunday Church School

The worship services of the Sunday church schools are separated into distinct types. Those of the first type include in a single service persons of all ages and experience. These schools usually have an opening and a closing exercise at each Sunday session.

Services of this type are used by about 90 per cent. of the 608 Sunday church schools. The distribution of time in these schools usually gives thirty minutes each for the opening exercises, the class work and the closing exercises. Services of the second type are improved by an attempt to adapt them to differences in age and experience by grading instead of resting upon the assumption that a common service is suitable for all persons regardless of age. About a tenth of the 608 churches follow this form of worship. In these schools, the services are usually held by departments; and the distribution of time is fifty minutes for class work, fifteen minutes for reports and preparation for worship, and twenty-five minutes for actual worship. One very good reason for grading worship is shown in the schools studied. The content of the worship in which all age-groups are included shows that the younger people suffer because, although they outnumber the adults, the services are planned mainly in terms of adult desires and experiences.

The purposeful use of songs as a means of bringing the worshipper to a realization of the church's wealth of history and belief, and of giving him at the same time an appreciation of religious music, is gradually overshadowing other uses suggested by custom or the necessity to "pep up" the service.

The schools in the 608 churches, either by choice or through a lack of knowledge and appreciation, make a wide use of hymns that express, almost wholly, adult ideas of religion and life which the children have had little or no opportunity to experience and are therefore unlikely to understand.

The schools use such songs as "Sweet Hour of Prayer," "Nearer My God to Thee," "Stand Up, Stand Up, For Jesus," "What a Friend We Have in Jesus," "I Came to the Garden Alone," "I Need Thee Every Hour," "Nothing Between," and others that are distinctly based upon adult experience. It is unlikely that the experiences of persons even fifteen or seventeen years of age would enable them to understand fully the religious significance in such songs. Songs like "All Nature's Works His Praise Declare," "Praise to God and Thanks We Bring," and "Little Voices Through the Temple Stealing," are probably more suitable for younger folk. It is, therefore, pleasant to report that several churches were found using songs of this type.

THE PRAYERS

There are many interpretations of the value of prayer as an element of public worship, among which at least these two may prove generally acceptable. (1) That the public prayer should be social rather than individualistic in its tone and conception, and should assist the worshippers to include others besides themselves in their hopes for higher life. (2) That the prayer should be intelligible to the worshippers.

The prayers used in the schools are in many instances almost entirely addressed to the minds of adults rather than those of children. Two prayers are presented here. These come from a group of stenographic reports of school services in the churches studied.

Prayer by a Superintendent

We thank Thee, Heavenly Father, for this great and grand opportunity; that You have spared us to turn out to the House of worship and hear Thy word once more. Have mercy upon us; bless the Sabbath school this morning; bless the teachers who are trying to instruct the little ones in Thy way as You have said; "Suffer the little children to come unto me, and forbid them not, for of such is the Kingdom of Heaven." Have mercy upon us. We are thankful that we are able to stand together and testify that we have seen another bright morning, while thousands have gone upward and onward. Bless all, Our Heavenly Father, that we are duty bound to pray for. Then, our Heavenly Father, when we have finished our work on earth; when there is no more space between the living and the dead, raise us up to Thy Kingdom. In Jesus' name, Amen.

Prayer by a Superintendent

O, Gracious Father, we again assemble in Thy house of worship, asking Thee to have mercy upon us. Lead us in the path that we should go. Teach us by Thy precepts those things worthy of knowing and worthy of a place in Thy Kingdom. Lead us in the path where righteousness is. Guide us away from those things which beset worries not only in this life, but in the life hereafter. Bless the children who have come and their parents at home working, striving, slaving in order that the lives of these children may be more worthy. Bless those without shelter, clothing and food. May we ask Thee to take care of the sick; get into the hearts of those people in the world who know Thee not. May they see Thee in their doings and do unto others as they would have others do unto them. Get into their hearts. Teach them Thy way. May the coming of these children here be a coming worthy of the life they have spent. These blessings we ask in the name of Thee, who has taught us when we pray to say: (Recital of Lord's Prayer in concert.)

GENERAL LESSON REVIEWS AND TALKS

A large part of the time of the closing exercise in virtually 90 per cent. of the 608 schools is devoted to lesson reviews. This procedure naturally, and often rightly, is based upon the assumption that every one has studied the same biblical lesson texts. The reviews seem to be regarded as necessities, although observations reveal that the reviewers seldom present the material even as interestingly as it has already been presented in the classes. Evidently it is hoped that the persons present will all have the same idea of the lesson, and that the conduct of all will be similarly changed. It is doubtful, however, that such an objective can be achieved in a service in which ages vary as widely as from six to seventy. If, however, the work of the classes were accepted as well done, the need of reviews would disappear.

A number of schools, probably a tenth, do not have general lesson reviews, and devote the time to planned services of worship. General observations of these two methods in the churches studied indicates that the latter method seems to produce more satisfactory results. There is usually less noise and moving about. The service proceeds with a greater sense of its achieving its purpose. The pupil participation appears to arise out of interest rather than coercion.

PUPIL PARTICIPATION

The services of worship of the schools are dominated by adult leadership. Duties such as passing and collecting song books and lesson materials, and the running of errands are given over to younger pupils. In many schools in which the services are not well planned, the pupils are permitted to select the songs as they are needed; but very rarely indeed are the younger pupils members of the worship committee or other subordinate activity groups in which they may learn by doing.

The Junior Church

The junior church, an adaptation to the church program during the last one and a half decades, has not become a common activity in the Negro church. Junior church work follows no generally accepted pattern. Each church promoted its junior work according to its own ideas. The thirteen junior churches studied are services or organizations for boys and girls and young people which attempt to serve the religious life of the young folk as the regular church service serves the adult people. The memberships of these churches range between fifty and seventy-five children.

TERM "JUNIOR" NOT CLEARLY DEFINED

If the term "junior" were used in a technical sense, it would cause the Junior Church to serve those individuals between the ages of 9 and 11 as distinguished from those of the primary, intermediate, or other age-group. In practice, however, these services include all persons who come. In fact, it includes all those who do not join naturally in the adult service. For this reason it would probably be better if it were called the "Junior Worship Service of the Church," and the adult service called the "Senior Worship Service of the Church."

WHEN CHURCHES FOR THE JUNIORS MEET

The junior churches of this study meet on days or nights during the week and on Sunday mornings. Two of the thirteen are known to meet during the week. The remaining eleven of the organizations meet on Sunday morning.

In a few of these, the juniors join with the adults in the opening of the adult service. They join in the singing and the prayers; and just before the sermon they go to their own room for a story or talk from their leader. In other instances the pastor talks to the juniors before they are excused from the adult service.

The most acceptable arrangement appears to be for the juniors to meet in their own room for the entire service. In this case they have their own pastor, a choir, a governing board of officers, a secretary, a treasury, ushers and other duplicates of the adult service. As to the time limit for these churches, there seems to be agreement in practice that they should not be more than an hour long.

These worship services are conducted by the minister of the church or his assistant. Most of these leaders have had no formal preparation for this work.

The Regular Public Worship Services

The bearing of the historical development of the church and of the race upon Negro church worship has already been indicated in this chapter. In presenting a discussion of the regular public-worship services, it is therefore necessary only to point out some more immediate facts.

Public worship is generally deemed by the church to be of major importance. Hence the buildings are all primarily meeting houses; the largest and best equipped room is the auditorium for public worship. The minister is very often judged upon his ability as a preacher in these services. The services draw the largest regular attendance, between a quarter and a half of the membership, of any activity in the church. And the time allotted to them is the best at the disposal of the church.

Consideration of the elements of the service of worship may serve to illuminate this work of the church.

SONGS, CHOIRS, INSTRUMENTS

In urban churches the services of worship usually include a number of musical selections. Among them are the old and new hymns of the church and the spirituals. Singing, in many of the churches, is lead by vested choirs, with the assistance of pipe organs and in few instances of brass, reed, or string instruments. In some services, older people occasionally break into song, especially following the sermons. However, in the very formal type of service this seldom if ever happens.

In all of the services, hymns expressing strength arising from dependence upon God are apparently very acceptable. Usually all of the people in the congregation join with the choir in singing those hymns that are familiar to them. Hymnals are used by most churches. However, in a few churches the worshippers depend largely upon memory.

The choirs use a variety of anthems in addition to leading the congregations in the singing of spirituals and hymns. Of the 609 urban churches about 85 per cent. have choirs.

PRAYERS

The prayers in the services of worship are offered by both ministers and laymen. They appear to follow a pattern in which many of the attitudes toward God and the present world-order are recurrent.

The Attitude Toward God

God is all powerful and ever present. He is very close to the individual, just as a friend or any living individual may be. He is also to be feared and appeased; and unlimited gratefulness belongs to Him for all good things.

(1) Gracious Father, the father of us all and of our Lord and Savior, Jesus Christ, our elder brother. We thank Thee from the depths of our hearts that we are allowed to be present this morning within these consecrated walls. We thank Thee that this

opportunity to worship Thee is denied no man but that every man and woman and child who believes can fall down and worship Thee. Lord, we come to Thee pleading no merits of our own. At best we are but poor feeble worms of dust, asking mercy that Thou abide with us. Sanctify our whole being. We know that we are short, Lord, but we are coming up to the throne of mercy pleading that Thou will make us the kind of servants that Thou would have us be. Banish from our minds everything that destroys our faith in Thee.

(2) Oh God, our Heavenly Father, we come to Thee this morning, so thankful that Thou hast allowed us the privilege of coming before Thee. Thankful, O Lord, that Thou hast called us the sons of God. Thankful, that Thou hast chosen us out of the world to be Thy followers and hast led us in the paths of truth and light.

(3) Dear Lord, we are gathered here this blessed morning to sing praises to Thee and ask Thy forgiveness of our many sins since we gathered together on last Sunday morning. We want to thank Thee for all Thy blessings bestowed upon us. Help us always to be thankful of Thy kindness. Guide our footsteps toward right and righteousness always. Give us strength to go forward in life and do the world's work for Thee. Bless all that are gathered here this morning. Bless those that are afflicted.

God Dwells in the Church

(1) We have come today, Father, into Thy Holy presence. We pray, Father, that as we gather here, we shall be conscious of Thy abiding presence, and that there shall be great rejoicing because Thou art with us. Abide with us. We thank Thee for this privilege.

(2) Lord, our Heavenly Father, we meet with you this morning to give Thee thanks for the past blessings Thou hast bestowed upon us. We pray Thee sincerely for help; get into our wondering minds and faltering steps. We earnestly pray your blessings upon this great congregation. We pray Thy blessings upon the choir, preaching the gospel through song. Help them wake up to the understanding of their duty. We ask Thy blessings upon the personnel of this church.

Dependence Upon God

(1) Lord, Thou knowest we can do nothing tangible without Thy assistance. We beg Thee, O Gracious God, give of Thy supernatural strength and power from on high, that we may do better. We ask Thy blessing for the speaker this morning; that his message will thrill our humble souls; strengthen him; help his family that they will be able to accomplish in every way their undertakings. We pray a prayer for the poor and needy, the sick and afflicted; we ask Thee to help all of us that we may do better for Thy glory.

(2) But we ask Thee for Thy holy privilege. We know we can do nothing without Thy aid or assistance. Make us conscious of the fact that we are all Thy children in that vineyard, striving to work out our souls' salvations. We ask Thee, give us the spirit of Christ and determination to press onward and upward. We ask Thee to give us, Father, grace, hope, patience, and keep our feet in the straight and narrow path and ever to be willing to do the task Thou hast assigned to us.

(3) Help us, O Blessed Savior, that we may surrender ourselves to Thee, that we may come with humbler hearts. We come to Thee because we feel that we need Thee, we feel that we have need of Thee as never before. In these times when there is so much mistrust, in these times when sons and daughters are turning against their parents, and when there is so much suffering in this world, will Thou bless this pastor and give him courage this morning. Help us that we may give courage to some discouraged heart, help them so that they may not give up all hopes.

Biblical References in Prayers

(1) When we consider Thy mercies, we say as David, what is man that Thou are mindful of him, and the son of man that Thou visited him? For Thou hast made him a little lower than the angels and crowned him with glory and honor.

(2) We thank Thee that because of Thy wonderful blessings men no longer have to lay at the pool and wait for the troubling of the waters, but that men and women may come and be reclaimed and fall out of their sinful ways.

Anticipating Another World

Other-worldly expressions occur in the closing sentences of some of the prayers.

(1) And when we are called from time to eternity, we will not go before the justice bar wanting, but having done the things commendable in Thy presence forever and ever. Amen.

(2) Bless Thy children, and when we come to press a dying pillow may we hear the sweet voice of Him, who taught us to say, Our——

Lord's Prayer chanted by the choir, Amen.

(3) Bless all for whom we are duty bound to pray. Bless the unemployed, bless the suffering everywhere. Then, dear Father, when we have finished our work, when all our work is over here and when we can do no more for Thy Kingdom among the children of men, bring us into Thy presence where all the redeemed of God are blessed. Amen.

The Present World

References to the present world-order are more often general than special.

(1) We pray for the sick. Bless the low in spirit. Bless this city of ours, O Lord. Bless this country and the world over. Bless the conditions of this country, we ask Thee. Give us peace and love and charity towards all mankind. Give us power. Give us a greater desire to serve Thee. We ask in Thy name.

(2) Some have come this morning because of bereavement over the loss of a loved one, some have come because of the economic depression that is prevalent and they haven't the necessary comforts of life.

As one listens to these prayers, and as one reads them, they are impressive primarily because there is a deep ring of sincerity in each of them.

Announcements

In some services, the making of announcements or the reading of notices consumes quite a large part of the time. Many of the church announcements and notices given by the reading clerk are repeated and emphasized at other times during the same service by the pastor.

Bulletin boards or weekly church papers and printed bulletins are used by many churches to acquaint the members with the notices. Twenty-two of the 609 urban churches studied have weekly or monthly papers.

Announcements in the churches that give them a place in the worship program, include financial, social, business, church program and other notices. The value of this practice has not been thoroughly tested; and not all of the churches equally emphasize it. The announcements usually precede the sermon, although reiterations may follow the sermon. The following from stenographic reports are typical.

(1) (Summary of Announcements.) The pastor announced a church conference meeting on ————. All the members were urgently requested to be present. He stated the purpose of the conference was to discuss financial matters pertaining to the church, and to fill certain vacancies in the church offices.

The pastor also announced that a worthy individual, a member of the church had been ill for some time, but had not desired to request assistance. He, therefore, requested that a contribution be lifted to assist this member. This contribution was taken. Hymn—"Grace Enough for Me."

(2) (Verbatim Announcements.) It is very warm this morning so we are going to rush through the announcements.

The ———— Club will please meet in the Gymnasium directly after the close of the services.

The ———— Club will hold their meeting Tuesday evening at 8 P. M. at the home of Mrs. ————.

The ———— Club will hold their weekly meeting, Wednesday evening at 8:30 P. M. They are urging all members to be present as there will be business of importance.

The Junior Church is extending a special invitation to you to be present at their musical to be given this afternoon at 3:00

P. M. We urge the parents to be there to encourage these children.

Miss ———— wishes to meet all those wishing to go to ———— after the services.

Mr. ———— died ————. He was the brother of ————. Funeral date will be given later.

Will everyone please vacate as soon as possible after services so that the Sunday school will be able to meet.

Further remarks in regard to the announcements by pastor.

This little bunch of sunshine wants to make an announcement. (A little girl made an announcement in connection with the Junior Church Musical.)

Announcement by chorister:

Friends, do not forget tonight, we have our regular monthly musical and we want you all out. There will be much pleasure in store for you in spite of the weather.

Remarks by pastor:

If you do not get here on time tonight you will have to stand and standing won't be very comfortable.

You ought not to miss the Junior Church Service this afternoon. May I call your attention to the membership cards, they are now in the hands of the Bureau of Information. We will be very glad to have you get them there and leave your contribution.

Next Tuesday night we are expecting a very interesting night. I hear it is to be a double header. The choir will start singing at 7:30 P. M. If you want to hear the beginning you had better be here on time. Following the meeting we will have the Concert by the orchestra under the auspices of the ———— Club.

Next Sunday will be ————.

In the morning we will have our regular morning services. In the afternoon we will have memorial services by the citizens. There will be many prominent men here. In the evening the young people will bring their tribute.

The ———— Department is having a fruit sale, and they are selling this fruit almost at cost price.

Sister ———— called and said her brother was very sick, and would be very glad to have you visit him at home.

There will be a program here tomorrow night given by ———. Admission 10 cents.

Mr. ——— left these fans here yesterday, and with it $1.00 for today's collection. He would like for you to patronize his place of business. There are several helpful hints on these fans, you will read them and at the end of the services you will please leave fans here. At times we all walk off with the fans by mistake, but let's try and remember to leave these here.

Listen friends, I want to tell you this very quietly. On ——— occurs the birthday of ———. It would be very nice if each one would send her a card.

Taking of collection.

Remarks by pastor:

Let each one of us go down in our pockets and get $1.00. This hot weather does not cut down our expenses very much. We want to send another payment on our financial obligations. We are behind in our obligations. While you are getting your contribution ready, Sister ——— has Church ——— which she would like you to relieve her of. You will find in them an account of the ———.

(Ushers take up collection. The choir sings "The Wonder of His Word.")

Prayer after collection by pastor:

Our Heavenly Father we are thanking Thee for this collection and your many blessings to us in the past, and that in the future they may not be less. Bless those that helped to contribute to this cause. Help them in these times of strife. May we use this contribution in Thy name. Amen.

Remarks by pastor:

You will recall that I asked you to patronize ———. During that month you are credited with $305.17. You also remember that the church was to receive five per cent. I am turning over a check for $17.14.

Many people find the worship services lacking in effectiveness because the continuity of the service is broken by long, over-emphasized remarks and announcements. Churches might profit by more intelligent use of printed or posted bulletins.

INVITATIONS TO CHURCH-MEMBERSHIP

Usually at the close of the sermon the minister or his assistant "opens the doors of the church" as an invitation to persons wishing to become members; or to those who are not "professed Christians" to accept Christianity and church-membership. These invitations vary from brief and simple statements to long statements and the use of music, as the following samples reveal:

I suppose there are those here who do not know Christ this morning. But my friends even though you have a historical knowledge of Him you need an experimental knowledge of him. If you know him both historically and experimentally but have no specific church home won't you come this morning? What's the use of living if you can't make life better? You can't make it better unless you know Jesus Christ. If you do not wish to join this particular church give us the name and address of the one you would like to join and we will send you there. Won't you please come today before it is too late? (Choir sings "Saviour Lead Me"—Baptism of a member—Choir sings "In the Garden.")

I want to open the doors of the church this morning. I want to see if there is a man or woman who feels that his or her ways please God; that he will triumph over anything with which he comes in contact. We will now sing.

Hymn—"Bye and Bye." Two persons joined the church, one being baptized.

The pastor stated the object of his sermon to be "to strengthen the Christian faith." He then requested that as many of the congregation, both members of the church and visitors, who had acquiesced in his stand, to rise. The entire congregation stood up.

Is there anyone who wants to join the church this morning? Come right on now. Let us sing that song, "He's the One." Won't somebody come right on now? Come on!

Hymn—"He's the One."

In conclusion, the worship activities may be summarized by pointing out that in the worship of the Sunday church school the interpretation of religion in terms of the experiences of children and youth is no doubt overshadowed by adult ideas and the appeal to adult satisfactions. Whereas in the public worship, although there is an apparent profound sense of the nearness of God, there is probably an under-emphasis upon the practical application of Christianity to life.

The organized teaching and worship activities by no means absorb the entire attention of the churches. They share the program with fellowship and community activities.

CHAPTER IX

Fellowship and Community Activities

Many churches make use of fellowship activities among their own members, and community activities outside the church, as means of furthering the development of their members and rendering a service to the people of the entire neighborhood. The fellowship activities include clubs and recreational work for the different age- and sex-groups. While all of these are in a way social, some emphasize either the financial or the educational interests of the church. They also include interchurch relations, which are generally embraced under the term "comity." The community activities include various types of social service, such as work to reduce juvenile delinquency.

Fellowship Activities

In the fellowship activities especially, the churches develop a sense of family unity among the members and satisfy the hunger of the youth for recreation and sociability, and of newcomers for friendship. These activities also provide opportunities to enlist and train the members in various ways.

CLUBS

Organized clubs for educational, social and financial purposes are found in almost every church. Of the 609 urban churches studied, 348 reported an average of six clubs each. Usually the larger the church the larger the number of clubs. In a church with heavy financial responsibilities, the number of clubs may exceed the number found in another church with the same number of members but without heavy financial burdens. Although it is difficult to say exactly how many

154

clubs have finances as their major interest, the study showed that practically all adult clubs make regular contributions to the church treasury. These contributions do not usually include, or substitute for, the individual contributions of club members to the church.

Church clubs customarily hold weekly meetings, in which both social and business activities are conducted. In a majority of the churches these clubs meet in the homes of members more often than at the church; a procedure that keeps down the expense for lighting, heating, and cleaning the building, and lessens the likelihood of conflicts in respect to meeting-places. Club meetings held in private homes are also assured a larger attendance because the homes are less formal and often nearer than the church building to the residences of many members.

RECREATIONAL WORK

Formal recreational work is not well developed in the Negro churches. In many instances where churches have advertised recreational work as a part of the program, the actual promotion of this work has been short-lived. In many cities the community recreational agencies, including the Y. M. C. A. and city recreational facilities, have increased their efforts to such an extent that churches have been unable to compete either in gaining the attention of the people or in obtaining financial support for the work. About 73 per cent. of the 609 urban churches have no form of recreational work, and 14 per cent. have only one activity, while 13 per cent. have two or more kinds.

Recreational equipment, including gymnasiums or playgrounds, is owned by thirty of the 609 churches.

POLLING MINISTERIAL ATTITUDE ON RECREATION

A poll of the ministers upon their approval or disapproval of various types of recreational work shows that 455, or

74.7 per cent., are in favor of general recreational activities.

When it was asked whether dancing, card-playing and moving-pictures were approved or disapproved, 590 replies revealed three distinctive attitudes. Dancing was disapproved in 72 per cent. of the replies; 8 per cent. of them favored it; and 20 per cent. maintained a neutral position. Card-playing was opposed in 70 per cent. of the replies; 10.6 per cent. approved it; and 19.4 per cent. assumed a neutral attitude. Moving-pictures were opposed by 62 per cent., and approved by 14 per cent.; while 24 per cent. assumed a neutral attitude.

Light is thrown on these attitudes by the reasons given in 228 of the replies. In 72 replies the reason stated for disapproval was the possibility that cards, dancing, and moving-pictures would lead to gambling and immorality. Thirty held that these things were against the rules of the church, and twenty-eight that they were all right if supervised.

Dancing, cards, and movies were ordinarily either sinful, worldly, traditionally bad, or at least worthy of condemnation. Other attitudes, and reasons given for the positions held, suggested that they were: "a personal matter," "of no social value," "against the scriptures," "of a nature to lessen the interest of individuals in the church," and "to be taken moderately." Others who replied, spoke of offering a substitute for these activities; some said that the people do much worse things; and, that they must have amusements. One reply, which indicated complete resignation, was, "you cannot stop them."

Obviously the church is in a period of transition in thought and practice regarding the activities of dancing, card-playing and the movies. That the movies are the more acceptable seemed evident from conversation with ministers and church people; as well as from the 590 replies, 14 per cent. of which approved movies and 24 per cent. of which were neutral. The attitude toward dancing and card-playing was far more unfavorable.

As an active community institution, the church is necessarily affected by its environment. Some individual churches have sought community contacts by performing special kinds of social work. Many have coöperated with other churches, or with community institutions and agencies, through ministerial alliances and associations; in religious educational activities; in coöperative humanitarian movements; in social welfare, poor relief, and the like; and in obtaining preventative and corrective legislation and administration in civic affairs.

Virtually all of the 591 ministers of this study are connected with some kind of a local ministerial body. It has already been indicated that a number of the 609 churches, especially in the northern cities, have been affiliated with community religious educational work. Churches generally also contributed to the Y. M. C. A. and Y. W. C. A. movements, the Community Chest, the Urban League, and the N. A. A. C. P.

However, church coöperation and work with governmental agencies, public schools, or commercialized amusements, has been very limited, so far as could be ascertained in this study.

Union services, or joint meetings of two or more churches are held for various purposes. In some localities these union meetings follow denominational affiliations. When this is the case, Methodists meet with Methodists, Baptists with Baptists, and so on. But there is an encouraging gradual increase in coöperative efforts without regard to denominational affiliations. Approximately 100 per cent. of the 609 churches of this study engage in them.

Almost every local church is represented by its minister in a city ministerial body. In each of the twelve urban localities, there were one or more denominational ministerial bodies. Wherever any one denomination was not represented by enough churches to have a distinct body, its local representatives joined with those whose religious practices permitted of the closest friendly relations.

INTERDENOMINATIONAL ALLIANCES

Another popular form of coöperation among Negro churches occurs when there are interdenominational ministerial meetings. In six of the twelve cities studied there are interdenominational alliances or meetings. Except in Charleston, South Carolina, there is a significant lack of a strong and vital program for these meetings. The result is that ordinarily the attendance is not dependable, and the work to be done is not well planned, so that it is difficult in some places to keep up the meetings throughout the year.

Interracial Fellowship

AS NEGRO MINISTERS SEE IT

Church coöperation across racial lines is very interesting. Very few Negro ministers ever have contact with white ministers on any basis of equal sharing. Coöperation between Negroes and whites does not usually mean the same as coöperation between Negroes and Negroes or whites and whites. Between Negroes and whites coöperation usually means that whites will give and the Negroes will receive.

Do Negro ministers exchange pulpits with white ministers? "No," is the general answer from Negroes; and not more than 150 ministers of this study answered "Yes." Do Negro churches have white speakers as their guests? And to this question a majority of the Negro ministers answered "Yes." Do Negroes speak in white churches as guests? "No," is again the general answer from Negroes.

It is, however, interesting to note that in the matter of music, though there is practically no exchange, the Negro musicians and singers are frequently called to white churches to render service, while white singers and musicians seldom enter Negro churches for this purpose.

The Negro ministers interviewed in the course of this study have interesting comments to make on this relationship. They think that, in a general way, the white minister does not care to deal with Negroes. On the other hand, the Negroes are not begging for this contact, but feel it their Christian duty to give a cordial response whenever an invitation comes.

The exchange of pulpits, according to the Negro minister, was for a long time considered as a novelty, an entertainment by both Negro and white churches. What the ministers said mattered very little, and they did not expect an invitation to return until the next special Sunday.

Some ministers say that it is all a farce and they see little good in white and Negro coöperation. Others, happily, see the good of interracial coöperation if it ever becomes a real coöperation on the basis of mutual exchange, that is, a mutual exchange of something other than pulpits.

Ignorance of one another is recognized by these Negro ministers as one of the obstacles. One minister gave this very fine comment: "I had no faith in the white man's religion until I began to associate with them." Another said, "The exchange of pulpits would be good if it were not confined to the large churches."

In Chicago, Detroit, Philadelphia, Cincinnati, and Baltimore, there are active city Church Federations which in some phase of their work recognize the Negro. Usually this phase is either the Interracial Sunday event, or through the department of religious education.

Negro participation in Church Federation programs almost invariably comes under the heading of a special committee or program. It is seldom that Negro participation is anticipated as a natural part of the federation program. Whether this is owing to the reluctance of the Negro or to the customs of interracial activity has not been conclusively determined. Although all the Federations observed had special committees affecting Negroes, some of them place Negroes on standing committees as the examples reveal.

In Detroit, Negroes are members of five committees, including the Advisory Cabinet, and the committees on Comity, Evangelism, Religious Education, and Public Affairs. Negro women have been invited into the women's work. This speaks well for the Detroit church council; but it does not mean that the coöperation is perfect. Negroes have not yet appeared on the Lenten season program; and there are other points at which coöperation does not break through racial lines.

In Chicago, Negroes are on several committees of the Church Federation, although the Race Relations Committee and participation in special meetings are their main interests. In Cincinnati, the Negroes are not very active in the work of the Federation. However, there are Negro members of Committees on Interracial Coöperation, Evangelism, Religious Education, Social Service, and the Juvenile Court. The Federation pays the salary of a Negro religious worker in the Juvenile Court. The Federation maintains a system of endorsement for Negro churches wishing to solicit funds from white firms. There are supposed to be about sixty Negro churches affiliated with the Cincinnati Federation.

On Race Relations Sunday in Chicago in 1931, eighty-one white and thirty-one Negro churches participated in the exchange and sharing of pulpits. The reports of the ministers on this activity are quite favorable. In Detroit, Cincinnati, and Philadelphia, this activity receives very little support.

AS THE WHITE MINISTERS SEE IT

White ministers representing both the North and the South were queried on the kind of fellowship their churches had with Negro churches. Replies were received from 720 ministers; about 36 per cent. of the churches they represented being either located near or in Negro neighborhoods. (See Appendix Tables 23 to 26.)

Not all of the questions asked were answered by each minister. Of 559 who replied to the request that they state instances in which all or a part of their congregation had coöperated in a common project with some Negro congregation, 53 per cent. replied "Never." The 47 per cent. returning affirmative answers revealed that most of them interpreted "coöperation" to mean simply contact.

Their replies indicated a variety of these contacts; of exchanges of musical organizations, contributions to various Negro church projects, and exchanges of pulpits. A very few actually coöperated in a true sense in community religious educational work.

According to the replies of 558 white ministers, only two cases were reported in which Negro churches refused to coöperate with white churches. It is also interesting that many say the Negroes never had a chance to refuse; they were not asked.

It is generally assumed that white churches help Negro churches; but 56 per cent. of 587 claimed never to have helped Negro churches financially.

In what definite manner has the question of race been included in your church program during the past year?, the ministers were asked. Their replies show that 38 per cent. of 567 have not included questions of race at all. Some included it in sermons, mission-study groups, and young-people's discussion groups. Only 173 answered whether the experiment was to be repeated. Of these 90 per cent. answered "Yes."

In reply to the question: Does your congregation encourage the idea of developing fraternal relations or Christian fellowship between Negroes and whites, 50 per cent. of 510 answered "No," and 40 per cent. "Yes." The remaining 10 per cent. of the answers were evasive.

On the question of recommending means for improving
the interracial aspects of the ministry and the church, several
surprises came forth. Men in the North and South reacted
contrary to the way people of their locality are characteristi-
cally supposed to react. The replies show a reasonable di-
vergence of opinion and attitude.

REPLIES FROM THE SOUTH

The replies included recommendations for more coöperation through Christian councils; mutual help and sympathy;
teaching and preaching God's attitude; better-trained Negro
leadership; more fellowship on the part of the young people
of both races; do away with prejudice; keeping white busy-
bodies and fanatics quiet on the subject; oppose colored and
white people worshipping together; no need for improve-
ment; coöperation, but not for social equality.

REPLIES FROM THE NORTH

The ministers in the North recommended, among others
the following things: greater exchange of pulpits; joint ministers' meetings; each doing his job coöperating with the
other; scientific study of race relations; common sense; invite
cultured Negroes to white churches, and more first-hand contact with best of races, and equal facilities for education,
worship and recreation; improve educational advantages for
colored ministers; much effort in this direction is doing harm;
whites need new conception of the brotherhood of man;
higher standards for Negro ministers educationally and
morally; have Negroes behave and act like decent human
beings; train and educate each in his own church; reading
Negro papers; better housing and living conditions; stronger
status of the Negro church; have Negro members.

Since these recommendations reveal very little difference in
thinking and attitude on the part of the white ministers,

whether of the North or the South, it may be concluded that white opinion is fairly well generalized.

However, there is some distinction, as the investigators know from their own experiences, between the expression of these attitudes in the North and in the South. The South suffers no inhibitions toward attempting to put the Negro where he belongs. In the North, although the feeling of the South is apparently shared, the Negro does not usually anticipate an overt expression of this attitude.

In further response to this question, some white ministers took the opportunity to extend their remarks. Excerpts from these remarks appear below without reference to geographical locality. The responses, like those already quoted, serve to illuminate these generalized attitudes.

THE MIXED FEELINGS OF THE WHITE MINISTRY

The question is—What would you recommend as a means of improving the interracial aspects of the ministry and the church?

The replies are:

Contact with cultured Negroes; sense of superiority visibly diminishes before the Negro with poise, brains and unprejudiced spirit. He makes whites of less ability feel humble, and demands respect because of his qualities.

Whites need a new (true) conception of the brotherhood of man. White man feels his superiority and makes this work complex.

Both must cultivate sympathetic attitude toward each other's problems and position. This is suggested from very practical and intimate knowledge.

Delegations from clubs, and pulpit-exchange would be helpful; also special projects of help such as financing daily vacation Bible schools.

Try to get two races together on intellectual rather than social basis.

Exchange of pulpits on Race Relations Sunday, and visiting of

Sunday school by white and Negro classes; also give plays in other race's church.

Avoid emphasizing differences by too much talk, and practice Christian and fraternal fellowship as a matter of course.

Seek to get parents to avoid making derogatory statements about other races before children, as calling the maid names, and preventing them from playing with other races, etc. I feel that most unsocial attitudes are thus engendered in the early years, and reconditioning is difficult.

Let Negro be proud of race and his racial history. Compel recognition.

Teach each race to value itself; to respect and help each other as much as possible; to deal honestly and fairly in all matters, but to keep absolutely apart socially. Separate schools, especially in grade and high school, would in my judgment help both races.

Segregation. Negroes should have their definite localities in cities. The churches of the whites and the government should assist them in their educational, religious and social program. There must be coöperation.

Our feeling here is that there is only one way to handle the Negro problem and that is complete segregation with no possible encroaching on white territory. Give him his section, schools, churches, etc., and see that he stays there.

It cannot be done; irresponsible people by the hundreds would make a social outcast of us; parsonages and churches burned; "niggers" would be killed—not by the better element but by robed and hooded hoodlums. (Not knights of the Ku Klux Klan.)

The Church and Its Community

The Negro church today is often challenged to do things that need to be done in the community. Individuals interested in social welfare often charge the church with being incompetent because it does not assume to satisfy many of the non-religious community needs.

In reality, however, the church is so limited by lack of funds, equipment and personnel that it could not adequately assume all of the responsibilities the public might place upon it. On the other hand, in cities where there are social-welfare agencies, it would not pay the church to compete with them. Further, and of great importance, is the fact that the church could probably very profitably spend its time, energy, and funds to intensify its own activities.

TWO METHODS OPEN TO THE CHURCH

There are two methods, among others, which the church may use to meet the challenge of its community. First, it may coöperate with existing agencies. The details of such coöperative activity will grow out of the particular locality, the kind of agencies, and the capacity of the particular church or churches. Secondly, it may serve its community by its contribution to the conduct and ideals of its members to the full extent of its own activities. Consideration of one major community problem, juvenile delinquency, illustrates these methods.

Juvenile delinquency results from the maladjustment of children to the home and to the community. It is usually the result of the broken home or of the low economic status of the family; and is sometimes traceable to conditions in a poor (semi-underworld) or "protected" anti-social neighborhood. Other factors such as ignorance, parental indifference, and inadequate recreation are also contributing.

The number of delinquents in the juvenile courts since 1928 was obtained in seven of the twelve cities of this study (see Appendix, Table 27). The officers of these courts were also interviewed.

The majority of the delinquents came from homes that had been broken. A large number lived with their mothers, many of whom worked away from home to gain support. A considerable number of the delinquents lived with relatives, or with persons not members of their immediate families. The juvenile courts usually take charge of children between the ages of nine and sixteen and have concurrent jurisdiction over them beyond the age of sixteen. The courts must use the remedial resources which are available, and they are limited in their ability to prescribe corrective treatment for the juveniles. It is surprising how well they have dealt with them under the handicaps.

CHILDREN NOT ESSENTIALLY BAD

The children who are brought to the juvenile courts, according to the reports, are not essentially bad. They are victims in many instances of poor training and poor environment. Except for the mentally defective, they are fairly normal children who are handicapped because the homes and neighborhoods from which they come prevent a wholesome development. The delinquents are not generally guilty of major crimes. They are brought to court for minor crimes and the possibility of saving them from further crime does not seem to be remote.

In almost every city the Negro juvenile delinquents represent a larger percentage of the total juvenile delinquency than the Negro population does of the total population.[1] The result is that Negro probation officers and workers are often overworked. It is the testimony of a majority of these officers that when Negroes are approached for help, the responses are evasive and generally cold.

THE TASK OF THE CHURCH

In the way of helping to remedy an already bad situation, the church through its organized teaching and other activities may assist the probation officers in family case-work.

The church also might agitate for the creation of organizations for the protection of children who are under-privileged; for the establishment of homes for children, for playgrounds, recreation, and proper care of child life. In most of the cities

---

[1] See Appendix Table 27.

the facilities available to Negro children in parks, play-grounds, supervised recreation and homes are very inadequate.

It seems quite possible for the church to reduce delinquency by helping to bring about the purification of neighborhoods in which protected vice is permitted. Many of these neighborhoods produce an alarmingly high percentage of juvenile delinquency.

CHAPTER X

Financing Negro Churches

Many people believe that the Negro churches have no systematic way of handling finance; that the Negro race has too much money invested in church buildings; that it spends too much money in the current running of its churches; and that virtually all Negro churches are heavily in debt. Criticisms such as these, which emanate from the masses, appear in the Negro press, and frequently are voiced by Negro leaders, imply an intimate and fundamental knowledge of the financial status of Negro churches.

But since no systematic study of the contemporary Negro church has been made, it is safe to conclude that these criticisms are not based on facts carefully gathered. Then, too, it is sometimes said that the money spent on Negro churches would be more beneficially used if it were invested in Negro business, in which case the money would be productive of a more adequate economic life for the race.

This assumption implies that Negroes who give their nickels, dimes, and quarters for the support of Negro churches would just as readily give these amounts in support of some kind of Negro business. It signifies also that a technique for diverting and using this church money for business could not only be worked out in theory, but that the method would be sound and practicable.

Some light might be shed on the subject if the public were to know, in part at least, the answers to the following questions: How much does the Negro actually spend annually on his church? How much does the average member give for the support of the church? Is the large church an asset financially? What is the value of Negro church property? What is the per capita indebtedness of the Negro church? How rapidly does the Negro church rid itself of its indebtedness? What is the method of financing the Negro church? What is the average salary of the Negro urban pastor? What proportion of the churches furnish parsonages for the ministers? Are church clerks and secretaries paid? What is the average salary paid to organists and choir directors? What is the source of income of the Negro church? Is the Negro church self-supporting?

No promise is made that the questions raised will here be answered satisfactorily and completely; but they will be discussed in the light of the data collected by the *Federal Census of Religious Bodies,* as well as those gathered on 609 urban churches; and it is the purpose of the writers to stimulate the public, if possible, to further thought and intelligent inquiry regarding the financing of Negro churches.

How Much Do Negro Churches Spend?

The *Federal Census of Religious Bodies* show that 39,245, or 92.2 per cent., of all Negro churches, reported expenditures in the year 1926; and that they expended $43,024,256. In 1916, 37,660, or 95.1 per cent., of all Negro churches reported expenses; and the total expenditures for that year amounted to $18,529,827, an increase in expenditures of 132.2 per cent. in 1926 over those of 1916. This increase in expenditures of Negro churches for the ten years is lower than the average of 148.5 per cent. for all churches—Negro and white.

Accepting as approximately correct the census figures as to the number of Negro churches in the United States and the amount that 92.2 per cent. of them expended in 1926, it is safe to estimate that the 42,585 Negro churches spent in that year $46,673,160; or an average of approximately $1,096 per church, an increase of 122.8 per cent. over the average of

1916. The national averages for all churches was $1,613 in 1916, but $3,783 in 1926—an increase of 134.5 per cent. Thus in Negro churches the percentage of increase in total expenditures, and the increase in the average expenditure per church from 1916 to 1926, are lower than the increase for all churches.

On the basis of a total expenditure of $46,684,896 in 1926 and a membership of 5,203,487, the Negro churches in the United States, urban and rural, spent in 1926 approximately $8.09 per member.

Of the 10,158 urban churches, 9,642, or slightly less than 95 per cent., reported their expenditures to the Government in 1926—a total of $26,402,536, or an average of $2,738 per church. If the 516 urban churches that did not report their expenditures spent on the average $2,738 per church, then the 10,158 urban churches spent in 1926 a total of $27,815,344, or approximately $12.42 per member.

The Expenditures of 609 Urban Churches in 1930

The data of this study were collected during the period of depression; and the financial status of the 609 churches revealed in this writing should not be accepted as a normal record of Negro church finance. The Negro church lives by the toil of its members, most of whom are laborers; and when they are unemployed and their wages reduced, the Negro church obviously suffers. That the churches were running at a lower ebb financially when these facts were gathered, as compared with more prosperous years immediately preceding 1929, was the unanimous testimony of the officials of 609 churches. However, without reference to what was or what will be, it is the purpose here to set forth the financial condition of these churches at the particular time of the field work. In 1930 the 609 churches raised $2,986,965; and it was spent as Table VII indicates.

TABLE VII—DISTRIBUTION OF EXPENDITURES OF 609 CHURCHES,
1930

	Amount	Per Cent.
Salaries	$1,289,818	43.2
Interest and Reduction of Church Debt	683,856	22.9
Benevolences and miscellaneous items such as Insurance, Light, Heat, Rent, Publicity, Balance, etc.	627,395	21.0
Church Overhead, including Education and Missions	196,478	6.6
Repairs and Upkeep	187,418	6.3
	$2,984,965	100.0

LITTLE MONEY FOR EXPANSION

Salaries, interest and reduction of church debts, repairs and upkeep, items such as insurance, light, heat, church rent, and much of the money included in church overhead, are bare necessities. This leaves an exceedingly small amount of expenditures for the expansion of the church program. Furthermore, the money spent in bare necessities is necessarily spread thinly over a wide area, in spite of the fact that there are very few paid church workers. Salaries are small, as will be shown later. The amount spent in reducing church debt is meager in the light of the total indebtedness. The amount spent for repairs and upkeep is more meager still, when one considers property evaluation of over nineteen million dollars. Thus, the barriers set up against the development of a more effective church program are formidable in view of the actual financial situation.

AVERAGE EXPENDITURE PER CHURCH

On the basis of the $2,984,965, an approximate average of $4,901.42 was raised by each of the 609 churches. Grouping the churches according to the amount of money raised, 115 raised less than $1,000 each, or a total of $61,403; 297 raised amounts ranging from $1,000 to $5,000, or a total of $767,-456; 120 raised amounts ranging from $5,000 to $10,000, or a total of $817,690; 46 raised from $10,000 to $15,000, or

$544,687; 11 churches raised amounts ranging from $15,000 to $20,000, a total of $186,269; 9 raised from $20,000 to $25,000, a total of $188,032; and 11 raised more than $25,000, making a total of $419,428.

EXPENDITURE PER MEMBER

In 1930 the expenditure of the 609 churches, which had a reported total membership of 357,169, was approximately $2,984,965. Therefore these urban churches averaged in expenditure in 1930 $8.36 per member, or sixteen cents a week for each reported member.

COMPARISONS

On the basis of the Government figures, the average Negro urban church spent $2,738 in 1926, or $12.42 per member. The averages in this study for 1930 are $4,901.42 per church, or $8.36 per member. Two points by way of explanation are necessary. It was pointed out in the chapter on membership that the churches of this report are more than average. It probably holds true with respect to finance; for a few churches raising sums in excess of $25,000 annually would give a relatively higher average per church than the Government's report, in which a higher per cent. of churches raising small sums are included. Furthermore, in the churches with large memberships, though they raise more money, the per capita expenditure tends to decrease in the excessively large church, as will be shown later.

THE RESPONSIBILITY OF THE FEW

In view of the fact, as shown in chapter v, that the financial burden of the churches under discussion is borne by less than half of the membership, it follows of necessity that the financial obligation of the regular contributors is more than doubled by the delinquency of those members who do not contribute. Setting the number of regular contributors, 156,352, over against the $2,984,965 raised in 1930, the churches raised $19.09 for each regular contributor, or an average of less than thirty-seven cents a week.

The responsibility of the church is more accurately revealed in the light of the thirty-seven cents weekly expenditure than if considered in the light of the sixteen cents. In most of the churches the minority carries on the work of the church. Perhaps the minister was not wholly mistaken who said: "The membership of my church can be divided into three classes. One-third of them are members in name only. Their names could be dropped from the roll and the work of the church would move on unimpaired. The second one-third give and attend on special occasions. The work of the church financially and otherwise is carried on by the last one-third."

THE NORTH RAISES MORE MONEY PER CHURCH AND MORE PER MEMBER

The 251 churches studied in the North raised $1,741,761 in 1930 with a reported membership of 198,867. The average per church was $6,939.29, and the average per member was $8.76. The 358 churches studied in the South reported a membership of 158,302, and raised $1,243,204. Thus the South averaged in 1930 only $3,472.64 per church, and only $7.85 per member.

EFFECT OF VERY LARGE MEMBERSHIP ON CHURCH FINANCES

The findings of this study show that in 1930 the highest amount raised per capita was $12.27 by the 390 churches with memberships of less than 500. The 551 churches with fewer than 1,500 members show a per capita contribution of $10.53. It was $5.88 in the 43 churches with enrollments between 1,500 and 3,000, and $5.41 in the 15 churches that reported enrollments beyond 3,000 (see Table 28 in the Appendix).

The evidence produced here and in chapter v does not mean that large contributions per capita are necessarily desirable, nor that small churches of fewer than 500 members are advocated; it does not mean that in large churches large per capita sums are not given; but it certainly does show that in churches with enrollments beyond 2,000 the greater are the chances that a smaller percentage of the memberships will attend and support the church financially.

It is significantly established, so far as this study goes, that as the membership increases the greater are the probabilities that the percentage of contributors and the percentage of those who attend will decrease; greater also is the likelihood that the larger churches will raise less money per member.

THE NUMBER OF CHURCHES OWNED

Of the 609 churches included in this study, 541, or 88.8 per cent., own their buildings or are buying them; 62 churches, or 10.2 per cent., are renting; and 6, or 1.0 per cent., are accounted for as follows: two are company-owned, one is owned by the pastor, one by a city mission, one by a white church, and the other one is a gift.

THE ESTIMATED VALUE OF NEGRO CHURCH PROPERTY

According to the *Federal Census of Religious Bodies,* the value of 94.8 per cent. of all Negro churches in the United States was $56,636,159 in 1906; in 1916 the value of 93.7 per cent. of all Negro churches was reported to be $86,809,-970; in 1926 only 87.7 per cent. of the churches reported, but the total value had risen to $205,782,628. These figures show an increase in value of Negro church property of 53.3 per cent. from 1906 to 1916, and an increase of 137 per cent. from 1916 to 1926. The edifice value per church increased from $1,635 in 1906 to $5,510 in 1926, compared with national averages for all denominations of $6,788 and $18,920. Thus the average edifice value of each Negro church is less than one-third of the average value of all churches in the United States. If 87.7 per cent. of all Negro churches were valued at $205,782,628 in 1926, then the 100 per cent. can be estimated to have been $234,643,350, or an investment of $45.09 per member.

THE ESTIMATED VALUE OF NEGRO URBAN CHURCHES

In 1926 the Federal Government received reports from 8,952 of the 9,124 Negro urban churches reporting church edifices. The total value was calculated to be $145,730,958, or an average of $16,279 per church, which is considerably less than one-third of $53,538, the average value of urban churches for the whole country.

The 541 churches of this study that own or are buying their buildings reported an evaluation of $15,373,278. The total property value, including extra lots, houses, old-folk homes and the like, was reported to be $19,869,183.86; an average of $36,726.77, or a represented investment of $57.04 per member.

The Indebtedness of Negro Churches

Of the 541 churches that own or are buying their edifices, 386, or 71.3 per cent., have indebtedness. The total indebtedness of the 386 churches at the time of this investigation was $5,142,051.

It was pointed out in the chapter on membership that regular contributors constitute 43.8 per cent. of the reported membership. On this basis, the average indebtedness per contributor is more than double—for example, in Charleston, it would be more than $5.76 per contributor, and more than $51.22 in Detroit.

TABLE VIII—CHURCH INDEBTEDNESS, BY CITIES

Cities	Number of Churches Owned or Buying	No. in Debt	Per Cent. in Debt	Total Indebtedness	Reported Membership of Indebted Churches	Average Indebtedness per Member
Atlanta.....	47	34	72	$ 229,755	23,930	$ 9.60
Baltimore...	48	45	94	682,622	28,250	24.16
Birmingham	52	39	75	378,338	26,352	14.36
Charleston..	46	8	17	9,576	3,378	2.83
Chicago....	37	25	68	1,132,919	44,585	25.41
Cincinnati..	39	25	64	372,958	14,892	25.04
Detroit.....	32	27	84	724,674	28,287	25.62
Houston....	48	34	71	123,972	14,036	8.83
Memphis...	50	30	60	134,826	13,649	9.88
New Orleans	48	43	90	248,465	10,496	23.67
Philadelphia	44	36	82	789,800	53,846	14.67
Richmond...	50	40	80	314,146	22,976	13.67
Total.....	541	386	71.3	$5,142,051	284,677	$18.06

INDEBTEDNESS AND PERCENTAGE OF CHURCHES IN DEBT COMPARATIVELY HIGH

The average indebtedness of $18.06 per member recorded in Table VIII is higher than the indebtedness per adult member for the country at large. "In 1906 the debts of churches in centers of 25,000 and over were equivalent to $6.15 per adult member, compared with $14.31 now" (1926).[1]

In this study of the 541 churches that own or are buying their property, 386, or 71.3 per cent. of them, are in debt. Of the total number of churches, 609 in number, 63 per cent. of them are in debt. This, too, is comparatively high. Quoting again from Mr. Fry: "Analysis shows that there has been an increase in the proportion of churches in debt. In 1906 the relative number was 18.1 per cent. compared with 21.7 in 1916 and 21.8 in 1926. . . ."

Since Mr. Fry probably includes the rural and small towns

---

[1] Fry, C. Luther, *The U. S. Looks At Its Churches* (New York: Institute of Social and Religious Research, 1930), p. 87.

in this latter quotation, it is more than likely that the percentage of churches in debt for cities 25,000 and more would be slightly modified. At any rate, it seems clear that the indebtedness per member, and the percentage of churches in debt, for this study are appreciably higher than they are for the country at large.

DISTRIBUTION OF DEBT

Of the 386 churches in debt, 176, or 45.6 per cent., owe less than $5,000; 152, or 39.4 per cent., owe between $5,000 and $25,000; and 58, or 15.0 per cent., owe more than $25,000. For details see Table 29 in the Appendix.

TABLE IX—DEBTS OF 21 CHURCHES THAT OWE
$50,000 OR MORE

$ 50,000	2
52,000	3
55,000	1
60,000	2
62,000	1
64,000	1
65,000	2
66,000	1
70,000	1
72,000	1
75,000	1
85,000	1
99,602	1
105,000	1
127,000	1
160,000	1
	21

THIRTEEN YEARS REQUIRED TO FREE CHURCH OF DEBT

In 1930, of the 386 churches that had debts, 251, or 65 per cent., paid interest and reduced the principal; 98, or 25.4 per cent., paid the interest only; while 37, or 9.6 per cent., paid neither interest nor principal. Table VII showed that $683,856, or 22.9 per cent. of the total raised in 1930, was spent for interest and reduction of church debt. The 386 indebted churches raised in 1930, $2,425,365; and spent

$683,856, or 28 per cent. of the amount raised, for interest and reduction of church debt. The total amount paid for the reduction of church debt was $375,332, slightly more than the interest on the total indebtedness at 6 per cent. per annum. In reality the principal was actually reduced by $375,332. If this should happen to be the rate at which the principal is reduced annually, it would take thirteen and one-half years for the churches to become free from debt.

To take extreme cases, churches that owe less than $1,000 might easily clear themselves of debt within a year or two. On the other hand, a church that owes $160,000 pays $9,600 a year for interest at the minimum rate of 6 per cent., or $800 a month, or $26.30 a day. In 1930 this particular church paid on its indebtedness $5,000, which is less by $4,600 than the amount needed for interest alone. In 1930 this church spent $4,000 for repairs and upkeep. It is difficult to visualize a Negro congregation of 800 people anywhere in America that would be able to reduce substantially each year a principal that is now $160,000. The average indebtedness per member in this church is $200.

It is almost safe to conclude that the whole debt will not be paid by the present membership. Twenty-five years would be a short time allotted for the complete amortization of a debt of such magnitude for a Negro congregation. The amount of money paid by Negroes for churches will probably never be known. Many churches similar to the one just described pay for years only the interest, or pay so little on the principal that its effect in reducing the debt is almost negligible. From year to year, the principal remains almost the same.

MIGRATION INCREASED CHURCH INDEBTEDNESS IN THE NORTH

The migration of Negroes from the South produced a crisis in the church life of Negroes in the North. It has already been pointed out how relatively small memberships became comparatively large memberships almost over night. As an example of how some churches grew chiefly from migration, Olivet Baptist Church in Chicago took in between 1916 and 1921, inclusive, 11,144 members by letter and Christian experience.[2] In 1916 Olivet Baptist Church moved into larger quarters at 31st Street and South Parkway, which made it possible for the church to serve more helpfully its great increase in membership resulting from the migration.

One pastor whose church is heavily in debt, states that he bought another church because his membership was increasing very rapidly owing to the coming of the migrants from the South.

This study makes clear the fact that neighborhoods that change their racial complexion also change the ownership and possession of churches. In many northern cities, such as Chicago and Detroit, as the Negroes moved into a section the white people moved out and often left churches for sale. Thus, facing the problem of inadequate housing facilities for an increasing membership, many a Negro church considered it a unique opportunity to purchase a church that was being vacated by white people rather than to take the time to build a new church. It is not surprising then that many Negro churches during the migratory period became heavily involved in debt because they felt the urgent need to purchase new quarters for their members. Some churches that started in a house or a store-front grew so rapidly that the need to purchase larger quarters gave impetus to the idea of buying a building from a Jewish congregation. Such is the case of the Pilgrim Baptist Church, one of the most outstanding Baptist churches in Chicago.

The situation just described accounts in part for the fact that the northern churches are more heavily in debt than the churches of the South. The northern churches were en-

---

[2] *Greetings of Olivet Baptist Church—Celebrating the 72 Anniversary, 1922.*

deavoring to meet an emergency which they considered to be of grave import.

PURCHASED CHURCHES

In the five northern cities studied, 158 churches have debts. Eighty-five, or 53.8 per cent. of this number, were purchased from white congregations. Sixty-eight, or 80 per cent. of the purchased churches on which there is indebtedness, were bought during the migratory period, between 1915 and 1928. In Baltimore, 30 of the 45 churches in debt were purchased from white congregations, and 23 of the 30 were purchased after 1915. In Cincinnati, of the 39 owned churches, 25 are in debt. All except 4 of them were bought during the period of migration. In Detroit, all 12 of the purchased churches were bought between 1915 and 1928.

Add to this the fact that there was a church building fad during the same period in the majority of the cities studied, Charleston, S. C., being the most noted exception, and one can readily see how migration increased the church debt in the North. Of the 158 churches that are in debt, 73, or 46.2 per cent., erected their own buildings; while 53.8 per cent. purchased their churches from Jewish or other white congregations. Of the 73 congregations that erected churches, 46, or 63 per cent., built during the migratory period, 1915 to 1928. In other words, 114, or 72.2 per cent., of the 158 indebted churches have either purchased or erected buildings since 1915.

INCREASED INCOME NOT COMMENSURATE WITH INCREASED MEMBERSHIPS

It is the testimony of scores of ministers that the great increase in membership did not justify the increased financial outlay in church building. Many of the migrants were transitory—they came into the community as roomers and renters and moved frequently. Quite a number passed on to other cities after five or six months. Not a few lost church connections altogether in the northern community, which was so unlike the rural South from which many of them came. One pastor comments thus: "As a result of increased numbers owing to the migration, we had to find a new place. Our financial obligations were trebly increased; but really the financial help of migrants was not commensurate with their numbers. These people, many of them, came from the rural South with the habit of giving ten and twenty-five cents a month."

Effect of Purchase of Churches on Race Relations

It is the opinion of some people that during the migratory period the wild financing of some Negro churches that purchased property from white congregations impaired interracial church relations. Many Negroes and whites who were interviewed during the investigation believe that Negro leaders were unwise in purchasing expensive Jewish synagogues and churches from other white congregations; especially when considered in the light of the Negro's earning power and his ability to pay. Equally unwise, they think, were the officials of some of the white churches to expect and require Negroes to pay as much as some of them did pay and are paying for the purchased churches.

No claim of deliberate unfairness is made here. In a number of instances the churches were sold at very reasonable rates; and often the white churches gave every possible consideration to the Negro congregation. On the other hand, there is ample evidence to show that too much was charged for some of these churches in view of the fact that the neighborhoods had already become, or were rapidly becoming, Negro, and of their own accord white people had moved out. From their point of view, the churches were no longer valuable to them. Then, too, the moving of Negroes into white sections often furnished white congregations an occasion to

get rid of churches that did not meet the modern require-
ments for religious education; hence an opportunity to get
rid of these out-of-date churches with apparent advantage to
themselves and to the Negro congregations as well; especially
so, they thought, since the migrants were coming in great
numbers. If perchance they had not sold these churches to
Negroes, they would no doubt have been forced to sell them
for much less—since a church building can seldom be used
for anything but a church.

At this point, Negro pastors and officials might have acted
more wisely, knowing as they do and did that the Negro
belongs to the under-privileged economic group in American
society. Vision and economic foresight might have enabled
them to see that they were placing debts on their congregations which would be burdens, in some instances, upon the
unborn children of their present members. The time element
was not properly appraised. As one critic puts it, "the Negro
officials were not so much disturbed about the total cost; they
were willing to buy if they could pay down little and have
the monthly or yearly payments apparently light. It was not
how much it costs, but how long do we have to pay for it."
In addition to all this, it seems obvious that church rivalry
and competition entered the situation—one congregation trying to out-do the other. The church across the way had
bought or built a big church; so this church felt obliged to act
similarly. Pastoral competition also played a part.

RESULTING STRAIN ON INTERRACIAL RELATIONS

In normal times it was difficult for these churches to meet
their obligations. This difficulty multiplied within recent
years because of what is known as "the depression." Consequently Negroes found themselves unable to meet their church
payments. The white church creditors were not always as
considerate as the Negro congregations felt a Christian church
should be. Many white people, as a result of these transac-

tions, came to feel that Negroes were and are an irresponsible lot and cannot be depended upon to live up to their obligations. These expressions cropped out again and again in interviews with whites and Negroes in Chicago, Detroit, Cincinnati and Baltimore. Some very frank and uncomplimentary things were said to the interviewers by Negroes and white people concerning each other because of these transactions. All of this straining of relationship might have been avoided if the several factors of the problem had been taken into account: The economic insecurity of the Negro race; the fact that if these churches had not been sold to Negroes, they would in many cases have been sold for little more than the value of the lots; and the further fact that some of the white congregations were getting rid of out-of-date and undesirable churches.

Church Indebtedness Compared with Property Evaluation

Strikingly significant is it to note that the total indebtedness of all churches reporting to the Government in 1926 was 11.3 per cent. of the total value of church edifices. In the present study, the total indebtedness of 386 churches is more than 25 per cent. of the total value of the church property of 541 churches, and approximately 33.3 per cent. of the value of the 541 church buildings.

Ways of Church Financing

An appreciable number of the 609 churches operate under a carefully planned budget. A growing number have their books audited annually. In these churches, financing is no secret; books are usually accessible to members at all times and to visitors who have genuine motives. It is possible to find a few churches of this character in each of the twelve cities studied. In the majority of cases, however, this is not true. Furthermore, the number of churches that raise most or all of their funds in a systematic way is negligible. The money raised through pledges or subscriptions and the regular public offering during services is rarely if ever sufficient to meet the financial needs of the church. Various methods are used in raising money.

It frequently happens that every auxiliary or organization of the church is primarily a money-raising organization. In one outstanding church more than $20,000 is raised through the circles of the church, which is approximately half the amount the church raised in 1930. These circles have their own secretaries and treasurers and report to the church the amount raised, always reserving the right to keep an adequate sum for their own expense. Another church received $1,698 from its Sunday school.

In making out the budget, the rally is usually named as one of the principal sources of income. Not only is this true relative to the raising of funds for building or church debt, but with respect to current expenses as well. It is a common occurrence for a large church to raise several thousand dollars a year through rallies.

Entertainment, soliciting, contests, musicals, singing over the radio, distinct emotional appeals through the sermon for funds, after-collections, special appeals to the Sunday school and young people's organizations, special collections at revival times, and money raised through prayer meetings are some of the methods employed by churches to raise the necessary funds.

ABUSE IN SOME OF THE METHODS USED

Many pastors preach their most emotional sermons on those Sundays when they hope to raise the largest sum of money. In some churches, on first Sundays when it is expected that the largest sums of money for the month, including most of the pastors' salaries, will be raised, the ministers not infrequently seem to strive to "shout" the people most. Ministers who do this seem to feel that it is easier to get their people to respond on the impulse of emotions than it is to train their members to give because of duty and because giving is a part of worship. It was an outstanding pastor of a nationally known church in a great city who said to another pastor in a church rally after a visiting minister, the chief of "whoopers," had successfully shouted the people—"Now is the time to take your collection."

The lack of a systematic method of financing the majority of the churches of this report accounts for the use of methods that are often undesirable. The long-drawn-out appeal for five dollars more; for ninety-five cents to make the collection even; three, four, and sometimes five collections during one service; soliciting, selling on the streets, and deliberate emotional appeals in the sermons are all methods that defeat the effort to train the people to give regularly and systematically. The method often defeats its own end. It is not unusual, in churches that have several after-collections, to hear people say that they will give a nickel or dime this time because the plate will be passed once or twice more. In cases of this kind, the individual probably gives the same amount whether there is one collection or three.

Salary of Negro Pastors

Opinions as to how well Negro ministers are paid differ widely. Many people are certain that the average Negro pastor receives so little that to make ends meet he must supplement his church salary by earnings from another job, or by an income from a business of his own, or he must resort to questionable methods of making a livelihood. On the other side are those who believe that no men in the race are quite as secure economically as that group of Negro ministers who are the pastors of reasonably large churches; who receive free rent, light and heat, and often free cars and other gifts from their congregations.

At this point, the salaries of 588 pastors representing 599

churches, and the number of them that have parsonages, should prove illuminating. Of the 588 pastors, 202, or 34.4 per cent., received less than $1,000 each for salary; 206, or 35.0 per cent., received salaries ranging from $1,000 to $2,000; 125, or 21.3 per cent., received salaries ranging from $2,000 to $3,000; 46, or 7.8 per cent., received less than $4,000 but more than $3,000; 5, or 0.8 per cent., received between $4,000 and $5,000; and only 4, or 0.7 per cent., received salaries embracing from $5,000 to $6,000. (See Table 30 in the Appendix.)

The 588 salaries paid by 599 churches total $871,132, an average of $1,481.52 a year per pastor, and an average of $1,454.31 for each of the 599 churches. It was the opinion of the majority of the pastors that they would receive much less in 1931 than they did in 1930. Many of them had voluntarily reduced their own salaries. Many others reported that already in 1931 the churches were hundreds of dollars behind in their salaries and there was no hope of their receiving the salary already overdue.

The Number of Pastors with Parsonages

Of the 202 pastors who received salaries of less than $1,000, 66, or 32.7 per cent., had homes furnished them by the churches; of the 206 whose salaries were from $1,000 to $2,000, 128, or 62.1 per cent., had parsonages; 125 pastors received salaries ranging between $2,000 and $3,000, and 104, or 83.2 per cent., had parsonages; of the 46 pastors whose salaries were from $3,000 to $4,000, 29, or 63.0 per cent., were living in homes provided by their churches; the 5 pastors who were getting salaries ranging between $4,000 to $5,000 all had homes provided them; and two of the four $5,000 pastors had parsonages. Thus 334, or 55.8 per cent., of the 599 churches furnish homes for their ministers.

These facts indicate that the smaller the salary the less

likely it is that the church will furnish a home for the minister. The smallest percentage of pastors with parsonages is found among the 202 who get salaries of less than $1,000.

PASTORS OF THE NORTH BETTER PAID

Of the $871,132 received in salaries by 588 pastors, $434,-825 is the aggregate amount paid to 244 pastors of the North. This represents an approximate average of $1,782.07 for each of the 244 pastors in Baltimore, Philadelphia, Cincinnati, Chicago and Detroit. Of the 244 pastors, 144, or 59.0 per cent., have parsonages provided by their churches. The 344 southern pastors received in 1930, $436,307, or an approximate average of $1,268.33 for the pastors in Charleston, Atlanta, Birmingham, Memphis, New Orleans, Houston and Richmond. Of the 344 ministers, 191, or 55.5 per cent., have homes furnished them. Thus the northern pastor not only receives a higher salary, but the percentage of churches that furnish parsonages is higher in the North than it is in the South. Nevertheless, Birmingham leads the twelve cities with 43 of the 55 churches studied, or 78.2 per cent. of them, providing homes for their ministers. Philadelphia leads the North with 37, or 74 per cent., of 50 churches furnishing homes.

ASSISTANT PASTORS NOT IN DEMAND

Nineteen, or 3.1 per cent., of the 609 churches have paid assistant pastors. These nineteen churches pay twenty-one assistant pastors an aggregate amount of $15,396, which gives an average of $733 per assistant. It appears that, occupationally speaking, the assistant pastorship is not a fertile field in Negro churches; possibly because of the large number of local ministers in almost every city who are anxious and willing to serve in this capacity for an occasional donation in order that they may have the opportunity to appear before the people once in a while.

NEGRO PASTORS ARE PAID LESS THAN WHITE PASTORS

Data relative to the salaries of white ministers in the twelve cities comprising this study were not collected. Nevertheless, a probable clue as to how the salaries received by the white pastors compare with those paid to Negro pastors should be of some value, and the comparisons are made for what they are worth. The facts concerning the white ministers are given by H. Paul Douglass in *1,000 City Churches,*[3] and deal with the salaries of 286 white ministers of the slightly adapted churches in cities with a population of 100,000 or more. These salaries are contrasted with the 588 salaries of this study. (See Table 31 in the Appendix.)

It is in the salary ranges from $1,000 to $3,000 that the comparisons are most nearly equal; 33.2 per cent. of the white pastors and 35.0 of the Negro pastors received salaries ranging from $1,000 to $2,000; 24.5 per cent. of the white pastors and 21.3 per cent. of the Negro pastors received salaries ranging from $2,000 to $3,000. But the Negroes lead by a large percentage in the lowest salary-scale under $1,000 —34.4 per cent. of the Negroes receive less than $1,000 as against only 3.9 per cent. of the whites. In the highest salary scales from $3,000 and above, the whites lead by a vast majority; such as 38.4 per cent. of the whites have salaries $3,000 and above and only 9.3 per cent. of the colored. Not one Negro pastor receives a salary of $6,000; 9.1 per cent. of the white pastors receive more than $6,000.

Since the study of the Negro church does include the highest-salaried pastors in the twelve cities included in the study, it is fair to compare the Negro salaries with a higher-salaried group of white ministers as reported by Mr. Douglass, who gives the salaries of 136 pastors of the internally adapted

---

[3] *1,000 City Churches* (New York: Institute of Social and Religious Research, 1926), p. 103.

churches in cities of 100,000 or more. (See Table 31 in the Appendix.)

As in the previous quotations, the Negroes lead in the number of salaries less than $1,000, and the whites have an appreciably higher percentage in salaries above $3,000. Of the Negro pastors of this study, 34.4 per cent. receive salaries of less than $1,000; no white pastor in this group gets as little as $1,000. Of the 136 white pastors reported here, 93, or 68.4 per cent., get salaries of $3,000 and above; among the 588 Negro pastors, only 55, or 9.3 per cent., are recipients of salaries of $3,000 and above; 22.8 per cent. of the white pastors are paid $6,000 or more; not one in the Negro church study gets $6,000.

NEGRO MINISTER NOT HIGHLY PAID

If the salaries represented here are typical of what the Negro ministers receive generally, it cannot be argued that they are highly paid. The vast majority, 410, or 69.4 per cent., of the ministers of this study get less than $2,000 a year. The situation is not radically changed when one considers a free home, because the smaller the salary, the less likely that the church will furnish a parsonage. It is probably true that the average Negro minister is as well-off economically as the average teacher or social worker, or as the average salaried Negro professional man for that matter; but that is not much to say. It is also to be doubted that the Negro pastor is exceptionally well-off because of what he gets from the congregation in excess of his salary and parsonage. The large number of ministers who supplement their earnings by teaching school, selling insurance, holding office in lodges and fraternities, or by promoting business of their own, serves to substantiate the point here advanced. The number of Negro pastors who are economically able to devote all their time to the church is alarmingly small.

Inadequate Secretarial Help

How well church records are kept depends almost wholly upon the extent of secretarial help and the salaries the secretaries receive. Of the 609 churches, 289 have paid secretaries and 22 have clerks only—that is, 311, or 51 per cent., of the churches have paid secretaries or clerks, leaving 298, or 49 per cent., without paid secretaries or clerks. These 311 churches have a secretarial staff of 390 workers. The 390 secretaries were paid in 1930, $66,804; an average of $171.29 a year, or $14.27 a month. In other words, the 609 churches spent for secretarial help in 1930 an average of $109.69 per church, or the meager sum of $9.14 per month.

POORLY KEPT RECORDS EXPLAINED

Only 6.4 per cent. of the 609 churches pay their secretaries more than $400 a year. Only three, or slightly less than half of one per cent., of the 609 churches pay as much as $1,200 a year; and this amount should be considered the minimum that a competent secretary or clerk should receive. Of the total number of churches, 49 per cent. pay their secretaries nothing at all; 93.6 per cent. pay less than $400, or the secretaries serve gratis. In the light of these astonishing facts, it is not surprising that complete church records are often not available, and that in many instances the available records are unintelligible. If the value attached to an office is to be partly determined by the amount of money invested in that office, then it must be concluded that in the vast majority of the 609 churches, carefully and adequately kept records are not considered of much importance. Furthermore, salaries paid secretaries indicate that the churches have not considered it necessary to get a person trained in secretarial technique and procedure to keep the records of the church. Ordinarily it is some church-member, not necessarily competent, who accepts the work as a side-line while his or her basic earnings come from other sources.

RECORDS NOT AS IMPORTANT AS MUSIC

The churches have been more concerned about music than they have about records. Of the 609 churches, 516, or 84.7 per cent., have paid organists, and 132 of these have choir directors as well. This percentage is to be set over against the 51 per cent. of the 609 churches with paid secretaries. In 1930 these churches spent $137,353 for music, including 527 organists, 4 assistant organists, 134 choir directors, 1 assistant choir director, 1 organ boy, and 4 singers—a total musical staff of 671 persons. The amount spent for music, $137,353, is more than double the amount, $66,804.06, spent on 390 persons for secretarial or clerical service.

A Challenge to the Negro Church

In every case where the church pays enough to enable the worker to spend at least half of his or her time in the secretarial work of the church, the financial and other records of the church were in fair order and intelligible. It is the testimony of scores of officials that with paid secretarial help, the finance of the church increases, and the people have more confidence since they know how the church money is being spent. As one secretary of a Birmingham church puts it: "It means a great deal to the members of this church to know that this office is open five hours a day and that any member of the church has access to my records."

It is the opinion of the writers that the 197 churches that raise more than $5,000 a year could afford to pay some one a minimum of $1,200 a year to keep the church office open daily and to keep the records in order. This would be an appreciable increase over the less than one-half of one per cent. that pay $1,200 a year for secretarial help. At least 194 churches, in addition to the three, could well afford to pay a competent person a minimum of $1,200 a year as church clerk or secretary. Within the next decade, hundreds of

Negroes will probably find employment in Negro churches as paid secretaries, musical directors, directors of religious education, and other activities that the Negro church must carry on if it is to be an effective institution.

The Negro Church Is Self-supporting

In the main, the Negro church is a self-supporting institution. It is true that much money is collected for local church support from a few white people who are friendly to a particular Negro pastor, or by Negro members who work in the homes or businesses of white people. Since this is more or less sporadic giving to solicitors, it is not possible to determine the amount given through this channel. Observation and statements from church officials tend to prove that, though these amounts are helpful and appreciated, they are, nevertheless, negligible when compared with the money paid by the members and the amount raised among Negroes themselves.

ORGANIZED SOURCES OF SUPPORT

There is an organized source of support, however, which cannot be neglected. Church officials were asked to name the organized sources from which the churches have received financial aid during the past four years. Seventy-one, or 11.7 per cent., of the 609 churches received aid through definitely organized channels. Included in this 11.7 per cent. are such churches as the Protestant Episcopal, Presbyterian, Congregational, and Methodist Episcopal, whose organic relationship to the parent body makes them more likely to get aid from it than are churches of some other denominations. Aside from aid received in this way, Negro denominations, such as the Colored Methodist Episcopal, the African Methodist Episcopal and the African Methodist Episcopal Zion, help local churches in some areas. Included in this 11.7 per cent. are also a few instances where white Baptist churches made a substantial donation to Negro Baptist churches. Of the 609 churches, 538, or 88.3 per cent., claim to have received no appreciable help from outside sources during the last four years. It is not too much to assert that, for the most part, Negro churches are supported out of the meager earnings of Negro people—the dollars, half-dollars, quarters, dimes and nickels of the toiling multitude of Negro workers.

Economic Status of the Race in Relation to Church Finance

Little hope comes from the assumption that because Negro congregations are large they can easily afford to expand indefinitely their programs. It was pointed out in the chapter on membership that it was the consensus of opinion of pastors and church officials of the study that 94.4 per cent. of the congregations are composed of either domestic servants, laborers, or a combination of both, and that only 2.4 per cent. of the congregations have a majority of their members skilled tradesmen, business and professional people.

These opinions, for the race as a whole, are supported statistically by Government reports. The most reliable information available on the occupational distribution of Negroes in the United States shows that four and a half million Negroes are "gainfully employed," and that two millions of these are making their living on farms. Of this number 232,000 Negroes are said to own farms, 500,000 are operating farms as tenants or managers, and one million and a quarter are just laborers or croppers. One million are industrial laborers, approximately a quarter of a million of them skilled or semiskilled; and one million are in domestic service. There are 100,000 listed in the professions, of which over three-fourths are teachers and preachers. There are only 4,000 practicing physicians, 5,000 nurses, 1,500 dentists and 1,000 lawyers. Seventy thousand are reputed to be engaged in business, which of course includes many small hucksters and pedlars and a number of persons with hair-dressing shops, restaurants, boarding-houses, and the like.

Leaving out the 2,000,000 that earn their living on the farm, since the city church is under discussion, there are 2,500,000 Negroes gainfully employed other than on the farm. Of this number only 420,000, or approximately 16.8 per cent., are business, professional, skilled, or semi-skilled workers, which probably leaves 83.2 per cent. or more who are common laborers and domestics.

Many things might be suggested that might relieve the financial load in Negro churches and place more money at the disposal of the local church—but only two will be mentioned here: The first is the consolidation of Negro churches, which will be discussed in chapter xi; and the second is better financial methods of distributing the church load over a larger area. It is gratifying to note that a few churches are beginning to do this, and are succeeding in getting a large per cent. of the congregation to give small amounts regularly and consistently. Moore Street Baptist Church of Richmond, Virginia, is an example. The records show that 987 of a membership of 1,200 have given small amounts rather consistently throughout the year. The Negro church, with better methods of financing and with an effective comity program at work, might go far to relieve its own situation.

It is doubtful that the Negro masses who in the main support Negro churches would give their money similarly to Negro business. Negro churches raise millions because millions of Negroes give small sums and get some kind of recognition in their church. Such business loyalty is yet to be developed. The first step is to be sought in the realm of church consolidation—fewer and better churches—and in raising the level of intelligence of the masses to coöperative group action in business.

Summation

1. That the average member gives little to the church in that the average expenditure per church totals sixteen cents a week for each reported member.

2. That 386, or 71.3 per cent., of the churches have indebtedness; and that on the basis of the payments in 1930, it will take 13½ years for these churches to free themselves of debt.

3. That debts are high when compared with property evaluations and with church indebtedness for the country as a whole; that debts are high, in many churches, when considered in the light of the memberships' earning power; that section (North and South) makes a difference relative to church indebtedness and the amount of money raised; that salaries vary according to the region of the country; that a few of the outstanding churches are free from debt.

4. That the buying of ready-built churches in the North during the migratory period strained church race-relations and hobbled the congregations with excessive debts.

5. That the larger the congregation the greater are the probabilities that the contribution per member will be less.

6. That the necessities of the church for salaries, interest, debts, heat, light, and the like, consume so much of the money raised that little is left for a church expansion program.

7. That Negro pastors, in the main, are meagerly paid.

8. That the vast majority of churches have no systematic way of raising funds.

9. That church records are poorly kept in the majority of the churches, almost wholly because paid secretarial help is inadequate; but in those churches that pay secretaries fair salaries and have their books audited, the records are better-kept.

10. That the Negro church, on the whole, is a self-supporting institution.

The Significance of this Financial Situation for Program Building

The chapter on program reveals the fact that, though much is being done, there is much to be done. This chapter makes it clear that the expansion of the program of the Negro church will, in the very nature of things, be slow. A church here and there will be able to do effective teaching or community service; but for many the pangs of debt will haunt them for years to come.

THE CHURCH AND COMMUNITY WORK

Before expanding their programs by building gymnasiums, hiring social workers, etc., these churches should first see to it that pastors are well paid, trained secretaries hired to keep adequate records, and that they prepare to do an effective job in the church schools by hiring workers to direct religious education. One of the weakest spots in the Negro church is the comparatively few trained and spiritually qualified people available for work in the church schools. The large proportion of the churches could reorganize their financial systems through trained clerks and planned budget systems so as to be able to attend to those things that are primarily the function of the church and coöperate with other agencies in the community that are looking after social and recreational work. It is more important, for example, that a church have its recreational work carried on at the Y. M. C. A. (if there is one) or that it coöperate with social agencies in matters of relief and family adjustment, and that it concentrate on the teaching function of the church, than it is for it to try to build a gymnasium or pay a social worker while the task of raising the religious intelligence of the young people goes neglected.

The church has no competition in the teaching of religion. But in social and recreational work, many communities are better organized to do it than the church; of course a high degree of coöperation is imperative. Ministers should have something to offer over and above that which social workers give. An appreciable number of social workers believe that ministers could help social agencies vitally if more ministers understood the social, economic and psychological factors that disintegrate the lives of clients, and if the ministers would be accessible to clients as spiritual advisers, a necessary function in the agency's effort to rehabilitate the individual. It is the opinion of the authors, however, that even in neglected areas, a church should enter these fields only until the community assumes its full responsibility. The church, because the financial strength of the Negro will allow it to do only so much, should confine its activities first and foremost to those areas that are specifically its own.

CHAPTER XI

Is the Negro Overchurched?

In an earlier chapter, attention has been called to the social, economic and psychological factors that gave rise to the larger number of Negro churches than of white in proportion to population; also to the propensity of some Negro leaders to start new churches regardless of the number in the same neighborhood. It is not strange, therefore, that it has been widely assumed and publicly proclaimed that the Negro is overchurched. The multiplicity of Negro churches has indeed become a subject of ridicule and laughter for many people, both Negroes and whites, who apparently have no knowledge or appreciation of the social and economic factors that gave rise to it. Until now no attempt has been made to discover the factors that determine overchurching. No one has established the point in church organization beyond which the people of a community dare not go without having too many churches.

No promise is made that anyone will know, after reading the findings of this study on the subject, whether the Negro is or is not overchurched. Future writers may not agree with the methods employed here. It is the purpose, therefore, not to reach definite conclusions, but merely to discuss the Negro church situation in the light of certain data which the authors believe one must consider in any effort to establish a norm or yardstick whereby overchurching may be determined. If as a result of this analysis the public is stimulated to further inquiry on the subject, and if Negro church leaders are so challenged that they begin to work out a coöperative plan of future church development, this part of the present study will have achieved its objective.

Factors to be Considered in Discussing Overchurching

The total number of Negro urban churches in the United States will be considered in the light of the adult urban membership. The total number of churches will be considered in the light of the total amount of funds raised by urban churches in 1926. The economic status of the race will also be discussed in connection with the total number of Negro urban churches. This discussion of the church situation for the United States at large will be followed by a more detailed analysis of the church situation in the twelve cities included in this study. The number of churches in each city will be related to the Negro adult population of that city and to the number of adults who are church-members. The financial status of the churches as of 1930 will be a vital factor in the discussion. In addition to a recognition of church finance, as far as possible the occupational status of the Negroes in each city will be given. On the basis of the findings of this study, the number of members discovered to be the most beneficial to a church financially, and the amount of money needed to maintain an adequate staff will be considered important factors in the attempt to determine the extent of overchurching among Negroes. Clearly the discussion will center primarily in the economic realm and secondarily in that of membership.

CHURCH DEFINED

Churches are included in this study that would not be recognized by denominational officials. For example, it is a rule in the Baptist church that it takes three ordained Baptist ministers and seven baptized laymen to organize a Baptist church. Many Baptist churches have been organized without adherence to this regulation. For the purpose of this study such churches, though unofficially organized, are included, because *church* is defined here as a place where a group of people assemble for worship—to sing, pray, and have preaching.

STORE-FRONT AND HOUSE CHURCHES RECOGNIZED

It has frequently been urged that store-front and house churches are of little consequence, and for that reason should not be included in a study of this character. The writers do not adhere to this view, because there are too many of the store-front churches for them to be completely ignored; and contrary to current opinion, the house and store-front churches are not necessarily short-lived. In not a few instances, services have been carried on for years in a store-front or house church. If there is enough there to keep the church alive over a long period, one cannot fairly brush it aside as insignificant.

Furthermore, where the church is short-lived, it is often short-lived only with respect to situation at a given point; the church proper may exist for a long time, but move from one store-front to another, or from one house to another. A few of the outstanding churches of this study had their beginnings in a house or store-front, especially during the migratory period. Then too, in all churches, human values are involved. To say that the store-front or house church is too insignificant to be taken seriously is equivalent to saying that the people of these churches are of little worth.

DETERMINING THE ADULT CHURCH-MEMBERSHIP

On the basis of the 1930 Government census, the number of adults 13 years of age and above, male and female, was computed for each of the twelve cities included in this study. Since all adults are not church-members, it was imperative to use some standard by which one may determine the number of adults who are church-members. It is now possible through the work of the Institute of Social and Religious Research, to estimate with a high degree of accuracy the number of adults who have their names on church rolls.

An analysis of the 1926 Government religious census shows that for the United States as a whole, 58 per cent. of the urban adults 13 years of age and over have their names on church rolls; that 59 per cent. of adults in cities with populations of 100,000 and above are churched; that 62 per cent. of the adults in the South Atlantic states have their names on church rolls; and that 46 per cent. of the adult Negro men, and 73 per cent. of adult Negro women, are churched.[1] It is assumed here that there is little variation in the percentage of 1930 and that of 1926. Therefore, the basis of calculation for this study is that 46 per cent. of Negro men 13 years of age and above, and 73 per cent. of Negro women 13 years old and above, are church-members. It must be kept in mind that these percentages are worked out for the United States as a whole, including the rural areas. If the rural areas were segregated from the urban, the 46 and 73 per cent. would be slightly altered; but not enough to modify the main conclusions of this chapter. It is assumed here that the urban ratios of male and female membership in the twelve cities studied are like those in the national average given by Mr. Fry.

The Number of Negro Adult Members per Urban Church in the U. S.

As previously indicated, there are 10,156 Negro urban churches in the United States with a total membership of 2,238,871, or an average of 220 members per church. It is difficult, perhaps impossible, to determine with precision how many members a church should have. It depends largely upon the loyalty of its members and their economic status. It is to be questioned whether the average Negro church with only 220 members is able to raise a sufficient amount of money to do a very effective piece of church work. Especially is this so when the 220 cannot all be relied upon to give systematic financial support. If the findings of this study should prove applicable to all Negro urban churches then less than 50 per

[1] Fry, C. Luther, *The U. S. Looks at Its Churches* (New York: Institute of Social and Religious Research, 1930), ch. ii.

cent. of the reported membership can be relied upon to contribute regularly.

That the membership of 220 is financially sufficient is further doubted because of the two and a half million Negroes gainfully employed in urban centers in the United States, one million are in domestic service; one million are industrial workers; a quarter of a million are skilled or semi-skilled workers; 100,000 are in the professions; and only 70,000 are engaged in business, including the smallest kind of business. In other words, only 20 per cent. of the urban Negroes gainfully employed are engaged in semi-skilled, skilled or professional work, or in business, leaving 80 per cent. to be engaged in common labor or domestic work. If the semi-skilled workers were included with the common laborers, domestic workers, etc., the 80 per cent. would be increased.

Again, if the facts of this study can be relied upon to apply to the urban church for the country at large, 220 members per church are too few to enable the average church to have at its disposal sufficient funds to carry on a vigorous, healthy program. The highest amount spent per member by any of the 609 churches of this study was $12.27, and it was expended by the churches with memberships of less than 500. Assuming that each of the 220 members were regular contributors, the average urban church would have for its annual expenditure $2,699.40. One can readily see that this is hardly enough to make it possible for a church to employ a well-trained minister. One gets nearer to the heart of the problem, however, if one considers actual expenditures by all churches for 1926.

The Average Expenditure per Urban Church in the U. S. in 1926

According to the *Federal Census of Religious Bodies,* 95 per cent. of all Negro urban churches, or 9,642, spent in 1926 a total of $26,402,536; an average annual expenditure of

$2,738 per church, or $12.42 for each reported member. Just what proportion of the $2,738 was spent in salaries, the figures of the *Federal Census of Religious Bodies* do not indicate. In the 609 urban churches of this study, approximately 43 per cent. of the total expenditures was expended in salaries. If this percentage should hold for all Negro urban churches, the average Negro urban church spent for all salaries in 1926 only $1,177.34. If the whole amount were paid to the pastor, the church could not expect a very able minister; and certainly the church could not hire any other worker; while to expand or make effective its program on $2,738 would be wholly out of the question.

It is quite clear that if the average amount was only $2,738 in 1926, many churches raised very large sums while others raised very small amounts. A high percentage of the 10,156 urban churches had at their disposal in 1926 far less than $2,738.

These averages of 220 members and $2,738 per urban church are far less than those for all the churches in the United States. The *Federal Census of Religious Bodies* makes plain that for the country at large the average number of members to an urban church was 546 in 1926, and that the average urban church expended that year $10,000.

Situation in Southern Cities

An analysis of the church situation in the seven southern cities of this study should throw further light on the topic of overchurching among Negroes. Table X gives the adult church-membership in these southern cities.

HOUSTON THE MOST CHURCHED

According to the 1930 census, Houston has 51,009 Negro adults. If the ideal obtained and all of these were church-members, there would be a church in Houston for each 319 Negro adults 13 years of age and above. The total Negro population

TABLE X—ADULT CHURCH-MEMBERSHIP IN SEVEN SOUTHERN CITIES

City	Adult Members	Number of Churches	Adult Members Per Church
Houston	29,712	160	186
Charleston	12,657	61	207
Birmingham	45,957	216	213
Atlanta	42,684	184	232
New Orleans	60,468	222	272
Richmond	24,358	89	274
Memphis	47,286	143	331
Total	263,122	1,075	245

of Houston is 63,337; and this gives the city a church for each 396 Negroes including children and babies. But since the ideal does not obtain, in that only 29,712 of Houston's adult population are churched, one must rely upon the 186 adults per church.

In this study the amount per member expended by churches of 500 members and fewer in 1930 was $12.27. With an average of 186 adult members per church and $12.27 per member, the average Houston church would have for expenditures of all kinds, $2,282.22. If 43 per cent. of this amount was spent in salaries, the average Houston church spent approximately $981.35 for all salaries in 1930. Even if the whole amount had been spent in salaries, the sum would have been insufficient to maintain an adequate staff of paid workers.

Fifty churches were studied in Houston for this report. Of that number, 29, or slightly less than 60 per cent. of them, raised less than $3,000 in 1930—amounts ranging from a few hundred dollars to $3,000. These twenty-nine churches had on the average far less than $1,000 for salaries of all kinds.

In the light of these facts, it seems to be clear that the available church money in Houston is very thinly spread over a very wide area; so much so that most of the churches of Houston must barely exist. Table XI shows conclusively that

TABLE XI—NEGRO CHURCHES IN SEVEN SOUTHERN CITIES IN
RELATION TO THE ADULT POPULATION, CHURCH-MEMBER-
SHIP AND EXPENDITURE

	Adult Population (13 years and over)	No. of Churches	Adults per Church	Adult Church-Membership	Adult Members per Church	Estimated Expenditure per Church*
Atlanta	69,512	184	378	42,684	232	$2,846.64
Birmingham ..	75,978	216	352	45,957	213	2,613.51
Charleston ...	20,545	61	337	12,657	207	2,539.89
Houston......	51,009	160	319	29,712	186	2,282.22
Memphis	77,987	143	545	47,286	331	4,061.37
New Orleans .	99,425	222	448	60,468	272	3,337.44
Richmond ...	40,055	89	450	24,358	274	3,361.98

* At $12.27 per member, the average spent in 1930 by churches of 500 members and fewer in this study.

essentially the same situation obtains in the other six cities.
Roughly speaking, the average for all the Negro churches
in the seven cities would be $3,000. On the basis of Table
VII in the chapter on finance, the expenditure would be as
follows: for salaries $1,296; for interest and reduction of
church debt $687; for benevolences and miscellaneous items
such as insurance, light, heat, rent, publicity, $630; for church
overhead, including education and missions, $198; and ap-
proximately $189 for repairs and upkeep.

THE ACTUAL EXPENDITURE OF 358 CHURCHES IN 1930

Confining the discussion specifically to the 358 churches
studied in the seven southern cities, the chapter on finance
reveals that these churches raised and spent in 1930 approximately $1,243,204, or an average of a little more than $3,472
per church. It was spent in this manner: salaries $1,493;
interest and reduction of church debt approximateley $798;
benevolences and miscellaneous items $729; church overhead,
including education and missions, $226; and approximately
$226 for repairs and upkeep.

A ONE-MAN STAFF

It is plain that most of the southern churches of this study
can do only an ordinary, or less than ordinary, piece of work

with only $3,472 at their disposal. It is true that many of the 609 churches raised relatively large amounts, as is pointed out in the chapter on finance, and as will be indicated again later in this chapter. On the other hand, the majority of them raised relatively small sums. The average salary paid to each of the 344 pastors of the southern churches of this study was $1,268. The average for all salaries was $1,492, only $224 more than the average for the pastors. Not only must most of the Negro southern churches of this study rely upon a paid staff of one man, the pastor, but in most instances there must be reliance upon a poorly paid pastor.

Economic Status of the Race in Relation to Overchurching

It is common knowledge that the Negro church is supported for the most part by domestic workers and by common and semi-skilled laborers. To say that approximately 80 per cent. or more of the Negroes in the urban South belong to these two classes would be conservative. Perhaps the most recent statement as to what the Negro common laborer receives in wages in the seven southern cities of this study is given by Paul K. Edwards, Professor of Economics in Fisk University. He gives the "wages paid male Negro laborers as of about January 1, 1930, in certain types of occupations in which large numbers of Negroes were employed."

In Memphis, these Negroes received weekly wages ranging from $15 to $20; in Birmingham, from $12 as porter in a store to $36 as worker in the coal mines; in Houston, from $21 to $27 as laborers in cotton compresses, manufacturing and construction; in New Orleans, a weekly wage ranging from $15 to $20; in Atlanta, from $10 to $14 as construction workers to $18 as truck drivers; the laborers in Charleston received weekly from $5, the lowest paid the porter in a store, to $21, the highest paid a stevedore; and in Richmond, the weekly wages were from $12 as coal-yard laborers to $18 as workers in a meat-packing plant.[2]

The Negro in Richmond, Virginia, the report of the Negro Welfare Survey Committee, asserts that over 60 per cent. of the Negro families of Richmond had in 1929 from all sources only $20 a week or less on which to live.

Furthermore, Mr. Edwards, on the basis of 1,029 families in Nashville, estimated the purchasing power of each Nashville Negro to be $347 in 1929, or for the family $1,266.55— an average of 3.65 persons to the family. He accepted this as a reasonable basis from which to approximate roughly the total purchasing power of the Negro in the seventeen largest cities of the South, which includes the seven southern cities studied in this report.[3] If Nashville should prove typical of the seven southern cities of this study, the following quotation is a revelation:

Of the 75 per cent. or more of Negro families in Nashville whose heads were engaged in either common and semi-skilled labor or its equivalent, approximately 40 per cent. were earning less than $900 per annum in 1929; more than 80 per cent. were receiving less than $1,500; and 95 per cent. were making less than $2,100. Of the 13 per cent. whose heads were employed at skilled labor, about 38 per cent. were earning less than $1,200 per annum; 50 per cent. were receiving less than $1,500; and 75 per cent. were making less than $2,100. Of the 5 per cent. of families whose heads were engaged in business enterprises according to the 1920 census, more than 60 per cent. were earning under $1,500 per year, and 77 per cent. less than $2,100. Of the 3 per cent. professional families, about 65 per cent. were earning less than $2,100. Disregarding occupation classes, and considering all Negro families as one unit, . . . the great majority fall into the lower income groups. . . . Cumulated, these

---

[2] Edwards, Paul K., *The Southern Urban Negro as a Consumer* (New York: Prentice-Hall, 1932), p. 28.
[3] *Ibid,* pp. 32 ff.

percentages show that more than one-tenth of the Negro families of Nashville were struggling along in 1929 upon incomes of less than $500; that considerably more than half were earning less than $1,200; and that only about 10 per cent. had incomes of $2,100 and above.[4]

For the purpose of this discussion, it is also important to know how the Negro spends his income. Again, if Nashville is typical for the South, the following quotation is illuminating:

Of the total annual earnings of the average family, 27.2 per cent. was expended for food; 14.9 per cent. for clothing; 12.4 per cent. for rent; 4.7 per cent. for fuel and light; 1.4 per cent. for furniture and household furnishings; 31.9 per cent. for miscellaneous purposes not otherwise accounted for, and 7.5 per cent. was saved.[5]

The 7.5 per cent., Mr. Edwards points out, includes significant investment in insurance.

These facts probably indicate that the Negro's income hardly permits him to support well the many churches that exist in these seven cities. Either there must be consolidation if the number of vigorous, effective churches is to be increased to meet the urgent church needs of today, or the vast majority of Negro churches will struggle along, barely existing, with insufficient funds to produce a constructive program.

CHURCH INDEBTEDNESS IN RELATION TO OVERCHURCHING

The meager earnings of the race, the small amount the average church raises, and the indebtedness of the churches of this study, furnish proof that the Negro is highly churched in these seven cities. In Atlanta, 34, or 72 per cent., of the 47 churches that own or are buying their property are in debt, averaging $9.60 per member. In Birmingham, 39, or

[4] *Ibid*, pp. 44-45.
[5] *Ibid*, p. 42.

75 per cent., of 52 of the churches are in debt, an average indebtedness of $14.35 per member. In Houston, 34, or 71 per cent., of 48 churches are in debt, and the average indebtedness is $8.83 per member. In Memphis, 30, or 60 per cent., of the 50 churches are in debt, and the average indebtedness per member is $9.87. Of the 48 Negro churches in New Orleans 43, or 90 per cent., are in debt, the average being $23.67 per member. In Richmond, 40, or 80 per cent., of the 50 Negro churches are in debt, an average of $13.67 per member. In only Charleston, S. C., are the churches practically free from debt; there 8, or 17 per cent., of the 46 churches have indebtedness, and $2.83 is the low average per member.

The overchurching cannot be isolated from the factors of meager incomes and church indebtedness; because it is the people of low incomes who must struggle along to meet current expenses and pay off these church debts.

THE BAPTISTS LEAD IN NUMBER OF CHURCHES

The Baptists lead in number of churches and of church buildings in each of the seven southern cities. Of the 1,075 churches in the seven cities, the Baptists have 661, or 61.5 per cent., of the churches; leaving 414, or 38.5 per cent., for all the other denominations combined. The African Methodist Episcopal denomination ranks second with 102 churches, or 9.5 per cent. of the 1,075. Strangely enough, some form of Holy or Sanctified church ranks third, with 95 churches in the seven cities, thus leading the Methodist Episcopal churches which take fourth place. The Spiritualists, in sixth place, are also apparently gaining ground in the South.

NEGROES ARE MORE CHURCHED IN THE SOUTH THAN WHITES

The Negroes of Atlanta constitute approximately 33 per cent. of the total population. They have 57.5 per cent. of the churches. Atlanta has a white population of 180,291 and

136 white churches.[6] It has a Negro population of 90,075, and 184 Negro churches.

TABLE XII—CHURCHES IN SEVEN SOUTHERN CITIES, BY DENOMINATIONS

Denominations	Number of Churches	Per Cent.
Baptist	661	61.5
African Methodist Episcopal	102	9.5
Holiness	95	8.8
Methodist Episcopal	50	4.7
Colored Methodist Episcopal	37	3.4
Spiritualist	36	3.3
Catholic	17	1.6
Episcopal	16	1.5
African Methodist Episcopal Zion	13	1.2
Presbyterian	12	1.1
Congregational	11	1.0
Other Methodist	7	0.6
Christian	6	0.6
Seventh Day Adventist	6	0.6
Lutheran	5	0.5
Evangelical	1	0.1
Total	1,075	100.0

Counting as churches only the 138 that have church edifices, the Negroes of Atlanta have slightly more than 50 per cent. of the churches. If the white people of Atlanta had proportionately as many churches as the Negroes have, white Atlanta would have 368 churches rather than 136. If the Negroes of Atlanta had proportionately as few churches as the whites, they would have 68 churches instead of 184.

Birmingham has a total population of 259,678 and a Negro population of 99,077. Negroes constitute 38 per cent. of the population. They own or have 53 per cent. of the churches. The whites have 188 churches; the Negroes have 216 churches. To equal the Negroes in the number of churches,

---

[6] Data as to the number of white churches in ten of the twelve cities were obtained either from the executive secretary of the Federation of Churches or from the *City Directory* after all Negro churches had been located and the number compared with the number in the *City Directory*. If the *City Directory* was approximately correct in the number of Negro churches, it was assumed that it was equally correct with respect to the number of white churches.

Birmingham whites would have to have around 350 churches instead of 188. If the Negroes had as few proportionately as the whites, they would have something like 116 churches instead of 216, a reduction of almost one-half. Counting only the 175 Negro churches with church buildings, the whites have only 13 churches more than the Negroes have.

In Charleston, South Carolina, the Negroes have approximately the same number of churches as the whites; but they have a population of 5,501 less than the whites.

The Negro population of New Orleans is 28 per cent. of

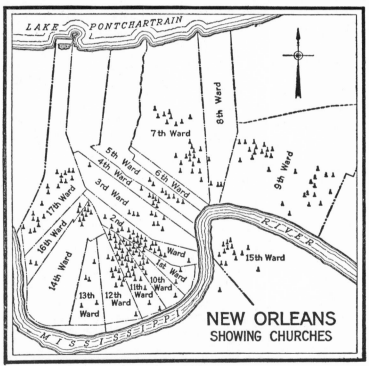

Map I

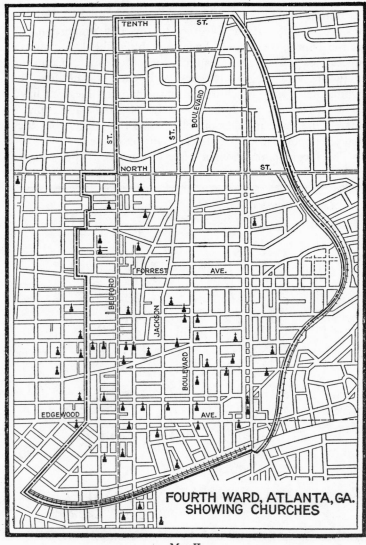

Map II

the total. New Orleans has approximately 424 churches. Of this number 222, or 52 per cent., are Negro churches. If the Negroes of New Orleans had as few churches as the whites in proportion to population they would have 80.

Memphis has a total population of 253,143; 96,550, or 38 per cent., are Negroes. Though constituting a little more than one-third of the population, Negroes have actually as many churches.

Richmond has a total population of 182,929; it has a Negro population of 52,988, which is 29 per cent. of the total; but the Negroes own 38 per cent. of the churches. If the white people of Richmond had as many churches as the Negroes, in proportion to population, they would have 218 churches, or 74 more than they have at present. If the Negroes had as few churches as the whites, they would have 59 churches instead of 89.

In Houston the Negro population is slightly more than 21 per cent. of the total population, but the Negro has slightly less than 47 per cent. of the churches.

The evidence produced in regard to the question of over-churching in these seven southern cities seems to be conclusive that when the number of churches is set over against the available church funds, the amount is so negligible that most churches must continue to operate with a poorly paid staff, sponsoring a program that is highly ineffective. Maps I and II are illustrative of the way churches are located in southern cities.

Situation in Northern Cities

Since in the North there have been large numbers of Negroes only in recent years, it is interesting to consider over-churching in the North and compare the findings with those for the South.

TABLE XIII—CHURCHES IN FIVE NORTHERN CITIES, BY
DENOMINATIONS

Denomination	Number of Churches	Per Cent.
Baptist	466	45.3
Holiness	244	23.7
Spiritualist	78	7.6
African Methodist Episcopal	77	7.5
Methodist Episcopal	43	4.2
African Methodist Episcopal Zion	19	1.8
Colored Methodist Episcopal	19	1.8
Presbyterian	15	1.4
Episcopal	14	1.3
Catholic	12	1.2
Christian	9	0.9
Community	7	0.7
Seventh Day Adventist	6	0.6
Lutheran	4	0.4
Congregational	3	0.3
Evangelical	3	0.3
Unity	3	0.3
Methodist, other than above	2	0.2
Universal	2	0.2
African Orthodox	1	0.1
Kodesh Church	1	0.1
Friends Church	1	0.1
Total	1,029	100.0

Cincinnati

The situation in Cincinnati may be taken by way of illustration. According to the 1930 Census, Cincinnati has a Negro population of 47,818. It has 112 churches, or a church for each 427 Negroes. Counting only adults, those 13 years old and over, Cincinnati has an adult Negro population of 37,594, or a church for each 336 adults. But considering only the 22,341 who have their names on church rolls, there is a church in Cincinnati for each 199 adult members. If the Cincinnati churches spent in 1930 sums that equaled $12.27 for each adult enrolled member, the average church had for expenditures $2,441.73. Of the 51 Cincinnati churches studied, 30, or approximately three-fifths, raised less than $3,000 in 1930.

The situation in the other northern cities is similar, as Table XIV shows.

The average for the five cities would be $4,257.69. On the basis of Table VII in the chapter on finance, the expenditure would be as follows: Salaries $1,839; interest and reduction of church debt, $975; benevolences, and miscellaneous items such as heat, light, publicity, insurance, rent, $894; church overhead, including education and mission, $281; repairs and upkeep, approximately $268.

TABLE XIV—NEGRO CHURCHES IN FIVE NORTHERN CITIES, IN RELATION TO THE ADULT POPULATION, CHURCH-MEMBERSHIP AND EXPENDITURE

	Adult Population (13 years and over)	No. of Churches	Adults per Church	Adult Church-Membership	Adult Members per Church	Estimated Expenditure per Church*
Cincinnati ..	37,594	112	336	22,341	199	$2,441.73
Chicago	190,469	344	554	113,602	330	4,049.10
Baltimore ...	110,114	186	592	65,654	353	4,331.31
Detroit	94,421	146	647	53,123	364	4,466.28
Philadelphia..	171,803	241	713	102,522	425	5,214.75

* At $12.27 per member, the average spent in 1930 by churches of 500 members and fewer in this study.

THE AVERAGE EXPENDITURE OF 251 NORTHERN CHURCHES IN 1930

The 251 churches of the North raised $1,741,761, or an average of $6,939 per church. It was spent in this manner: salaries of all kinds, $2,984; interest and reduction of church debt, $1,596; benevolences, and miscellaneous items such as heat, light, insurance, rent, and publicity, $1,457; church overhead, including education and missions, $451; and approximately $451 for repairs and upkeep.

The average expenditure of $6,939 per church in the 251 northern churches, and the average of $3,472 per church in the 358 southern churches for 1930, are contrasted below:

TABLE XV—CONTRASTING EXPENDITURE IN THE NORTHERN AND SOUTHERN CHURCH

Object	North	South
All Salaries	$2,984	$1,493
Interest and reduction of Church Debt................	1,596	798
Benevolences, Heat, Light, Insurance, Rent, Publicity.....	1,457	729
Church Overhead, including Education and Missions.....	451	226
Upkeep and Repairs...............................	451	226
Total..	$6,939	$3,472

It is quite clear that the northern church raises approximately twice as much money as the southern church and pays twice as much for salaries. These facts indicate that the North is better prepared to maintain a trained ministry than the South, and is in a better position to expand its paid staff by including others besides the pastor. That the North is slightly more able to secure a trained ministry is borne out in reality in chapter iii. There it was pointed out that the northern pastors of this study are slightly better-trained than those of the South.

INSUFFICIENT FUNDS FOR AN ADEQUATELY PAID STAFF AND AN
EFFECTIVE CHURCH PROGRAM

Even in the North, $2,984 to be expended in salaries is not a large sum. In this study, the 244 pastors of the North received annual salaries averaging $1,782. On the basis of $2,984 for all salaries, there is left $1,202 after the pastor is. paid; and certainly a competent church clerk should not receive less than $1,200 a year. The average northern church of this study is barely able to maintain a full-time, paid staff of two people. What usually happens is that the average church has one regularly employed person, the pastor. Small sums (not enough to be called salaries) are distributed among several or many people, such as choir director, organist, clerk, secretary, and the like. The average Negro church has a paid staff of one man. It is not surprising that Negro churches with effective, constructive programs are usually confined to one or a very few churches in each large city.

Further substantiation of the fact that the majority of the churches of this study have too little money to build a vigorous, effective church program is readily seen when one recalls that in the chapter on finance it was shown that 115, or more than 18 per cent., of the 609 churches studied raised less than $1,000 in 1930, or an average of $533 per church; that 297, or slightly less than 50 per cent., of the 609 churches raised amounts ranging from $1,000 to $5,000, or an average of $2,588 for each; and that 67.6 per cent. of the 609 churches raised $5,000 or less in 1930. What can a church do with $533? What can it do with $2,588? Certainly 68 per cent. of the churches of this study are seriouslv handicapped financially.

Suggestıng a Norm or Yardstick

The facts discovered, and the experience gained during the two years of intensive study of the Negro church, give the authors a basis for suggesting a yardstick that should be thought-provoking and helpful in a consideration of the question of overchurching among Negroes. In making this suggestion, the writers are conscious of the fact that there are notable exceptions to the rule given here; but they feel that the public should be given the benefits of the findings disclosed. The norm suggested here is based primarily on tables 16 and 28 in the Appendix.

Of the 609 churches covered by this report, 390 had memberships ranging from 500 down to less than 100. These 390 churches raised $869,604, or an average of $2,229.75 per church. Of the 609 investigated, 123 had memberships ranging between 500 and 1,000. These raised in 1930 approximately $792,852, or an average of $6,445.95 per church. Thirty-eight of the 609 churches had memberships ranging between 1,000 and 1,500; and these churches raised $421,-024, or an average of $11,079.58. Twenty-one churches had memberships ranging from 1,500 to 2,000; and they raised $250,779 in 1930, or an average of $11,941.86 per church.

A study of Table 28 in the Appendix shows that the amounts raised by the churches with memberships between 2,000 and 3,000 and between 3,500 and 4,000 are almost the same as the amounts raised by churches with memberships from 1,000 to 2,000; but that the churches with memberships between 3,000 and 3,500, and those with memberships of 4,000 and above, raised considerably more, $26,-652.50 and $30,435.56 per church respectively.

Although the amounts increase considerably in two instances in churches with memberships beyond 2,000, this is somewhat offset by the facts revealed in Table 16 in the Appendix. This table shows that the best churches, as to average attendance and the number of regular contributors, are those with memberships less than 2,000. Churches with fewer than 1,000 members, and those with memberships ranging from 1,000 to 2,000, have an average attendance of almost 49 per cent. of the reported membership; and approximately 49 per cent. are regular contributors; but beyond 2,000 there is a reduction of 17.0 per cent. in average attendance and 16.6 per cent. in the number of regular contributors. The norm or yardstick, therefore, lies between 500 and 2,000 members, and the finance of the churches with memberships ranging from 500 to 2,000 ranges between $6,446 and $11,942. The point advanced here is that those churches with budgets ranging from $6,446 to $11,942 are in a position to command a paid staff, which would make possible a more effective church program than most of the churches that have small memberships and less than $3,000 for all

TABLE XVI—NUMBER OF CHURCHES NEEDED ON BASIS OF 500 ADULT MEMBERS

City	Adult Members	Number Needed*	City Has Now	Excess
Houston	29,712	59	160	101
Cincinnati	22,341	45	112	67
Charleston	12,657	25	61	36
Birmingham	45,957	92	216	124
Atlanta	42,684	85	184	99
New Orleans	60,468	121	222	101
Richmond	24,358	49	89	40
Memphis	47,286	95	143	48
Chicago	113,602	227	344	117
Baltimore	65,654	131	186	55
Detroit	53,123	106	146	40
Philadelphia	102,522	205	241	36

* On a basis of 500 adult members per church.

operations. Using 500 as the minimum rather than the 2,000, the church situation in the twelve cities is as Table XVI indicates.

Store-Front and House Churches More Numerous in the North Than in the South

Interestingly enough, in these five northern cities store-front and house churches are more numerous than churches with church buildings. Only 444, or 43.1 per cent., of the 1,029 churches have church buildings. This leaves 585, or 56.9 per cent., that worship in houses, store-fronts, halls, houses made into churches, or theaters.

Of the 1,075 churches in the seven southern cities just referred to, 883, or 82.1 per cent., have church buildings, leaving only 192, or 17.9 per cent., in store-fronts, houses or halls. This wide difference is possibly explained by the fact that Negroes in large numbers have lived in the southern cities much longer than in northern cities; and by the further fact that so many Negroes went North during the migratory period that church homes could not be provided in sufficient numbers to meet the emergency. Another factor accounting for the large number of store-front and house churches in the North has been given in chapter v where it was pointed out how the psychological factor played a conspicuously important part in increasing the number of churches in northern centers. (See Table 33 in the Appendix.)

Four Northern Cities More Poorly Churched Than Overchurched

In Detroit, 66, or 45 per cent., of the Negro churches are store-front or house churches; in Chicago, 248, or 72.1 per cent.; in Baltimore, 101, or 54.3 per cent.; and in Philadelphia, 115, or slightly less than 48 per cent., are houses, store-fronts, halls or theaters. With these high percentages of store-front and house churches, it is only fair to say that these four cities are not so much overchurched as poorly churched. In these four cities, the problem is largely that of reducing greatly the enormous number of store-front and house churches and increasing slightly the number of churches constructed for church purposes; but there is also the further problem of properly locating churches.

The Baptists Also Lead in the Number of Churches in the North

As in the South, the Baptists lead. Of the 1,029 churches in the five northern cities, 466, or 45.3 per cent., are Baptist. The African Methodist Episcopal churches do not, as in the South, rank second, but the Holiness churches, with 244, or 23.7 per cent., of the 1,029. In the North, the Spiritualist churches take third place. The African Methodist Episcopal ranks fourth, having 77 churches in five cities, or 7.5 per cent. of the churches; and the Methodist Episcopal churches which were in fourth place in the South, are in the fifth place. The Colored Methodist Episcopal, along with the African Methodist Episcopal Zion, ranks sixth in the North and fifth in the South.

Negroes in the North More Highly Churched Than Whites

In Baltimore, Negroes make up 17.7 per cent. of the population, and have 21.5 per cent of the churches. They are slightly more churched than the whites.[7] If they had as few churches as the whites, there would be 145 Negro churches in Baltimore and not 186. Baltimore has 677 white churches and a white population of 662,768. The Negro population is 142,106.

---

[7] Data as to the number of white churches were obtained from the Executive Secretary of the Federation of Churches or from the *City Directory* after all Negro churches had been located and the number compared with the number found in the *City Directory*. If the directory was approximately correct in the number of Negro churches, it was assumed that it was equally correct in the number of white churches.

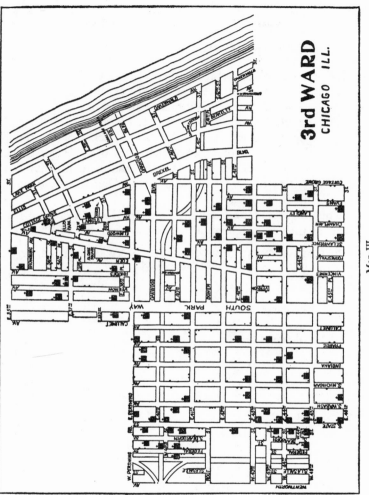

Map III

Cincinnati has a total population of 451,160. The Negro population is 47,818, or approximately 10.6 per cent., of the whole. Cincinnati has 347 churches. Of this number 112, or 32.3 per cent., are Negro churches. The Negro population is 10.6 per cent. of the total; but the Negro churches are 32.3 per cent. of the total number. If the whites of Cincinnati had as many churches per 10,000 as the Negroes have, the whites would have 945 churches instead of 235.

The population of Detroit was 1,568,662 in 1930; the Negro population is 120,066, or 7.7 per cent., of the total. Detroit has 610 churches, of which 146, or 23.9 per cent., are Negro churches. If white Detroit had as many churches per 10,000 as the Negroes have, white Detroit would have 1,762 churches instead of 464.

The Negroes of Philadelphia number 219,599, or 11.3 per cent. of the total population. The total number of churches

TABLE XVII—NUMBER OF CHURCHES IN TWELVE CITIES, BY DENOMINATIONS

Denomination	Number of Churches	Per Cent.
Baptist	1,127	53.6
Holiness	339	16.1
African Methodist Episcopal	179	8.5
Spiritualist	114	5.4
Methodist Episcopal	93	4.4
Colored Methodist Episcopal	56	2.7
African Methodist Episcopal Zion	32	1.5
Episcopal	30	1.4
Catholic	29	1.4
Presbyterian	27	1.3
Christian	15	0.7
Congregational	14	0.7
Seventh Day Adventist	12	0.6
Lutheran	9	0.4
Methodist, other than above	9	0.4
Community	7	0.3
Evangelical	4	0.2
Unity	3	0.1
Universal	2	0.1
African Orthodox	1	
Kodesh Church	1	0.2
Friends	1	
Total	2,104	100.0

is 981, of which 241, or slightly more than 24 per cent., are Negro churches.

Denominational Comparisons

In both the North and the South the Baptists lead in the number of churches. Of the 2,104 churches in the twelve cities, 1,127, or 53.6 per cent., are Baptist; and those of all the other twenty-one denominations combined number only 977, or 46.4 per cent. of the total. Owing to the large number of Holiness churches in the North, the Holiness churches take second place when the churches of the twelve cities are combined. The African Methodist Episcopal ranks third; but the Spiritualist takes fourth place, owing to the increased number of Spiritualist churches in the North.

THE SPIRITUALIST, HOLINESS AND BAPTIST DENOMINATIONS LEAD IN THE PERCENTAGE OF STORE-FRONT AND HOUSE CHURCHES

The four denominations that have the largest number of churches, as Table XVII shows, are the Baptist, the Holiness, the African Methodist Episcopal, and the Spiritualist. Of these four, the Spiritualists, with 114 churches, have the highest proportion, 97, or 85.1 per cent., store-fronts, houses or halls, leaving only 14.9 per cent. with church buildings.

The Holiness churches have the next highest proportion, with 240 of the entire 339, or 70.8 per cent., in houses or store-fronts, leaving 29.2 per cent. with church buildings. The Baptist denomination takes third place, with 363, or 32.3 per cent., of its 1,127 churches worshipping in halls, store-fronts, houses, theaters, etc., leaving 67.7 per cent. that worship in buildings erected for church purposes. The African Methodist Episcopal denomination has 179 churches in the twelve cities; and 29, or 16.2 per cent., are in store-fronts or houses. (See Table 33 in the Appendix.)

In What Way is the Negro Overchurched?

It is not because the average member pays too much money for the current support of the church that the Negro is overchurched. Sixteen cents a week for each enrolled member is not too much for a church to spend. The facts show that it is hardly enough. Even thirty-seven cents a week, the amount required per active member, is not excessive for thousands of people, many of whom spend more than thirty-seven cents a week for theaters, chewing gum, soft drinks, and the like, which cannot be classed as necessities.

Furthermore, when it is said that the average church spends sixteen cents a week for each reported member, or thirty-seven cents a week for each active member, one must take into account the amount of money raised through selling projects and that given by non-church people. In reality, the average contribution per member is less than sixteen or thirty-seven cents a week.

The Negro is overchurched primarily because the available church money is so thinly spread over so wide an area that the effectiveness of the church program is limited, except in rare instances. The problem of overchurching is further complicated because less than half of the members can be relied upon to support the church regularly, and this places a heavy burden on the faithful few. The problem is still further complicated in individual cases where the churches are heavily in debt, in which instances the burden of the faithful few is increased. In discussing overchurching, these factors must be constantly kept in mind.

Finally, the man who builds a church in an already sufficiently churched or overchurched area does not always recruit his members from among the unchurched people. He often recruits them from the churches in the community.

REFLECTING HIS ENVIRONMENT

The social, economic and psychological factors that gave birth and nurture to the Negro church, the restrictions in the environment and freedom in church areas, have all contributed to the multiplicity of Negro churches. That the Negro has more churches than he can maintain in healthy condition, no one can deny. A failure, however, to understand that there are many Negro churches, not so much because the Negro desired it but because he was largely forced to it by being shut out here and there from a larger participation in American life in other areas, is a failure to appreciate the survival struggles of a minority group in a civilization that has developed primarily to meet the needs of the majority.

But it is not enough to understand why there are so many Negro churches. Intelligent church planning with respect to the future is the most urgent need of Negro churches today.

The Dawn of a New Day

The circumstances that gave rise to the need for so great a number of Negro churches are not as compelling now as they were twenty-five or fifty years ago. The Negro is not as highly proscribed as he was. Before emancipation, and immediately following it, and on for years after the reconstruction period, the Negro was narrowly confined to two or three professions. This is not so today. Negroes are now found in scores of occupations. Many more avenues are open to them. New centers of culture are available which twenty-five or fifty years ago did not exist. The Negro is no longer almost wholly confined to the church for expression and leadership.

Although Negroes are still migrating to urban centers, the great emergency, for the present at least, is over; and wiser planning for the church housing of urban Negroes is possible.

Despite the apparent setbacks from time to time, there is evidence to show that the forces of interracial coöperation are constantly at work and the restrictions in the American environment are being slowly raised. These facts suggest new and intelligent planning with respect to the future church development among Negroes.

DEFINITE SOCIAL NEEDS

It is possible that the argument will be advanced that Negro churches meet a definite social need in the Negro community that is not met by churches of other racial groups, and thus the large number of churches is justifiable. Though much truth is contained in this argument, the economic phase cannot be left out; and, further, a church for each 500 adult members does not preclude the possibility of Negro churches meeting the social needs of the Negro community. Surely four or five store-front churches in one block on State Street in Chicago are not required to meet the social needs of Negroes in South Chicago. Forty-seven churches concentrated in the 4th ward in Atlanta, comprising an area of less than 1¼ square miles, are not required to meet the community needs of the Negroes in the 4th ward. This argument is further advanced by the fact that less than half of the population attends church regularly; and this is proved not only by statistics already quoted but by observation as one visits the churches. The number of churches that are packed from Sunday to Sunday is negligible. During the week, when people need churches for recreation, most of them are closed.

THE WAY OUT BY CONSOLIDATION

It is not the purpose in this study to suggest in detail the way out. But it is obvious that if Negroes are going to have a healthier church life, many of these churches must go out of existence; and one way out is by merging. The chapter on origin shows that only six churches of the 609 are the result of consolidation, and that only in one case was the merger one of outstanding significance. It is quite singular that in business and education the trend is toward consolidation, but that in religious and church work among Negroes the trend is toward expansion by the organizing of new churches, or in a few instances by splitting churches.

EDUCATION AND ECONOMICS DEMAND FEWER BUT BETTER NEGRO CHURCHES

Scores of churches in close proximity to one another and often of the same denomination, many with only a "handful of people," are doing the same type of work; in many instances they are doing it poorly, and in addition are competing against one another.

The economic status of the group, and the large number of churches in debt, also show the need for consolidation. Many of these churches must merge or die.

The teaching of religion is at a low ebb, primarily because workers in the church school are not trained. Consolidation should make the merged churches stronger to do a finer type of teaching in the church schools and throughout the entire church, because more leaders and more money would be available.

LEADERS RESPONSIBLE

In the twelve cities covered by this report, no effective method is being worked out to make fewer but better churches possible. It is almost safe to say that the need of merging Negro churches so far as actualities go, is foreign to the minds of Negro leaders who for the most part must take the lead in church consolidation. The Baptists, the Spiritualists, and the Holiness groups, which are the most active in dotting the streets with churches irrespective of need, are doing nothing to prohibit this promiscuous crowding together of churches.

Interdenominationally, the situation is not encouraging. Coöperation among the denominations through interdenominational ministerial associations is a frail effort. In most cities

where there are associations of the kind, they are weak and
their meetings are ill-attended; and practically nothing worth
while is being done. Charleston, South Carolina, is the only
possible exception among the twelve cities. In Charleston,
the Interdenominational Union is stronger than the separate
denominational bodies, and the denominations do not all have
separate unions. But even there, no plan is on foot to secure
fewer and better churches. In the other eleven cities, the
denominational associations are strong, but the interdenominational associations are not effective even where they exist.
The denominational emphasis is still very strong.

In the main, local church leaders, and the leaders in parent
national bodies, are responsible for this lack of coöperation
in local communities. Local committees, encouraged and
helped by the national bodies, should be organized to study
local church needs. There should not only be organized
committees within the denominations, but interdenominational committees should be organized to study the church
needs of whole cities. Such organizations should tend to
prohibit unwholesome competition among the denominations.

COMITY COMMITTEE

In addition to organizing to promote a more healthy church
life on the basis of the churches already in existence and with
a view of merging some of these if the conditions warrant it,
the establishment of churches in the future should follow a
procedure that has been carefully worked out by comity committees. Sentiment to this end could be molded by those
in authority, and by the intelligent lay leadership, so that
within a few years more intelligent action would be exercised
in regulating the number of churches to be conducted in a
given community.

It has been asserted several times in this volume that Negroes are more highly churched than white people. Yet white

Protestant bodies have gone a long way toward controlling the establishment of new churches. H. Paul Douglass writes:

Cooperative planning in church extension is an actual force in most of the major American cities and among the major Protestant denominations. Few churches have been organized or relocated during the last ten years without consciously facing the question, How will this affect the churches of other denominations? And a very large number of new or readjusted churches have resulted from deliberate joint agreements on the part of the Protestant forces.[8]

The comity process set up by the various city-wide councils or federations of churches does not generally take account of the comity needs of the local Negro churches. Thus, Dr. Douglass says: "Again, Negro churches, though rarely excluded in theory, are rarely included in fact within the working scope of comity practice." [9]

Challenge to Negro Church Leaders

In the judgment of the authors, if Negro churches are to be strengthened, there are four possible methods to that end: (1) It is conceivable that there will be a merging of Negro churches in certain communities, especially churches of the same denomination. (2) It is possible for the average church to increase the number of its active members, since less than half of the reported membership can be relied upon to support the church systematically and regularly. (3) Since only 46 per cent. of Negro male adults and 73 per cent. of Negro female adults are churched, wise evangelism might increase the number of Negroes in the church. (4) Comity committees could be created that would vitally affect the future church life of Negroes. It is the belief of the writers that the first and the last of these are the most urgent, and demand immediate attention.

[8] *Church Comity*, H. Paul Douglass (New York: Institute of Social and Religious Research, 1929), p. 14.
[9] *Ibid*, p. 10.

CHAPTER XII

The Membership of 185 Rural Churches

Despite the fact that more than half the Negro population of the United States is still to be found in rural areas, that more than 76 per cent. of all Negro churches and fully 56 per cent. of Negro church-members are rural, and that the Negro rural churches are so numerous that there is one for each 91 members, this study includes a much smaller number of rural than urban churches.

The reason for this has been partly accounted for in chapter v, where it was pointed out that the American Negroes, in quest of larger freedom in social, economic, civic and educational areas, are gradually becoming an urban people. It was shown there that since 1900, and especially since 1910, the Negro urban population has greatly increased, while the Negro rural population has decreased rather rapidly. It was also shown in that connection that as a result of the migration of Negroes from rural to urban sections, both the number of urban churches and memberships increased, especially in the North; and further that there is a larger concentration of Negro wealth and finance in metropolitan centers.

There are other factors, however, that account for this greater emphasis on the urban church. In the urban study, both the North and the South were included. The number of Negroes in the rural North is almost negligible—not a sufficiently large number to warrant a study of the Negro rural church in the North. There is not the diversity of types of churches in rural areas as in urban localities. The rural churches are more nearly the same in program, organization, leadership, cost of buildings, number of churches in debt, and membership size. A phase of this is demonstrated in chapter xiii where the messages of the rural minister are found to be more uniformly other-worldly. As to denominations, the urban churches are more representative than the rural. The rural Negro churches are primarily Methodist and Baptist. In the city, all Negro denominations are found.

Notwithstanding the fact that the rural material is less extensive than the urban, it presents an insight into the problems of the Negro church in the rural South. For reasons given in the Appendix, Peach County, Georgia; Orangeburg County, South Carolina; Montgomery County, Alabama; and Fort Bend County, Texas, with a total of 185 rural churches, were selected for study.

Rural Membership Smaller Than Urban

For the most part, the rural church has fewer members than the urban. It is much easier, therefore, to check the membership in rural churches than in those in the city. Often a deacon of long standing knows all the members, especially in a small rural church.

TABLE XVIII—MEMBERSHIP DISTRIBUTION OF 185 RURAL CHURCHES

Members	No. of Churches	Per Cent.
Less than 100	78	42.2
100 to 200	58	31.3
200 to 300	27	14.6
300 to 400	14	7.6
400 to 500	2	1.1
500 to 600	5	2.7
800	1	0.5
Total	185	100.0

In the urban study, 217, or 35.6 per cent., of the churches have memberships of less than 200. In the rural study, 78, or 42.2 per cent., have memberships of less than 100. In fact, 136, or 73.5 per cent., of the 185 rural churches have memberships of less than 200; and this is in striking contrast with the 35.6 per cent. of the urban churches with rolls of less than 200.

In the urban study, 392, or 64.4 per cent., of the churches, and in the rural study only 49, or 26.5 per cent., have memberships of 200 or more. In the urban study 130, or 21.3 per.cent., of the churches report 800 or more members enrolled, including a good many with several thousand members and a few with memberships of more than 5,000. In the rural study only one, or less than 1 per cent., had a membership of 800.

TABLE XIX—AVERAGE MEMBERSHIP PER CHURCH IN FOUR COUNTIES

Place	No. of Churches	Combined Membership	Average Per Church
Fort Bend, Texas	50	3,863	77
Peach County, Georgia	25	2,151	86
Montgomery, Alabama	57	8,491	149
Orangeburg, South Carolina	53	12,340	233
Total	185	26,845	145

The average is approximately 145 members per church for the 185 rural churches, while 586.5 is the average for the 609 urban churches. The average of 145 members in the rural churches of these four counties compares somewhat favorably with the membership per church in rural Virginia. Messrs. Ellison and Hamilton state that the Negro rural church in the state of Virginia has an average of 158 members.[1] The total membership of 26,845 in the 185 rural churches scarcely equals the combined membership of four large-sized urban churches.

Per Cent. of Regular Contributors Higher in the Rural Churches

The rural church differs from the urban in the percentage of active supporters in the total membership.

In Fort Bend County, 54.5 per cent. of the members are regular contributors; in Montgomery County, 51.3 per cent.,

---

[1] Hamilton, C. Horace, and Ellison, John M., *The Negro Church in Rural Virginia* (Blacksburg, Va.: The Virginia Polytechnic Institute), p. 8.

and in Orangeburg, 47.8 per cent. In the 160 churches of the three counties, 50.1 per cent. of the total membership is actively supporting the church with consistency. It is interesting to note that this is 6.3 per cent. higher than the percentage of regular givers in the urban churches, where the financial load is carried by only 56.3 per cent. of the membership.

Average Attendance Higher in the Rural Churches

Although the check on average attendance was not made with a degree of consistency to warrant statistical treatment, it was the opinion of the persons interviewed that the active members, those who actually support the church, are the ones who attend regularly. Then, too, if the check on average attendance in the urban study has any value for the rural study, it is safe to count the average number in attendance and the number of regular contributors as the same; for in the urban study 42.5 per cent. of the total membership of the 609 churches is listed as regular in attendance, whereas 43.8 per cent. is listed as contributing regularly, a slight variation of 1.3 per cent. Thus in the rural churches of this study, average attendance, as well as the per cent. of regular contributors, is undoubtedly higher than in the urban.

This is probably because people in the country do not have as many things to attract their attention away from the church as people in cities. The preaching services are far less frequent than in the city, and the members are more likely to attend on the one or two Sundays a month when preaching services are held. In the city, attendance by many members only one or two Sundays a month would greatly reduce the average attendance. In most rural churches there is no night service and this, too, tends to boost the average attendance of the day services.

Besides, it is more difficult for rural people to see their friends during the week than it is for urban people; thus regular preaching services in rural areas are social gatherings as well. In fact, the Negro rural church is possibly more of a social center than the Negro urban church.

Denominational Distribution of 185 Churches

Of the 185 churches, 125, or 67.6 per cent., are Baptist; 24, or 13.0 per cent., are Methodist Episcopal; 15, or 8.1 per cent., African Methodist Episcopal Zion; and the remaining 21, or 11.3 per cent., African Methodist Episcopal and Colored Methodist Episcopal. Presbyterian, Congregational and Protestant Episcopal churches are exceedingly rare among Negroes in rural areas.

Occupational Distribution of Members

FORT BEND

In Fort Bend County, Texas, it was the opinion of the officials of 26 of the 50 churches that renters are far in the lead in the occupational distribution of members. Officials of 22 churches gave it as their belief that renters held first place and owners second. In eight churches it was stated that owners of farms would constitute the majority of the membership; in three cases, day laborers were listed as constituting the majority; and in one case, share-croppers.

These opinions can be partly supported statistically. According to the 1930 census report, there are 361 Negroes in Fort Bend County who own their farms; 750 who rent farms; and 714 who are share-croppers. This distribution of Negro farmers in Fort Bend gives a total of 1,825; and shows that approximately 19.8 per cent. of the Negro farmers in the county are farm owners; 39.1 per cent. are share-croppers; and 41.1 per cent. are renters. In other words, not quite one in five owns his farm. It was not possible to check on the number of farm day laborers. This occupational distribution for the county as a whole must be fairly adequate for the occupational distribution of the members in the various churches.

PEACH COUNTY

In Peach County, according to the 1930 census report, 37 Negroes own their farms; 328 are share-croppers; and 123 are renters. Including renters, share-croppers and owners, there are 488 Negroes in Peach County who operate farms; and the percentage is as follows: owners, 7.6 per cent.; renters, 25.2 per cent.; and share-croppers, 67.2 per cent. Not one in ten owns his farm. If the many heads of families who are mere day laborers could be included in the calculation, the percentage of owners in the total Negro population would be much smaller than these figures indicate.

MONTGOMERY COUNTY

Montgomery County has 3,173 Negro owners, renters and croppers, according to the Government census report; and of this number 376, or 11.8 per cent., are owners; 610, or 19.2 per cent., are share-croppers; and 2,187, or 69 per cent., are renters.

ORANGEBURG COUNTY

The farm owners, renters, and share-croppers in Orangeburg County in 1930 totaled 4,711. The number of owners was 826, or 17.5 per cent. of the total; the croppers numbered 1,424, or 30.2 per cent.; and the renters 2,461, or 52.3 per cent.

As already indicated, the percentage of owners, renters and croppers in the total Negro population would probably be very small if the number of farm day laborers in each of the counties was known. The significance of this occupational distribution for church development will be discussed in the section on finance.

Effect of Migration on Membership

In Orangeburg County, the officials of 47 of the 53 churches studied stated emphatically that the migration of Negroes from the South to the North and from the country to the city had reduced both their memberships and the amount of money the churches had raised prior to the migratory movement, between 1914 and 1918 and 1921 and 1925.

In Peach County, the officials of 18 of the 25 churches expressed the view that migration had reduced their numbers and finances. In Montgomery County the officials of 57 churches laid emphasis on the same fact. Only in Fort Bend County was it the view that the migratory movement had only slightly reduced their numbers. A glance at the population figures of these counties in 1910, 1920 and 1930 may prove helpful at this point.

Orangeburg, South Carolina, had a Negro population of 36,794 in 1910 and 42,718 in 1920—an increase of 5,924. But there was a slight decrease of 2,078 in 1930, when the total was 40,640.

Montgomery County had in 1910, 56,867 Negroes; in 1920, 48,462. In 1930 the Negro population was 52,144, a decrease over 1910 but an increase over 1920.

In 1910 there were 11,422 Negroes in Fort Bend County; 9,996 in 1920, and 9,787 in 1930.

Peach County was not organized in 1920.

In reality the population figures do support the opinion that the number of Negroes who left these counties during the migration left the churches handicapped by reduced membership; but not so greatly handicapped as the authors had been led to believe.

The probable explanation of the situation is that the people who move into the counties are not as loyal to the church as were the migrants; and the instability of rural membership is probably more marked now than it was in 1910 and 1920. Probably also, good roads and automobiles are making the country people less attentive to the country church. In addition, the younger element in these counties may be less attracted to the church than the country young people were fifteen and twenty years ago. A lack of systematically kept church records of members from 1910 to 1930 makes checking at this point impossible.

Another item must be considered, especially in the case of Montgomery County, Alabama. In 1910, the Negro population of the city of Montgomery was 19,322; in 1920, it was 19,827; but in 1930 it had increased, by more than 10,000, to 29,970. The Negro population in the county as a whole increased only 3,681 from 1920 to 1930. If this great increase in the city over that in the county is to be explained in part by the moving of Negroes to the city from the neighboring open country, one can readily see how church-membership in the rural part of the county would decrease.

Recruiting Members

In the four counties studied, the principal method employed in recruiting members is the revival, which in most instances comes once a year. In the city church, every service is considered somewhat evangelical, in that the opportunity for joining is given each Sunday; and emphasis is placed on this method by virtue of the fact that many of the churches have grown to enormous size with revivals playing only minor parts. The revival is still the biggest event in the country churches for these four counties.

Comparing the data of the urban and the rural studies, this chapter reveals that the membership in rural churches is much smaller than in city churches; that the percentage of average attendance and that of regular contributors is higher in rural churches; that more denominations are found in cities than in rural areas; and that rural churches have lost members and money as the result of the migration from the country to the city. In the next chapter the rural ministry is discussed and compared with the urban ministry,

CHAPTER XIII

Some Aspects of the Negro Rural Ministry

Since more than half of the Negroes of the United States live in rural areas and since three-quarters of all Negro churches are rural, a study of the rural ministry is important. The 185 rural churches included in this inquiry are under the leadership of 134 pastors. Frequently the rural pastor has more than one charge, and this accounts for the fact that there are fewer pastors than churches. These charges may or may not be all in one county. A pastor may, in fact, have four churches, each in a different county.[1]

Education of Rural Ministers

A minister's ability to lead, as well as the quality of his message, is partly determined by his academic preparation. It is necessary then to study the academic background of the rural pastors included in this investigation, and to compare it with that of the urban pastors.

Table XX shows that only three of the 134 rural pastors

TABLE XX—DISTRIBUTION OF FORMAL TRAINING OF 134 PASTORS

Academic Background	Number	Per Cent.
A.B.	3	2.2
Some College	2	1.5
Normal	7	5.2
High School	45	33.6
Grammar School	77	57.5
Total	134	100.0

[1] When it is stated, as later on in the chapter, that one pastor has two, three, or four churches under his supervision, it does not necessarily follow that data were collected on all of them, because one or more of them may have been in a county that was not studied, or in that one of the four counties from which no data on this phase of the subject were obtained.

are college graduates, that twelve have attended college or normal school, that slightly more than 91 per cent. of them have had only high-school or grammar-school training, and that more than half are only of grammar-school rating. Only one has a B.D. degree, and none holds the B.Th. degree. Although many have had a few seminary courses, seminary degrees are very rare.

RURAL PASTORS MORE POORLY TRAINED

In the urban study, 20 per cent. of the pastors are college graduates; in the rural study less than 3 per cent. of the urban pastors, approximately 27 per cent., and of the rural pastors, approximately 58 per cent., are graduates of only the grammar school. In the cities 13 per cent., and in the country less than 1 per cent. of the pastors have B.D. degrees. B.Th. degrees are held by 5 per cent. of the city pastors, while no country pastor holds one.

That rural pastors are poorly trained is substantiated by other data. Arthur Raper in his study of Greene and Macon counties, Georgia, states:

The preachers in the rural Negro churches in Greene and Macon Counties have but little formal education. Five of them had never studied beyond the sixth and seventh grades; twelve had gotten past the eighth but not through the eleventh; two had taken special college courses and two had degrees, both of which were D.D. degrees. Not one had finished a regular four-year college course.

The 96 per cent. of the rural pastors of this study who are not graduates of either college or seminary is a larger proportion than that reported by Mr. Fry, who states that 83 per cent. of the rural Negro ministers of the entire country, representing three denominations, Baptists, African Methodist Episcopal and Colored Methodist Episcopal, are non-graduates.[2]

---

[2] Fry, C. Luther, *The U. S. Looks at Its Churches* (New York: Institute of Social and Religious Research), p. 66.

The figures of the present study compare more favorably with those reported by Mr. Fry in a particular area.

But in the West South Central Division, comprising the four states of Arkansas, Louisiana, Oklahoma and Texas, the proportions of non-graduates are much higher. In that area three-quarters of the urban and nearly nine-tenths of the rural Negro ministers did not class themselves as either college or seminary graduates.

In the four states, approximately 90 per cent. of the rural Negro pastors are non-graduates, while in this study, 96 per cent. of the ministers in the four counties are not graduates of either college or seminary. In comparing this material with that of the *Federal Census of Religious Bodies,* it must be borne in mind that it was proved in chapter iii that the official figures are too high. Since this is true in the case of urban pastors, it is highly probable that the report of the Federal census of the training of rural ministers is also too high.

TABLE XXI—AGES OF 120 PASTORS

Age-Group	No. of Pastors	Per Cent.
20–29	2	1.7
30–39	19	15.8
40–49	39	32.5
50–59	43	35.8
60 and above	17	14.2
	120	100.0

Table XXI shows that the number of pastors increases rather substantially from the 20 to 29 year age-group up through the group of men 40 to 49 years of age; that there is a less marked increase in the number in the 50 to 59 year group, and a decided decline in the last group—60 and above. The number of men in the 30 to 39 year group, compares favorably with the number 60 and above. Of the rural pastors checked on here, twenty-one, or 17.5 per cent., are under forty years of age; and ninety-nine, or 82.5 per cent., are forty or older.

The Rural Ministers Are Older

The number and percentages of urban and of rural ministers between the ages of twenty and fifty increase almost consistently; and the percentage of men sixty and older is almost the same, 14.2 per cent. in the rural communities, 13.9 in the cities. The variation comes in the 50 to 59 year group. In the rural counties, 35.8 per cent. of the pastors are between 50 and 59; in the cities, 27.1 per cent. are in this age-group. In the cities, a larger proportion, 37 per cent., of the pastors are in the 40 to 49 year group, as over against 32.5 per cent. in the rural counties.

In other words, the number of men begins to decrease at the age of fifty in the cities, and at the age of sixty in the rural counties.

If this is true for the United States generally, the cities, for the most part, have a younger ministry. Probably the younger men are less likely to go to rural areas owing, in part, to the fact that, being slightly better trained, they seek more lucrative fields.

A similar conclusion as to the age of Negro rural pastors was reached by Arthur Raper in his study of Macon and Greene counties. He writes:

It will be noticed that only one of the fifty churches was served by a preacher under 30 years of age, and but 13 by men under 40 years, whereas 19 were over 50. Forty to 60 is the most common age, which while having certain advantages indicates that the younger and better trained Negro preachers are not serving rural churches.

Years in the Ministry

Of the 134 pastors, 116 gave the number of years they have been in the ministry. Twenty-eight had served from one to ten years; forty-two from eleven to twenty years; thirty from twenty-one to thirty years; eleven from thirty-one to forty years; four from forty-one to fifty years; and one had been in ministerial work nearly sixty years.

As is true of city pastors, the largest number of rural men have been in the ministry from eleven to twenty years. Beyond twenty years the number declines consistently to one in the country and five in the city who have served more than a half century.

TURNOVER GREATER IN RURAL AREAS

The rural churches have a greater ministerial turnover than the urban churches. In this study, 15.1 per cent. of the rural churches and only 8.3 per cent. of the city churches reporting had had their pastors less than a year; while 22.1 per cent. of the former and 16.8 per cent. of the latter had had their present pastors a full year. Thus there is a higher percentage of rural men who have held their present pastorates a year or less, while the city men have the higher percentages in service during the longer periods.

The Number of Points Served

Of the 134 rural pastors, 130 gave the number of points served. Twenty-four, or 18.5 per cent., were serving only one point; fifty-one, or 39.2 per cent., were serving two points; forty-one, or 31.5 per cent., had charge of three churches; thirteen, or 10 per cent., of four; and only one was the pastor of five churches.

A comparison of these figures with those for the United States as a whole is of interest.

In all, returns were received from virtually 172,000 churches. Of this number approximately half reported that their pastors had charge of only one church. Slightly more than one church in five had pastors who divided their time between two churches, while an eighth of the churches stated that their ministers were serving three organizations. This leaves nearly one church in six with a pastor serving four or more churches. In fact, there were actually 4,130 churches out of 172,000 investigated which reported their pastors were serving seven or more churches.[3]

In no case do the pastors of this study serve more than five points, and only one serves five. But only 18.5 per cent. of the pastors serve only one church, as compared with 50 per cent. for the nation as a whole. Slightly more than 20 per cent. of the pastors for the 172,000 churches reported by Mr. Fry serve two churches; whereas 39.2 per cent. of the pastors in the four rural counties of this study serve two. For the country as a whole, 12 per cent. of the churches have pastors serving three points. In this study, 31.5 per cent. serve three. Speaking strictly of Negro country churches, the figures for the four counties here under discussion differ widely from those reported for 25,000 country churches of three Negro denominations representing the rural part of the United States.

Reports from almost 25,000 country churches of the three colored denominations show that half of them were served by pastors with but one charge each, while the 105,000 such churches of the eighteen white bodies reported only about two-fifths in the class with a minister to a church.[4]

It is the opinion of the present writers that if the *Federal Census of Religious Bodies* had checked or verified the reports of these 25,000 churches, it would have found a much smaller percentage of churches whose pastors served only one point. Experience gained in this study, and years of actual living in the rural South, would lead one to doubt the Federal census data at this point.

Within recent years a great deal has been said about the absentee pastor in the rural district and in the small town. The distance from the pastor's home to the church was ascertained for 159 of the 185 churches.

---

[3] Fry, C. Luther, *op. cit.,* p. 42.
[4] *Ibid,* p. 43.

TABLE XXII—DISTANCES OF PASTORS FROM CHURCH

	No. of Churches	Per Cent.
On the ground or in the immediate community........	9	5.7
1– 5 miles	29	18.2
6– 10 miles	24	15.1
11– 15 miles	18	11.4
16– 20 miles	29	18.2
21– 30 miles	24	15.1
31– 50 miles	15	9.4
51–100 miles	9	5.7
130 miles	1	0.6
300 miles	1	0.6
Total	159	100.0

A glance at the accompanying table shows that 23.9 per cent. of the 159 churches have pastors living within five miles; that 39.0 per cent. have pastors living within ten miles. The pastors of approximately 50 per cent. of the 159 churches live within fifteen miles; and those of the other 50 per cent. are farther away, with 16.3 per cent. living at a greater distance than thirty miles.

Sermons of Rural Pastors

As in the case of the urban pastors, it is important to know something of the type of message preached by rural pastors. Excerpts from three sermons follow:

—1—

HEAVEN THE OBJECTIVE

I want to tell Jesus my trials. I will not murmur or complain but I shall take it to my Father in prayer. Some day, I cannot tell how soon, but I know that some day I shall be like Jesus. I shall walk in His holy way. I shall be filled up with the love of God. When I shall cross the river Jordan—when I have run the last race—when I walk the streets of ——— the last time, when I close this hymn book and Bible, God shall say, "Well done, good and faithful servant, you have been faithful over a few things, I shall make you ruler over many. Enter into the joy of our Lord." My hands shall be like His hands—my feet shall be like His feet—my eyes shall be like His eyes. I shall be standing there looking over the road I have traveled and rejoice and shall be glad in my heart that I am like Him.

When I get there, not only shall I see Jesus, but all the old soldiers. Some of those who took sacrament at this very altar. I will say, "I know I have been redeemed and washed in the Blood of the Lamb." I shall be like Him. I shall see Him as He is. Everyone who has hope, purifies himself. We shall have to struggle on day after day in our life. We cannot give up because we want to be like Him. Though some may not believe and coöperate, I feel and believe that we shall all make ourselves like Christ and continue to hold on. Though many have died— though throughout this town many have passed away, those who still live are those whom God has blessed to live. I think sometimes that the young are dying as well as the old. The young are passing away, I say. We do not know how many of us will be living at the end of the year. We have only a few days now until 1930 passes away, but we do not know whose name shall be called before then. I hope to be able to say that I have run the race and kept the faith. I want to wear the crown that has been prepared for me. I want to keep the faith, and some day when this journey is over, Jesus will bid you come in and you shall be like Him. Sometime the perfect day will come. The bright sun will rise. You cannot tell what you are now, but some day you will know. We will be in the likeness of our Saviour. I hope that we will continue to go forward and that God will bless us and guide us.

May these words of encouragement inspire you to go forward and not give up the struggle. The battle is not to the strong, but to him who holds out to the end.

—2—

DOCTRINE OF THE HOLY SPIRIT

We are talking about the doctrine of the Holy Spirit. You can see some people in the street. They may be driving an automobile; they may be riding in something else; you may turn around and talk to them about the doctrine of the Holy Spirit and they will say, "I do not know about it, I do not understand it." We are doing things every day that we do not understand. You cannot understand how it is that you can go to your meal-bag and take out some meal from the bag. You make bread out of it; you cook it, and you eat it. It puts blood in you; it gives you strength; it gives you life. You cannot understand how it is that you go to the same meal-bag; you get out some more of the same meal; you give it to your cow; it gives you butter; it gives you beef steak; it puts blood in your veins; it gives you life. You cannot understand it, can you? But you go right on back to that same meal-bag and you get that same meal and give it to your hog; it gives you pork chops; it gives you blood in your veins. You cannot understand it, can you? Still you go right back to this same meal-bag; you take out some of this same meal; you give it to your chickens; it puts feathers on them; it gives you eggs; it puts blood in your veins. You cannot understand that, can you? You should not attempt to disclaim the Holy Spirit because you cannot understand it. You know how well you like to go to Saturday night parties; you never get tired; but you are always too tired when it comes time to go to church.

I want you to shout. Nowadays, people think it is a shame to shout; they are afraid to shout; they are afraid someone will laugh at them. They shout seldom, because someone will think they are drunk. They think it is a disgrace to shout. You ought to have the doctrine of the Holy Spirit and you would not be ashamed to shout. When your enemies try to crowd you down, you should think about the doctrine of the Holy Spirit. If you have this doctrine of the Holy Spirit when your enemies crowd you down, you will get along. I can hear Paul talking to Jesus. He had the gift of this doctrine. You must have the doctrine of the Holy Spirit. God will help you get this gift.

You remember Isaiah. He was a wonderful prophet. Isaiah said he had the doctrine of the Holy Spirit.

John said that you should know the doctrine of the church and the fundamental principles of the church. You talk about this denomination and that denomination because your mother and father belong to it, but you ought to know the fundamental principles of the church.

John knew the doctrine of the Holy Spirit. He understood it. God tells us to go into the world and preach the gospel to every creature. My Lord! My Lord! You ought to build up the King's Highway. John helped to build up the King's Highway. My God! My God! This great man has said to us, "Repent ye, for the kingdom of God is at hand." My Lord! My Lord! You women who come here, I wonder if the Spirit has been your guide. Has the Spirit been your leader? I say, I wonder has the Spirit been your guide! I heard my captain say that He was the Spirit. My Lord! My Lord! Talk about the Holy Spirit, it has struck me down in my heart. It has set the wheel turning in my heart. He will be my guide at the midnight hour. I am talking about the doctrine of the Holy Spirit. My mother talked to me about the doctrine of the Holy Spirit. She knew about it. When I am burdened, heavy-laden, and friendless in this world, He is my guide. He has made my spirit doctrinized. He will lead me to the Glory Land. The Spirit will lead me, I say. It has been my guide, and it will lead me to Heaven and immortal Glory.

Sometimes the devil tries to lead me. I send him away, and call in the doctrine of the Holy Spirit. God in Heaven will baptize me and He will save me. He will lead me through the chilly waters of Jordan. If you have the love of God in your heart, if you know about the doctrines of the Holy Spirit, you will be saved. He knows the plan of my salvation. My Lord! My Lord! I want you to journey on; I do not want you to turn back.

He was pierced in the side. He was nailed on Calvary's rugged cross. I can see them as they hung Him there. I can see them as they laid Him in the tomb. He brought light out of darkness. He died that we might have eternal life; that we might have a right to the tree of life. I know His blood has made me whole.

I indeed baptize you with water unto repentance; but He that cometh after me is mightier than I, whose shoes I am not worthy to bear: He shall baptize you with the Holy Ghost and with fire.

—3—

FORMAL TRAINING IS NOT ALL

Fools should not try to teach God's word. You have never
seen one do it well. Everybody cannot preach God's word.
There are many people who think they can preach it. Moses was
a man of experience, and he had been taught in the schools of
Egypt. I believe that God has selected a certain few to do a
certain thing. Colored people think that everybody can preach
and everyone wants to take up the collection. I saw a man
preaching the other day who had a lot of education. He did not
know how to preach. You can get your Bachelor of Arts and
your Master of Arts degrees, and you can pile up knowledge,
but still you will be a fool. Some fools can preach better than
these educated men. I think our men drive too fast to the schools
of theology and our students rush too rapidly. They will leave
Jesus behind. If you leave Him behind, your way will be dark.
If you leave Him behind, you will leave everything. You will
perish and you will die. Hairs may be white on your head, your
burden may be heavy, your friends may turn their backs on you,
but you will finally say on your knees, "Rock of Ages, Cleft for me.
Let me hide myself in Thee." You had better not leave Him
behind.

The life of Jesus sets a wonderful example. Jesus did not study
books. Peter, James, John, Philip and others were ignorant men.
They had knowledge of the law of Jesus Christ; but they did
not go to school. Jesus was contented to scatter His words on
the wind, but they fell in the hearts of the Disciples. They
climbed upon the rocks. They stood and listened to Him.

I may not know the eight parts of speech, but I know the Bible.
Glory to His Name! The Negro race is in a hurry. I listened
the other day at the conference to some of their awful ideas about
the church. Some of their ideas startled me. God's immensity
is so great that we cannot preach about it. I do not know where
heaven is. I only know that I am trying to go there. I want to
meet God in the morning. I am going to fight my way to
heaven. As I think of it, man is like a wild horse without a
bridle. If you had no bridle on the horse, there would be no

hope for you. If you can do something to guide him you will be all right. It is a pity these old men make these mistakes. We are all on our way to death, and we should be getting ready. You should not be stumbling all your life. An old man may look like a fool, but he has God on his side. God has some interest in old fools as well as in young fools.

Rural Messages More Uniformly Other-Worldly

It is not surprising that the rural messages are more consistently other-worldly than those that are preached in cities. It was pointed out in chapter iv that the other-worldly idea develops best among the people who fare worse in this world. For the most part, the rural Negro is not as well fixed economically as the urban Negro; his opportunity for social expression is less; and he is more highly proscribed than the urban Negro. There is also a higher percentage of illiteracy in rural areas; and rural pastors are more poorly trained than city pastors. All these factors tend to produce a larger proportion of other-worldly messages in rural sections.

The country preaching runs along lines of the magical and other-worldliness with scarcely a dissenting voice. But in the large cities there are always a few exceptional ministers who are endeavoring to teach their congregations that religion has also real practical value here in this world. In the country, religion is more of an opiate and an escape from life.

Outstanding Leadership Problems in Rural Areas

When the ministerial leadership in the rural church is contrasted with that in the urban church, the rural church suffers by comparison in four distinct ways:

1. MORE POORLY TRAINED MINISTRY

The Negro rural church, like the white rural church, has a ministry whose academic background is decidedly lower than that of the urban ministry. In this study, 20 per cent. of the urban pastors are college graduates, and only 2.2 per cent. of the rural pastors. In the urban section of the study, 13.4 per cent. of the pastors have earned B.D. degrees, while only one of the rural ministers has.

This situation is not hopeful. The rural church, as the chapter on finance shows, is not able to pay the man of college and seminary training a salary that is commensurate with the time and money he has spent in preparation. The inability of the rural church to pay a trained ministry is aggravated by the fact that the trained Negro is more sensitive to the restrictions and limitations that the open country and small town offer; so he is less likely to accept a pastorate in the small town or rural area than the man with practically no academic standing.

2. AN OLDER MINISTRY

It does not of necessity follow that a youthful ministry is an asset to the community; but the younger men are slightly better trained than the older ministers, a higher percentage of the younger ministers are to be found in the cities. The country church must not only content itself with a poorly trained ministry, but with a slightly older ministry as well.

3. GREATER TURNOVER IN RURAL CHURCHES

It has been pointed out that the turnover of ministers in the rural churches of this study is greater than that in the urban churches. Slightly more than 15 per cent. of the 185 rural churches, and only 8 per cent. of the 609 urban churches, reported that their pastors had been with them less than a year; while a much higher proportion of city than of rural churches has retained their present pastors for long periods.

It can probably be inferred that the rural pastor changes often because he is looking for a more lucrative field. Many rural pastors have the ambition to obtain a city church. Not infrequently in this study urban pastors were found who had worked themselves up through three or four country charges to a comparatively outstanding city church. In no case was it discovered that an outstanding urban pastor had gone to the pastorate of a rural church.

4. PREACHERS AND NOT PASTORS

It has been asserted, and with much truth, that Negro rural ministers are preachers and not pastors. This contention is to some extent supported by certain facts. Many of the pastors serve two, three, four and occasionally five churches. The strictly country church has preaching services one Sunday in the month. The rural church that has preaching two Sundays in the month is the exception. Furthermore, rural pastors usually live a considerable distance from their churches. Of 159 rural churches, only 5.7 per cent. have pastors who live close by, while 61.0 per cent. have pastors living from 11 to 300 miles away.

It may be urged that automobiles and paved roads have eliminated distance, and that the rural church gets real supervision from its pastor. In some instances this is probably true.

But it is also true that automobiles and paved roads make it possible for the Negro pastors to spend less time with their flocks. Before the days of the automobile, the pastor came at week-ends, by train or in a buggy, and lived around with the members. Now, he can leave the city or the town early Sunday morning and arrive in time for the eleven o'clock service, and leave for home immediately after the evening service (if there is one).

The four problems are distinctly rural; and must be effectively dealt with if the rural church is to have a more adequate ministry. The salary of the rural ministry is discussed in chapter xv.

CHAPTER XIV

Program of the Rural Churches

As religious, social and intellectual guides, the church, the fraternal order, and the school are the important rural institutions. Preeminence may be given to the church because, for a long time in many of the rural communities and sections, it dominated all other cultural activities. In a large number of rural sections the church is yet the strongest institution among Negroes; and its program is worthy of analysis.

The program of the rural churches is much like that of the urban churches some decades ago. Although the problems of life in country and city are comparable in seriousness, the reaction of the rural church to them is quite different from that of the urban church. The rural church holds closely to the traditional and orthodox soul-centered programs. The activities are limited to the most elementary forms of worship services, Sunday church schools, occasional prayer meetings, young people's work, and the yearly revival meetings.

Services of Worship

The Sunday services of worship are probably the most important of all. They are not held regularly every Sunday in most of the rural churches, but on the average twice a month.

TABLE XXIII—DISTRIBUTION OF SUNDAY SERVICES PER MONTH IN 185 RURAL CHURCHES

No. of Services Per Month	Number of Churches	Per Cent.
1	20	10.8
2	113	61.1
3	14	7.5
4	31	16.8
8	7	3.8
Total	185	100.0

For 79.4 per cent. of these churches the program must be of a kind that will continue to function even though the minister is absent one, two or three Sundays a month.

The Mid-week Service

The lay leadership of the churches in country areas must be responsible for the mid-week services. Owing to the poor lighting facilities, to the inconvenience of travel at night in the rural districts, and to the physical exhaustion of many people at the end of the day, possibly also because the programs are ineffective, these services are seldom held and are poorly attended. A total of seventy-nine of the 185 rural churches hold mid-week meetings. Twenty-eight of these hold one such meeting a month, and fifty-one of them hold four.

Revivals

The value of the revival or protracted meeting is less appealing in rural churches today than in former years. The churches do not all conduct revivals, and many that have them are simply complying with a custom. During the period of this study 140 of the churches held revivals.

Thirty-two churches each held more than one revival meeting. Of the 185 churches, 106 held only one meeting and 79 held no meetings at all. Where the revivals were held, an interesting attitude toward them was revealed by the ministers and church officials. According to most ministers, the revival no longer causes large numbers of "conversions." It is now used largely for reviving the church-membership.

There are others among these ministerial and official church families who consider the revival or protracted meeting worthless except that it is in accordance with custom. The type of evangelism that may be carried on in every service of the church is being substituted wherever possible for the revivals. This obtains because the "man who comes ordinarily is most

dependable"; and further because when the artificial enthusiasm aroused by the protracted meeting subsides, so does the
aroused activity of the church. Of the revivals held, 63 per
cent. lasted one week; 32 per cent. lasted two weeks; and 5
per cent. lasted three weeks.

This reflects a change from the old custom of continuing
these meetings at least two weeks. The landowners, a strong
minority group in the rural areas, are interested in having
good farmers busy on their land. If their workers, tenant-
farmers and share-croppers, dissipate their energy and "fire"
in the "big meeting," the farm work will suffer. It is reasonable to suppose that the landowners may have helped to
shorten the duration of protracted meetings.

Another rapidly passing feature of the revival or protracted
meeting is the professional evangelist. The regular pastor in
57 per cent., and a visiting pastor in 39 per cent. of the
church revivals, were substituted for the professional evangelist. The reasons given for this substitution were very
pointed. The evangelists as a group seem more interested in
money than in the individuals to be taught and led; and they
are also interested in the show of numbers, in quantity rather
than quality of work. On the other hand, there is greater
probability that the pastor of another church will enter sym-
pathetically into the effort, and that there will be greater
coöperation between him and the resident pastor.

The Sunday Church School

The rural churches place the Sunday church school next in
importance to the church service. The ministers are forced,
because of their absentee relationship, to leave much of the
work of this department to lay leadership. The total enrollment of schools in the 185 rural churches is 8,084, or 30 per
cent. of the total church-membership of 26,845.

The enrollment in the rural schools represents a smaller

percentage of the church-membership than the school enrollment in urban churches with memberships up to 2,000. In urban churches with memberships of less than 1,000, the school enrollment is 40.7 per cent.; and in churches with memberships between 1,000 and 2,000, the school enrollment is 31.3 per cent.

The actual distribution of the enrollment of 172 rural Sunday church schools shows that 59.8 per cent. of the schools have 49 persons or fewer; 33.7 per cent. have between 50 and 99; and 6.5 per cent. have between 100 and 199.

The attendance at the school sessions is no more encouraging than its enrollment. The average attendance for all the schools is 5,483, or 67.8 per cent. of the total enrollment. Although only slightly over half of those on the rolls attend regularly and no other activities are conducted for these people, neither the records nor the officials of these schools and churches revealed any organized effort to reach the 32.2 per cent. who do not attend regularly or at all.

It will be remembered that the data on urban church-membership and school enrollment show that as the total membership in either activity increases the total average attendance decreases. In the rural schools with not more than 49 persons enrolled, the average attendance is 73 per cent. of the enrollment; in those with 50 to 99 persons, 20 per cent.; and in those with 100 to 199 persons, it is 17 per cent.

The average attendance in the schools indirectly governs the number of classes and teachers needed. The organization of most of the schools does not anticipate the attendance, but instead is created or adapted at each session to meet the needs of the day's attendance. There are 627 teachers and workers in the rural Sunday church schools studied. Of these, 87 per cent. have only elementary or grade-school training; 11 per cent. have attended high school; 1 per cent. have attended normal schools, and 1 per cent. have been to college.

Consequently there is much work to be done in the training, supervision, and selection of teachers. In all except six of the churches, the supervision is done by the superintendent; while in the six churches, either the pastor or the pastor and the superintendent perform this duty. In many of the schools the teachers are selected either by a vote of the school or by a vote of the church.

The standards of teacher-selection are necessarily low, because of the limited number of trained people upon whom the churches may draw. The possibility of teachers receiving training after they are elected is remote, because the churches seldom have teachers' meetings or any kind of training classes. Only eighty-two, or 48 per cent., of the churches claim to conduct a teachers' meeting or workers' conference for their Sunday church school workers. Under these conditions the educational status of these rural workers will be a difficult one to improve.

The lesson materials used are the improved uniform type. These uniform lessons comprise the whole of the curriculum; and they are not adapted to the actual needs of the people. Usually the school session consists of opening and closing exercises, with a teaching period sandwiched between them. Differences in the ages of the pupils are but slightly recognized; and in most instances classifications within the school are made on size and ability to read. The literature for all those who read is practically the same. Those who do not read are placed in the picture-card classes.

There is no fundamental difference in the literature prepared for and used by these rural churches and that used in urban places. Since most of the illustrations in the printed material are in terms of urban life, there is little help for the teachers in offering an adequate lesson to rural people. With limited teaching ability and poor material to use, not too much can be expected from the workers of these schools.

Young People's Work

Young people's work in the rural churches is restricted to 74 church groups. Of this number, eight were inactive at the time visited. The young people's work in the rural community suffers from a number of ills. The most important impediment to progress is lack of purpose and adequate direction. The young people's groups have practically no program. If they attempt to teach the Bible, the Sunday church school is found to be doing a better job. If they put on debates, entertainments or discussions, the interest soon lags.

Physical Equipment for the Program

The indoor activities of 94 per cent. of the 185 rural churches are limited to one room, because this is all the church has. In 5 per cent. of the church buildings there are two rooms, and in 1 per cent. of them there are three.

In addition to the building, a church usually has at its disposal about an acre, or one and a half acres, of ground. In a large number of localities the churches share their ground space, and some even share their buildings, with the county school and the fraternal orders. Except for church entertainments and an occasional picnic, the rural church does not make use of this ground.

The auditoriums of the churches all contain about the same equipment, such as a pulpit, benches, and means for heating and lighting; and in a few, either a piano or a pump organ. Besides being the place of meeting for all the public services, it is often used for the community activities. Interior decorations are usually poor and not very cheerful.

The general condition of the church property is discouraging. Of the 185 churches, 59 per cent. are in need of general and major repairs to roofs, windows, doors, walls and floors. Except for the exceptionally well-maintained rural Negro church building, the atmosphere of deterioration seems to be general throughout the countryside.

Church programs, which must make use of these poorly appointed and unattractive structures, are necessarily greatly hampered.

Even in the eleven churches with extra rooms, the program remains limited because little use is made of the rooms. In probably nine of the eleven church buildings, these extra rooms were originally the pastor's study and the choir room. Although they may not now be used by pastor or choir, most of them are too small to be used for classes or other Sunday church school purposes.

The 185 churches have adequate seating capacity when the membership, the number of churches, and the population of each county are considered. There are churches that will seat 900 or more persons. The distribution of the total capacity of 54,441 is as follows: 99 churches will seat up to 300; 52 will seat between 300 and 500; 25 between 500 and 700; 8 between 700 and 900; and 1 will seat over 900.

The rural church program has about as few activities as it can have and yet maintain a church. The promotion of these few activities at present lacks force and vitality. Probably the chief fault lies in the absentee ministry. The rural church is ordinarily deprived of its ministerial leadership three-fourths of the time. With the exception of the days on which regular services are held, the church must depend upon its lay leadership, which is proscribed by a lack of training and experience. The church programs suffer, therefore, not only from lack of continuity, but also from leadership that cannot promote it or attract large support to it. A vigorous rural church program will demand a vigorous resident ministry. Under the present economic conditions the church can hardly command or maintain such leadership.

CHAPTER XV

Financial Status of the Rural Churches

According to the *Federal Census of Religious Bodies,* in 1926, 29,603, or slightly more than 91 per cent. of the 32,427 Negro rural churches, reported their expenditures. The total amount expended was $16,621,723, an average of $561 per church. On the basis of the expenditures of 91 per cent., it may be assumed that all Negro rural churches expended in 1926 approximately $18,191,547.

One of the basic problems of the rural church, that of little money, is here revealed. In 1926, the 10,158 urban Negro churches spent approximately $27,815,344, an average of $12.42 for each member. In the same year, the 32,427 rural churches expended approximately $18,191,547, an average of $6.14 for each member. The urban church has for its annual expenditure an approximate average of $2,738; the rural church has only $561. The average city church has almost five times as much money at its disposal as the average rural church. The highest amount raised by an urban church in this study was approximately $50,000; the highest amount raised in 1930 by a rural church was $1,500.

Expenditures of 185 Rural Churches

The financial statement of the 185 rural churches is likely to be more representative of the financial status of all the Negro rural churches than the financial statement of the 609 urban churches would be of all the Negro city churches. This is true because the economic crisis in the rural South is of longer duration than the present period of depression which began in 1929. The economic disturbance in the rural districts of the South reaches back to the World War and the

259

beginning of the boll-weevil ravages in 1914, 1915 and 1916. Church officials expressed the conviction that the migration of Negroes from the rural to the urban areas had greatly reduced both their numbers and funds, and that the rural church was operating financially below par. But since the depression in rural centers has existed for approximately fifteen years, the financial statements here are believed to be typical of the financial status of the average rural church.

In 1930, the 185 churches raised $80,573.56, or an approximate average of $435.53 for each. The separate amounts raised varied from less than $50 a year to $1,500 per year. The amount raised by the 609 urban churches varied from less than $100 to approximately $50,000 per year.

In Orangeburg County, fifty-three churches raised a total of $30,626, an average of $577.85 per church. In Montgomery County, the fifty-seven churches studied raised $20,776, an average of $364.49 per church. The fifty churches in Fort Bend County, Texas, raised on the average $400.32 in 1930, or a total of $20,016. In Peach County, Georgia, there are twenty-five Negro churches, and these raised a total of $9,156, an average of $366.24 per church.

TABLE XXIV—AVERAGE EXPENDITURES PER CHURCH IN FOUR COUNTIES

County	No. of Churches	Total Expended	Average Per Church
Orangeburg	53	$30,626	$577.85
Fort Bend	50	20,016	400.32
Peach	25	9,156	366.24
Montgomery	57	20,776	364.49
Total	185	$80,574	$435.54

The average expenditure per church, $435.54, compares favorably with the average of $561 for the 29,603 rural churches of the 1926 religious census.

EXPENDITURE PER MEMBER

It was pointed out in the chapter on membership that the 185 churches had a total membership of 26,845. Setting the total membership over against what they raised, $80,574, these churches in 1930 spent on the average $3.00 for each member enrolled; and this is slightly less than half the average per member in all Negro rural churches for the year 1926. Each active member, of course, contributed a much larger proportion than this.

TABLE XXV—DISTRIBUTION OF EXPENDITURES OF 185 CHURCHES, 1930

	Amount	Per Cent.
Pastors' Salaries	$48,694	60.4
Other Salaries (Janitors, Secretaries, Organists, Presiding Elders)	7,666	9.5
Repairs and Upkeep	5,162	6.4
Education and Mission	4,722	5.9
Interest and Reduction of Church Debt	1,621	2.0
Miscellaneous (Insurance, Light, Heat, Benevolences, Publicity, Balance of Church Overhead)	12,709	15.8
Total	$80,574	100.0

The Olivet and Pilgrim Baptist churches in Chicago, with a combined reported membership of 12,908, raised and expended in 1930 more money than the 185 rural churches combined. The Olivet and Pilgrim churches raised over $90,000 in 1930. As extreme as these two cases are, it is further proof that the outstanding Negro churches are to be found in cities. It has already been indicated that $1,500 was the highest amount raised by a rural church in this study in 1930.

EXPENDITURE FOR SALARIES

The accompanying table shows that $48,694, or 60 per cent. of the total amount expended in 1930 by the 185 churches, went for pastors' salaries. Approximately 70 per cent. was spent for salaries when those of janitors, secretaries, organists and presiding elders are included. The other 30 per cent. was spent for repairs and upkeep, education and missions, interest and reduction of church debt, and other items such as insurance, light, heat and the like. In the urban churches studied, 43.2 per cent. of all funds raised in 1930 was spent in salaries, in contrast with the 70 per cent. spent in salaries by the rural churches.

Clearly almost all of the money raised in the rural church must be spent for the necessities required to run the church. It is quite obvious that the average rural church has very little money, if any, for the expansion of its program.

Church Evaluation

The evaluation of 168 of the 185 church properties, including lots, was ascertained, as well as the evaluation of twelve parsonages. The total was $285,698, an approximate evaluation of $1,700 per church. The average city church of the 609 is valued at $36,726.77, representing an investment of $57.04 per member. The 168 rural churches represent an investment of $10.64 per member.

Rural Church Debt

In Orangeburg County, ten of the fifty-three churches, or 18.9 per cent. of them, have debts; a total of $1,725, or $172.50 per church. Of the fifty-seven churches in Montgomery County, seven, or 12.3 per cent., are in debt. The aggregate indebtedness of the seven churches is $3,240, or $462.86 per church. Fort Bend has seventeen, or 34 per cent., of the fifty churches in debt, presenting a total indebtedness of $4,589, or $269.94 per church. Peach County reports all of its churches free from debt. Of the 185 rural churches, therefore, thirty-four, or 18.4 per cent., are in debt; the total being $9,554, or $281 per church.

TABLE XXVI—CHURCH DEBT IN FOUR COUNTIES

County	No. of Churches	No. In Debt	Per Cent. In Debt	Total Debt	Debt Per Church
Peach	25	0	0	0	0
Orangeburg	53	10	18.9	$1,725	$172.50
Fort Bend	50	17	34.0	4,589	269.94
Montgomery	57	7	12.3	3,240	462.86
Total	185	34	18.4	$9,554	$281.00

PERCENTAGE OF CHURCHES IN DEBT LOWER IN RURAL AREAS

The rural churches are almost free from debt. For the most part, they are older and more cheaply built, usually of frame material. The rural people are not as well off economically as the city people and they are used to the simplest art and facilities for school and home as well as church. For these reasons, the church-building mania that has taken possession of many people in the city has not extended to the rural folk.

In the cities studied, 71.3 per cent. of the Negro churches that own or are purchasing their buildings have indebtedness; in the four rural counties, only 18.4 per cent. The average indebtedness for the 386 urban churches is $13,321.38; which is in striking contrast with the average of only $281.00 for the thirty-four rural churches.

Salaries of Rural Ministers

The salaries of the pastors of two of the 185 churches were not given. The total salary paid by the remaining 183 in 1930 was $48,694. On this basis, these churches paid their pastor, on the average, $266.09. It has already been pointed out, however, that many of these pastors serve more than one church. If the $266.09 represents the average paid per church, those who serve four churches would receive a salary of $1,064.36 yearly. If the rural pastor has four churches, which the majority do not have, the $1,064.36 would compare favorably with the average salary of the urban pastor, which in the study was found to be $1,481.52. It must be noted, however, that a rural minister's total salary is determined by the number of churches he serves. Then, too, quite a number of cases were found where pastors who serve relatively large churches in the city supplement their earning by serving one or two churches in the country. Hence preaching is often conducted only once or twice a month in many rural areas.

It is quite convenient for the city pastor to leave his city church during one of the eight preaching services in a month; or if the rural church is reasonably close, he can arrange his preaching in the afternoon for the country church. In this latter case, it is possible for an occasional pastor who gets $200 or $300 from a country church to draw at the same time a salary of $1,500 or $1,800 from his city church. However, in comparison with the number of pastors who have only rural and small-town churches and of those who serve both city and rural churches, the number of city pastors with rural charges is quite negligible.

Secretarial Service Highly Inadequate in Rural Churches

Of the 185 churches, 106 pay something to the church clerk or secretary; the total amount in 1930 being $1,588. This gives an average of $14.98 per secretary per year. It is needless to say that this is almost equivalent to a free-service secretarial staff. Many of the rural churches give the clerk or secretary only one dollar a month.

Custodians' Pay

Quite a number of the 185 churches, 130 in all, have some one to do janitorial service. A total of $2,178 was paid to 130 persons in 1930, an average of $16.75 per year per person.

Salary of Organist

In most instances, the organist serves free in the rural church, but is given a donation at times. Twenty churches paid to organists in 1930 a total of $959, an average of $47.95 a year for each organist.

Situation Not Hopeful

The financial situation in the rural church is not very hopeful. It can hardly be expected that the rural church will, with the present set-up, be able to command a trained ministry and develop an effective program. Life on the farm is less permanent with the Negro now than formerly. The Negro rural population is gradually decreasing, and rural church-membership seems to be less stable than that in the city. These facts alone make it very difficult for the rural church to make much progress. Economic stability is a necessary factor for real church development. If the church-members continue to move away, and if the number of Negro farm owners and prosperous renters does not increase, the rural church is likely to prove even less effective in the future than it is at present.

CHAPTER XVI

Overchurching in Rural Areas

The question of overchurching in rural areas, as well as in the cities, must be considered in the light of an increasing or decreasing population and the economic status of the people who make up the church-membership; and some attention must be paid to the permanency of residence of members. These three factors will now be considered.

A Decreasing Rural Population

That the Negro rural population is gradually decreasing need not be discussed in detail here, since this fact has been established in previous chapters. It was pointed out in chapter xii that the Negro population had decreased since 1910 in both Montgomery and Fort Bend counties; and that there was an increase in Orangeburg County in 1930 over that of 1910, but a decrease since 1920. Peach County was not organized in 1920.

T. J. Woofter, Jr., writing on the farm situation among Negroes, states that practically 50 per cent. of the farms in the four extreme southeastern states were operated by Negroes in 1910 and only about 45 per cent. in 1925; that the decrease of 96,000 farms during the five-year period, 1920 to 1925, was caused almost entirely by the migration of Negro farmers, the Negro farmers losing 84,000 of the farms and the white farmers 12,000.[1]

The Economic Status of the Rural Negro

Woofter states further that the number of Negro owners in the southeast decreased from 161,600 in 1910 to 145,900 in

---

[1] Woofter, T. J., Jr., *A Study of the Economic Status of the Negro* (Institute for Research and Social Science, University of North Carolina, June 1930), pp. 11 and 12.

1925; that the number of Negro renters likewise declined rapidly in the same period; and that the number of share-croppers, the half-share tenants, actually decreased. He goes on to say that the depression in the cotton areas has not only occasioned a decrease in the number of Negro farmers but has forced the masses, those remaining on the farms, downward in the scale. Here and there it is possible to find farmers who are making money; but the majority have been in serious financial straits. The proportion of Negro croppers to the total number of Negro farmers in the extreme southwestern states increased from 39 per cent. in 1920 to 46 per cent. in 1925.[2]

Of the 2,000,000 Negro farmers, it is calculated that 57.5 per cent. are laborers, 32.4 per cent. are tenants, and 10.1 per cent. are owners. There has been an actual decrease in the number of both Negro owners and renters.[3]

RURAL INCOME MEAGER

The incomes of Negro farmers are very low. Mr. Woofter points out that the average income in cash plus family living on St. Helena Island was only $420 in 1928; and Mr. Raper in his study of Macon and Greene counties, Georgia, shows that the average total income for Negro farmers in Greene County is $339 and in Macon County $448. A study of the North Carolina State Tax Commission made in 1927 shows that the average cash income for southern farmers was $556, and the average family living from the farm was $478, or a combined cash income plus family living of $1,034. The median or middle cash income was $250.[4] Of course, it is much less for Negroes. The large number of Negroes, 89.9 per cent., who do not own their farms is almost conclusive proof that the membership in the Negro rural church is not

---

[2] *Ibid*, pp. 12 and 13.

[3] Johnson, Charles S., *The Negro in American Civilization* (New York: Henry Holt & Company, 1930), p. 38.

[4] Woofter, T. J., *A Study of the Economic Status of the Negro*, p. 23.

very stationary, owing to the frequency of moving about in any particular county or out of the county altogether.

An analysis of the church situation in relation to the economic status of Negroes in the four counties studied should prove helpful. The data were obtained from the 1930 Government census. It is in the light of these data that over-churching in the four counties will be discussed.

Overchurching

PEACH COUNTY

The Negro population of Peach County was 6,565 in 1930. The number of Negro churches was 25. There is in Peach County, including children, a church for each 262 Negroes. The county has 4,561 Negro adults 13 years of age and over; consequently there is one church for each 182 adult Negroes. It is pointed out that in the rural United States only 52 per cent. of the adult people are churched.[5] If this is true of the Negroes of Peach County, its churches have only 2,372 adult members, or 95 for each church. This average of 95 adult members per church tallies closely with that for the Negro churches of Peach County, which was found in the present study to be 86 members per church. This compares favorably with the average of 83 adult Negroes per church in the entire rural part of the United States.

The ability of the Negroes in Peach County to support 25 churches, or the possibility of 86 members adequately supporting a church, has partly been answered in the chapter on finance, which showed that in 1930 the 25 churches raised on the average only $366.24 per church.

The financial ability to support these churches is also determined by the occupations of the Negroes. Only 37, or 7.6 per cent., of the farmers are farm owners; 123, or 25.2 per

[5] Fry, C. Luther, *The U. S. Looks At Its Churches* (New York: Institute of Social and Religious Research, 1930), p. 15.

cent., are renters; and 328, or 67.2 per cent., are share-croppers. It is the opinion of the farm demonstration agent, who has been in the county for more than a decade, that there are in addition fully 300 day laborers who get on the average less than 75 cents a day.

In 1925, the year Peach County was organized, there were 207 Negro share-croppers as against 328 in 1930, an increase of 58.5 per cent. There were 87 renters in 1925; and the number had increased to 123 in 1930, a 41 per cent. increase. In 1925, 27 Negroes owned their farms in Peach County, and in 1930, 37 owned their farms—an increase of 37 per cent.

These figures show that there has been a definite increase in owners, renters and croppers since 1925; but the percentage of increase in ownership is less than that of renters and share-croppers. This increase does not of necessity mean that economically the Negroes are better off now than in 1925; for farm values, including buildings, have depreciated from $4,980,617 in 1925 to $3,471,690 in 1930, a drop of more than 25 per cent. Land values alone have fallen from $3,681,762 in 1925 to $2,571,785 in 1930, a decline of more than 25 per cent. Furthermore, despite these increases, the farmers are not as well-off now as the farmers were in 1925, if the testimony of the farm demonstration agent, religious workers, and the educators of Peach County is to be literally accepted. It is certainly true that the low economic status of the people of Peach County will make it impossible for them to retain well-trained ministers; apparently they must continue to rely upon an untrained ministry. Church expansion programs can hardly be expected.

Obviously the consolidation of many of these churches would make it possible for them to launch better programs, and at the same time call a better-trained ministry. In Fort Valley, the county seat, the Negro population was 4,313 in 1930, and there were ten churches. Counting children and the unchurched, there is a church in Fort Valley for each 431 Negroes. In Peach County, 69.4 per cent. of the total population is made up of adults 13 years of age and above, which gives for Fort Valley 2,993 Negro adults of 13 years and over. On this basis, Fort Valley has a church for each 299 adult people. If only 52 per cent. of rural adults are churched, then Fort Valley, giving slightly more than 300 adult members per church, has a church for each 156 adult Negro members.

It would be most generous to say that five churches would amply take care of the Negro church needs of Fort Valley, giving 290 adult members per church. If the 500 per church minimum, which was the low minimum suggested for urban churches, be taken as the minimum here, six Negro churches would serve Fort Valley and take care of every adult Negro in town. In reality three churches, one for approximately each 500 adult members, would probably be sufficient. And 500 members per church in a small town is by no means equivalent to 500 members in the city.

Including children, Powersville, a small town in Peach County, has 528 Negro inhabitants. It has two churches, both in poor condition physically, one church for each 264 Negroes. Powersville has 366 adults 13 years of age and above; a church for each 183 Negro adults. Assuming that 52 per cent. of these are churched, there is a church for each 95 adult members.

ORANGEBURG COUNTY

In 1930 Orangeburg County had 40,640 Negroes and 109 churches, a church for each 373 persons. The adult Negroes number 25,591. If the ideal obtained and all persons 13 years of age or more were church-members, there would be a church in the county for each 235 adults. But the ideal does not obtain; and calculating on the basis of a 52 per cent. adult membership, Orangeburg has a church for each 122 adult Negro members. In these days of good roads, Orangeburg could well afford a reduction of fifty churches.

The fifty-three churches studied in the county raised an average of $577.85 per church; not a large sum with which to carry on the most needed activities. These amounts are somewhat indicative of whether the Negroes in Orangeburg County are economically able to support 109 churches.

Orangeburg Churches Weaker Economically Than a Decade Ago—A glance at the economic status of Negroes in the county should be of some advantage in determining the need of increasing or decreasing the number of churches. The number of Negroes who own farms has decreased appreciably since 1920. In that year, according to the United States Census returns, 1,129 Negroes owned their farms. In 1925 this number had dwindled to 919; and in 1930 to 826, a decrease of 26.8 per cent. in ten years.

If land-ownership is an indication of economic stability and independence, then it is clear that the churches in Orangeburg County have less to depend upon now than they had in 1920 and 1925. The economic situation indicates that fewer churches are needed. The number of renters, including croppers, decreased from 1920 to 1925, but increased from 1925 to 1930. Since 1925, land-ownership has decreased, and the number of renters has increased. There were 4,628 renters and croppers in 1920, 3,425 in 1925, and 3,885 in 1930; a decrease of 16 per cent. since 1920. The croppers have greatly increased since 1925—from 927 to 1,424 in 1930. Croppers increased 34.9 per cent. in five years; renters decreased 16 per cent. and owners 26.8 per cent. in the ten years between 1920 and 1930. It is evident that the churches of Orangeburg County have less to support them than they had five and ten years ago.

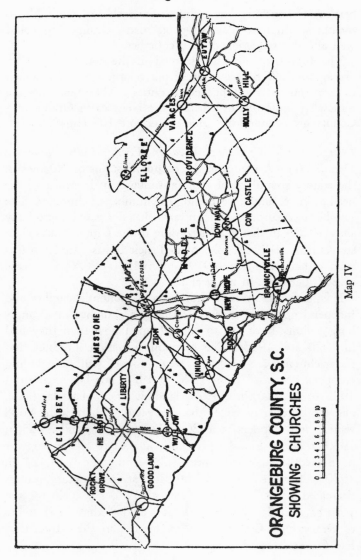

ORANGEBURG COUNTY, S.C.
SHOWING CHURCHES

0 1 2 3 4 5 6 7 8 9 10

Map IV

MONTGOMERY COUNTY, ALABAMA

The 1930 census reveals that in Montgomery County there were 22,174 Negroes. A careful count of churches in the county gives 67. Calculating on the basis of 22,174 people and 67 churches, the county has a church for approximately each 331 Negroes, including children. There are 15,403 adults 13 years of age and above. There is therefore a church for approximately each 230 Negro adults. Estimating 52 per cent. of the adults to be members of the church, there is a church for each 119 adult members.

The 57 churches studied in Montgomery County raised on the average in 1930, $364.49 per church; the smallest average of the four counties. On the basis of 500 adult members per church, the county could get along with about one-fifth of the number of churches it has at present. Allowing 238 adult members per church, and assuming that the amount of money raised per church would be double the present amount, the number of churches could be reduced by half, giving an average of $728.98 per church. If this were possible, the rural churches of Montgomery County could command a better-trained ministry.

The ability of the county to support 67 churches can be judged also by the occupational classification of its population since 1920. The number of Negro farm owners increased from 342 in 1920 to 410 in 1925; but decreased to 376 in 1930. The number of renters, including croppers, decreased slightly from 3,180 in 1920 to 3,135 in 1925; but the decrease was greater between 1925 and 1930—from 3,135 to 2,797. The share-croppers decreased from 720 in 1925 to 610 in 1930. Thus in this period the number of owners, renters and croppers decreased.

Here again, if ownership means anything, the churches in Montgomery County are slightly less independent than they were in 1925, to say nothing of what the years of depression have done to the financial status of the churches.

Fort Bend County had a population of 9,787 Negroes in 1930. It had 50 churches, or a church for each 196 people including children. Of the total Negro population, 7,164 were adults 13 years of age and above; so there is a church for approximately each 143 adults.

If 52 per cent. of these are churched, then Fort Bend has a church for approximately each 75 adult members. These 50 churches raised on an average of $400.32 in 1930.

The number of Negro farm owners in the county changed only slightly between 1920 and 1930. There were 363 owners in 1920, 388 in 1925, and 361 in 1930. The number of renters increased from 1,360 in 1920 to 1,470 in 1925; but slightly decreased to 1,464 in 1930—almost no change. Share-croppers increased slightly from 708 in 1925 to 714 in 1930.

Orangeburg County, S. C. and Montgomery County, Ala. present the best examples of the churches with probably less stability in their membership owing to decrease in the number of owners within the last five or ten years. In Montgomery County the renters, share-croppers, and owners decreased in number; while in Orangeburg County the renters and croppers greatly increased as the owners decreased. Fort Bend County has probably held its own within the last decade better than the other three counties.

Outstanding Problems of the Rural Church Suggest Church Merging

Possibly the most complicated problem confronting the rural church is the instability of its membership. The fact that the number of landowners is much smaller among rural Negroes than among rural whites makes the Negro church-membership more migratory and less stable than that of the rural whites. This lack of stability affects greatly the progress of the Negro rural church.

In Orangeburg County the total population is 63,864; the Negro population is 40,640. Although the Negroes constitute 63.6 per cent. of the population, they have only 35 per cent. of the farm owners. On the other hand, there are far more Negro than white renters; in fact, approximately 78 per cent. of all renters in Orangeburg County are Negroes: and there are more than four Negro croppers to each white cropper—1,424 Negroes and 321 whites.

The total population of Fort Bend County is 29,718; the Negro population is 9,787—slightly less than 33 per cent. of the total. About 33 per cent. of the farm owners are Negroes. In ownership the Negroes compare favorably with the whites. But constituting only 33 per cent. of the population, the Negroes constitute 46 per cent. of all renters and 53 per cent. of the total number of croppers.

Excluding Montgomery city, there are 32,596 people in Montgomery County; and of this number, 22,174, or 68 per cent., are Negroes; but only 44 per cent. of the farm owners are Negroes. Of the renters, including croppers, 88 per cent. are Negroes; and of the croppers alone, 90 per cent.

In Peach County, the Negroes are slightly more than 63.9 per cent. of the total population. Normally 63.9 per cent. of the owners, renters and croppers would be Negroes; but Negroes really own only 22 per cent. of the farms, while they constitute 77 per cent. of the renters and 87 per cent. of the croppers.

These figures show why it is difficult for the Negro rural church to maintain itself. Croppers and renters move frequently, more frequently now than formerly; often they move away from the church where they maintain membership, even when they remain in the county. Consequently the financial support of the church is less, and attendance declines.

Four factors tend to make Negro church life in rural areas somewhat precarious. One of these is the gradual decrease of the Negro rural population; another is the instability of rural church-members, owing to the small and decreasing number of farm owners. Still another factor is that, following the boll-weevil ravages, the Negro farmer has been worse off than before. No adequate adjustment to farm life has been made since the collapse of the one-crop system. The white landowners are less able and less willing to carry the Negro while the crop is being made; and finally, the rural Negro has become more sensitive to rural limitations, such as inferior educational opportunities, injustice in the courts, and a lack of adequate physical protection. It is easier now for the rural Negro to escape rural restrictions by seeking the larger freedom of an urban center. In the very nature of things, these forces make it impossible for the rural church to maintain a trained ministry.

If the rural church is ever to become a strong, healthy institution, these problems must be courageously grappled with and solved by the leading Negroes and whites, to the end that constructive measures may be instituted to effect necessary changes in the Negro rural church.

When the Negroes lived rather happily and contentedly on the farm, unattracted by city life; when cotton growing was the chief industry of the South and the white landlord advanced money for sustenance while the crops grew; when roads were not so good and modes of travel not so convenient; and when Negroes were less sensitive to proscriptions and more amenable to circumscription; the multiplicity of Negro rural churches was more of a necessity, and they could all be better supported than now. But life in the rural South has been completely revolutionized within the last eighteen years, and social and economic changes have profoundly affected the Negro rural church. A good many of these churches, once flourishing, are no longer needed and are economically unable to exist except at a poor dying rate.

The need for fewer churches and better ones is just as imperative, possibly more so, for the rural areas as it is for urban centers. If these churches do not consolidate, a large number of them will die of natural causes. On the basis of the facts of this study, this will be the inevitable outcome of many rural churches unless there is a check of city migration, a return of a large number of Negroes to the farm, and a rapid return of healthier days in the rural South.

It is the conviction of the authors that healthier days include the working out of a farm system by agricultural experts, encouraged and aided by the Federal Government, so that life on the farm will be made attractive, safe, and profitable for the Negro. They include a more vigorous program to improve the inadequate educational system under which most rural Negroes still live, and certainly a more humane treatment of him on the part of those who are intrusted with the task of administering the law.

CHAPTER XVII

The Genius of the Negro Church

Perhaps the reader feels that the analysis of the Negro church so far presented, though encouraging here and there, gives a rather dark picture; and that it offers nothing exceptionally promising for the future church life of 12,000,000 people.

The analysis reveals that the status of the Negro church is in part the result of the failure of American Christianity in the realm of race-relations; that the church's program, except in rare instances, is static, non-progressive, and fails to challenge the loyalty of many of the most critically-minded Negroes; that the vast majority of its pastors are poorly trained academically, and more poorly trained theologically; that more than half of the sermons analyzed are abstract, other-worldly, and imbued with a magical conception of religion; that in the church school less than one-tenth of the teachers are college graduates; that there are too many Negro churches; that the percentage of Negro churches in debt is high; that for the most part the Negro church is little concerned with juvenile delinquency and other social problems in its environment; that less than half of the reported membership can be relied upon to finance the church regularly and consistently; and that the rural church suffers most because of the instability and poverty of the rural Negroes.

Yet the authors believe that there is in the genius or the "soul" of the Negro church something that gives it life and vitality, that makes it stand out significantly above its buildings, creeds, rituals and doctrines, something that makes it a unique institution. For this reason, the writers, in this chapter, lean more heavily than in previous chapters upon the observations and personal experiences gained during the two-year, intensive study of the Negro church; and these are supplemented here and there by the experiences of the race.

The Church is the Negro's Very Own

The church was the first community or public organization that the Negro actually owned and completely controlled. And it is possibly true to this day that the Negro church is the most thoroughly owned and controlled public institution of the race. Nothing can compare with this ownership and control except ownership of the home and possibly control of the Negro Lodge. It is to be doubted whether Negro control is as complete in any other area of Negro life, except these two, as it is in the church.

A statement of this character may sound paradoxical in the light of the facts discovered in the chapter on finance, which show that 71.3 per cent. of the churches of this study are in debt. But churches are unique institutions, for which reason they enjoy special privileges.

Churches, unlike houses and business enterprises, are not very valuable to their creditors. Residence property, if taken from the buyer, is usually very valuable, and may return a profit. This is not true with churches. A church taken over by creditors is generally of little value to them and usually cannot be used for any other purpose. Ordinarily the financiers want the money and not the church; and they are not concerned with either the ownership or the control of the church. Another reason is the good reputation enjoyed by churches for eventually paying off their debts. Thus, for both of these reasons, indebtedness on churches generally does not involve loss of control to the creditors.

Furthermore, a glance through the chapter on finance shows that the huge total indebtedness of the Negro churches is more striking because of the high percentage of churches in debt than because of the amount of the indebtedness per church.

For example, 45.6 per cent. of the 386 churches in debt have an average indebtedness of less than $5,000; and only 15.0 per cent. of them have debts ranging between $25,000 and $160,000; with twenty-one owing $50,000 or more, and only three owing more than $100,000.

Even if indebtedness carried control, most of the churches would not be so heavily in debt as to warrant creditor-control. Therefore, whatever the Negro church is in the United States, it is largely the outcome of the Negro's own genius and his ability to organize. Like other institutions it has glaring defects; and improvements in many spheres are greatly needed.

It is equally true, however, that there are hundreds of Negro churches that operate sufficiently well to warrant the commendation of critical minds.

Not only is this institution controlled by Negroes, but nine-tenths of the local churches are self-supporting. A few Negro churches, organically connected with white churches, churches of Negro denominations, and several Baptist churches were helped in an organized way between 1927 and 1931; but during the same period, 88.3 per cent. of the churches of this study received no systematic organized support from outside sources. Certainly in the majority of cases the amounts received from outside sources were so negligible that the churches would continue to exist if the outside help were entirely cut off. Even in the cases of the 11.7 per cent. of churches that received some organized support due to denominational connections and otherwise, there was sufficient evidence to show that control of the church was primarily in the hands of the Negro congregations.

Through and through, with or without outside help, the Negro churches of this study are principally governed by Negroes. Many Negroes, though unable to own homes of their own, take a peculiar pride in their churches. It gives them a sense of ownership that can hardly exist with respect to any other institution in the community. Since thousands do not own their homes, they develop a loyalty and devotion to their churches that command respect and admiration. It is characteristic of the Negro church that the Negro owns it and that it is largely the product of his hand and brain.

Ownership and Control Provide Opportunity for the Common Man

With races and individuals, there must be an opportunity for the development of initiative and self-direction if real character is to be developed, and if hidden potentialities are to be brought to the fore. Certainly the Negro church has been the training school that has given the masses of the race opportunity to develop.

The opportunity found in the Negro church to be recognized, and to be "somebody," has stimulated the pride and preserved the self-respect of many Negroes who would have been entirely beaten by life, and possibly completely submerged. Everyone wants to receive recognition and feel that he is appreciated. The Negro church has supplied this need. A truck driver of average or more than ordinary qualities becomes the chairman of the Deacon Board. A hotel man of some ability is the superintendent of the Sunday church school of a rather important church. A woman who would be hardly noticed, socially or otherwise, becomes a leading woman in the missionary society. A girl of little training and less opportunity for training gets the chance to become the leading soprano in the choir of a great church. These people receive little or no recognition on their daily job. There is nothing to make them feel that they are "somebody." Frequently their souls are crushed and their personalities disregarded. Often they do not feel "at home" in the more sophisticated Negro group. But in the church on X Street, *she* is Mrs. Johnson, the Church Clerk; and *he* is Mr. Jones, the chairman of the Deacon Board.

It can be argued, and justly, that this untrained leadership is partly responsible for the fact that the Negro church has progressed so slowly. But still it is important that recognition and inspiriting opportunity have been given to people who would not have achieved the one or risen to the other elsewhere. Granted also that the same may be said of the churches of other racial groups, nevertheless it can hardly be denied that it is more accentuated among Negroes because they are more highly segregated and restricted in American life.

Freedom to Relax

The Negro church furnishes the masses, to a less extent now than formerly, an opportunity for self-expression that no other enterprise affords. Not expression in leadership as just described, but release from the restraint, strain and restriction of the daily grind. If in their church services Negroes show more emotion than members of some other racial groups, it can hardly be proved that they are by nature more expressive. The explanation lies in the environmental conditions under which they live. This is true because, as the Negro becomes more intellectual and less restricted in the American life, he becomes less expressive in emotion. A few churches in practically every large-sized American city show the truth of this. But the point urged here is, whatever one may think to the contrary and despite the advance made in the realm of improved race-relations, that as the Negro moves about in most areas of the American Commonwealth he is less free than other Americans. He not only feels, but he knows, that in many places he is not wanted. He knows that in most white churches of the United States he is not desired, even though a sign on the outside of the church may read "Welcome to All." He understands perfectly well that the welcome does not include him. He comprehends clearly that in many of them he would be ushered to the rear or to the gallery, or be refused admission altogether; and in some other instances he would be patronized and tolerated.

A sign on the outside of an important church in a metropolitan southern city reads thus: "We offer riches to the poorest, friendliness to the friendless, comfort to the sorrowing—a welcome to all, step in." But every Negro child in that city is aware of the fact that the invitation is not meant for him.

The Negro is conscious of the fact that in many courthouses, city halls, public parks, city auditoriums, institutions supported by the taxes of all the people, he is not a welcomed guest; and that special arrangements must be provided for him. He appreciates the fact that in privately owned stores in many sections, where the money of all groups is sought, places of comfort and relaxation are quite often not provided him; and, if they are, they are provided in such a way as to make him feel humiliated.

The Negro is not unmindful of the fact that as he elbows his way through the crowded thoroughfare, he must be just a little more careful than most people; and that if he were to do what others would be excused for doing, he would be condemned. He works on the job ever aware that to hold his position he must often go the second mile, do more and take more, and work for less money. He must be an epitome of politeness; must smile when ordinarily he would frown; must pretend that it is all right when the respect that is habitually given others is deliberately denied him.

In this tense situation, the Negro lives. In many instances he expresses himself in song, dance and laughter; but for thousands of Negroes this release from restraint, this complete freedom and relaxation for the sake of mere expression, if nothing more than a faint "Amen," a nodding of the head as the minister preaches, a feeling of oneness with the crowd in song and prayer, is to be found only in the Negro church. Here he gathers poise, courage and strength to make it through another week. Langston Hughes' "Negro Servant," though related to Harlem, is somewhat illustrative of what is portrayed here, and if the Negro church is kept in mind as well as Harlem, the idea expressed in this poem becomes more universal in its application.

All day, subdued, polite,
Kind, thoughtful to the faces that are white.
O, Tribal dance!
O, drum!
O, Veldt at night!
Forgotten watch-fires on a hill somewhere!
At six o'clock, or seven, or eight,
You're through.
You've worked all day.
Dark Harlem waits for you.
The el, the sub.
Pay-nights,
A taxi through the park.
O, drums of life in Harlem after dark!
O, dreams!
O, songs!
O, saxophones at night!
O, sweet relief from faces that are white!

—Quoted by permission of the publishers of *Opportunity*.

It might be urged that this kind of expression is not helpful; that it makes religion an escape from reality; that it serves as an opiate for the people. The possibilities are great that this is true, and that it does happen no one can deny. But whether it is true or not depends in a large measure upon what the minister provides and the kind of instruction he gives the people. If these expressions or outlets help the people to live, they can hardly be set aside as of no value.

Negro Church as Community Center

Three quotations are illustrative of the use of the Negro church as a social center. George E. Haynes writes:

The Negro as a worker makes contact with the white world when on his job, and receives information, instruction, and stimulus so far as his occupation influences his ways of life. All his leisure-time activities that condition intellectual development and emotional motivation under present conditions of segregated Negro life must find their channel mainly through the principal community agency the Negro has—his church.[1]

Forrester Washington states:

From the very beginning the Negro has had to make numerous approximations and substitutions to supply himself with decent recreational opportunities. In both city and country he has made of the Negro church a quasi community center.[2]

The Mayor's Interracial Committee of Detroit reports in its 1926 Survey:

The Negro has been humiliated in so many public and privately owned institutions and amusement places that he has resorted to the church as a place in which he can be sure of spending his leisure time peacefully. To a large extent it takes the place of the theatre, the dance hall, and similar amusement places, and fills the vacancy created by the failure of public and commercial places of recreation and amusement to give him a cordial welcome. Consequently, the average Negro church in Detroit keeps its doors open constantly for the use of the community. Numerous suppers, lectures, recitals, debates, plays, and the like are given by clubs and individuals from without and within the congregation.

The Church Has Encouraged Education and Nurtured Negro Business

Through the years, the Negro church through its ministry has encouraged Negroes to educate themselves. The rather naïve and blind faith that many Negro parents have had that

[1] Haynes, George E., *The Church and Negro Progress,* The Annals of the American Academy of Political and Social Science, November, 1928.

[2] Washington, Forrest B., *Recreational Facilities for the Negro,* The Annals of the American Academy of Political and Social Science, November, 1928.

education is a panacea for all ills came from the Negro pastors. Mostly illiterate, and greatly lacking in formal training himself, he has continually urged the parents of his congregation to sacrifice much in order that their children might enjoy a better day. Many a country boy or girl would never have had the chance to attend college if the pastor of his or her church had not urged it. Even in cases where Negro education was graciously supported by white people who were kindly and justly disposed toward the Negro, the Negro minister was often needed, and relied upon, to give sanction to and boost education. The parents did not always see the light; but the pastor insisted on it, and somehow the parents believed that the preacher knew. The existence of a large number of weak denominational schools as well as some strong ones is testimony to the fact that the Negro church has greatly encouraged education. Not only has the church urged Negroes to secure an education, but the church has nurtured and still nurtures Negro business. The great medium for the advertisement of Negro business is the church. Not only in sermons but in other ways, the authors were impressed with the way Negro pastors advise their people to help make strong Negro business such as insurance, banking, privately owned Negro enterprises and the like.

Democratic Fellowship

In the main, there are no social classes in the Negro church. In one or two city churches of the 609, there was evidence that some of the members were particular about the people who joined and wanted a "certain brand" for members. In a few cases there was a natural development whereby people of supposedly similar cultural levels assembled. But even in these churches, there are members who represent all grades of culture and varying occupational levels.

BRIDGING THE GAP

In practically all of the 609 churches there exists a thorough democratic spirit. The church is the place where the Negro banker, lawyer, professor, social worker, physician, dentist, and public-school teacher meet the skilled and semi-skilled tradesmen, the maid, the cook, the hotel man, the butler, the chauffeur and the common laborer; and mingle with them. The Negro church still furnishes the best opportunity for Negroes of different social strata and various cultural groups to associate together in a thoroughgoing democratic way.

The Negro race is young in emancipation. It has not had sufficient time to build churches of the wealthy nor of the cultured. As the race gets older in freedom, the number of college-trained business and professional people will inevitably increase. There will be more grouping and mingling among people of similar interest, and the tendency will be in the direction of a more rigid separation between Negroes of different interests and achievements. Up to this time, the Negro church has been one of the most outstanding channels through which this gulf between the "high" and the "low," the "trained" and the "untrained" has been bridged. It will continue to be for years to come; because the vast majority of Negroes who reach the business and professional classes are the sons and daughters of parents whose opportunities for training have been meager and who for the most part have kept this Negro church in operation.

The tendency is, and may continue to be, for the intellectual Negroes to break away from many of our churches because they are not attracted by services that differ so widely from those of the college and university. On the other hand, a good many of these more highly privileged Negroes see great possibilities in Negro churches, and work in them weekly; a goodly number of the Negro students are closely connected with the church. Of 2,594 students, professional and lay people whose attitudes toward the church were ascertained,

67 per cent. attend church weekly and 56 per cent. have specific church duties, such as work in the Sunday church school, singing in the choir or some other activity of the church.

As the writers moved about in sixteen communities during the period of the field work of the study, one thing stood out conspicuously—there was a warmth, a spontaneity in worship, and welcome that one could actually feel on entering most Negro churches. In most of them, the atmosphere is congenial and a timid or tense person is set at ease immediately. Perfect relaxation is possible. Frequently it is a hearty handshake by a member of the church, or a cordial greeting by the usher who seems to sense that this man is a stranger, or some word from the pastor in his sermon or at the end of the services. At any rate, the atmosphere is conducive to a feeling of "at-home-ness." To the ultra-sophisticated, it may seem naïve and primitive, but there is a virtue in it which the truly wise will not scorn.

Transcending Racial Barriers

The democratic fellowship that exists within the race transcends racial barriers in the church. The Negro church generally preaches love and tolerance toward all races and abides by these ideals in its practice. Members of other racial groups are welcomed in Negro churches. Other races experience no rebuffs, no discrimination. Chinese, Japanese, and white people are never deliberately given the back seats in Negro churches. They are never ushered to the gallery for worship. They are never refused admission to Negro churches. If there is any discrimination, it is usually to the advantage of the members of other racial groups. Precaution is taken in Negro churches to see that white visitors are given, not gallery seats, but often the very best seats in the house. The members of churches occupying front seats frequently give their seats to the visitors of other races. They give the stranger and the chance guest of different color, not the worst, but the best.

Negro Ministers Welcome White Ministers

White ministers are not barred from Negro pulpits.

In the interviews, a few Negro ministers expressed the conviction that they would be perfectly willing to have white ministers preach to their people provided they could preach for the white ministers. But in the vast majority of instances the Negro pastors were willing to have white pastors preach to their people even though they knew that the white ministers would not, or could not, have them preach in their pulpits.

In securing the services of white ministers, most Negro preachers experience no difficulty from their board or congregation. It was the unanimous testimony of the 600 pastors and officials interviewed that their people did not object to visiting white ministers.

Not a single case was observed by the investigators, in interviews and worship, where Negroes did not cordially receive members of other racial groups in their worship. As one minister expressed it: "My church is always glad to have members of any racial group worship with us and I know of no case where our visitors have experienced embarrassments in our church."

Negro ministers who do not invite white pastors because the white ministers cannot invite them, nevertheless insist that in their services no lines shall be drawn against white worshippers.

A Potentially Free Ministry

It is the firm conviction of the writers that the Negro pastor is one of the freest, as well as most influential, men on the American platform today. This is due to various causes, but chief among them is the factor of the long-time prestige of the Negro minister, the respect for him and for religion; and the poverty and the financial freedom of the Negro church.

It is not the aim of the writers to extol poverty or economic insecurity as a virtue per se. This cannot be done any more than wealth can be set up as a virtue of itself. But there is some virtue in being identified with the under-privileged. It is usually more likely that the man farthest down will advocate complete justice for all than that the man farthest up will. It is hardly possible for the most privileged to be as sensitive to the injustices, the restrictions and the limitations imposed upon the weak as it is for the weak themselves; or for him to feel these wrongs with the same degree of intensity as they are felt by the under-privileged. They who sit in the seat of the mighty, or those who are racially identified with the ruling class, are more likely to feel that they have too much to lose if they begin to champion too ardently the cause of the man farthest down. It is more difficult for them even to see the wrong. The danger is that they view the evil from lofty heights, if at all. They fear economic insecurity and social ostracism, which may come to them if they identify themselves too openly with the oppressed group.

Perhaps the white minister was correct when he said in an interracial seminar that if he were to take an open and vigorous stand in opposing economic and interracial evils the Negroes would have to give him a pastoral charge. Possibly, too, there is much truth in some of the answers given by many white pastors in response to questionnaires on inter-racial church coöperation, that their congregations would not tolerate an exchange of pulpits between Negro and white ministers.

On the other hand, the suffering man feels the sting more keenly and is more likely to complain. Being the under dog, he has nothing to lose and all to gain when he goes forth in the name of God advocating a square deal for all men. It is not an accident that possibly the most outstanding prophets of religion such as Jesus, Moses, Jeremiah, Isaiah, Micah, Hosea, Amos, and Ezekiel were members of an under-privileged race. It is not argued for a moment that prophets of the ruling class have not and do not exist; but often they must break with the ruling majority and identify themselves with those who suffer. It is simply argued that, all things considered, it is easier for the man who is down to see wrongs and injustices and in many cases easier for him to become an apostle of righteousness.

Thus, one of the main theses of this chapter is that it is a part of the genius of the Negro church that it is owned by a poor race, supported by its members and, further, that this fact alone gives the Negro minister an opportunity and freedom in his church life that ministers of some racial groups might well covet. If the Negro pastor sees fit to condemn from his pulpit practices with respect to low wages, long hours, the working of children in industry, the unfair treatment of women in factories, the denying to the worker the right to organize, and the injustices of an economic system built on competition, self-interest, and profit—he is more likely not to be censured, and less likely to lose his position than his white brother who preaches in the same city. It is more than likely that no committee will wait on him advising him to go slow. No leading financier will walk out of the church threatening never to return. To the contrary, it is highly possible that the Negro minister would receive many congratulations and "Amens" from his congregation if he were to preach such a gospel.

When the Negro pastor feels the urge to preach a thorough-going gospel of brotherhood, applying it to the Negroes, whites, Japanese, Chinese, and other races, it is gladly received by Negro audiences. It is taken for granted that Negro ministers will courageously oppose lynching, Jim Crow law, and discrimination in the expenditure of tax money, especially as applied to schools, parks, playgrounds, hospitals, and the like.

This fellowship and freedom inherent in the Negro church should be conducive to spiritual growth of a unique kind.

It furnishes the foundation for the Negro church and the Negro ministry to become truly Christian and prophetic in the truest sense. The Negro church has the potentialities to become possibly the greatest spiritual force in the United States. What the Negro church does and will do with these potentialities will depend in a large measure upon the leadership as expressed in the Negro pulpit.

APPENDICES

APPENDIX I

Methodology

The work required to achieve the results presented in this volume involved several separate but related procedures.

In order that churches in both the North and the South should be represented, cities in these sections were chosen on the basis of certain criteria. Among these were geographical location; center of industry or production; size of city, including Negro population; central or key city to a large area; racial stratification; point of concentration for Negro migration; crime records, educational center for Negroes; and religious complexion.

It is generally known, for example, that Atlanta, Ga., is important commercially because it is the southern central distributing point for a large number of manufacturers and producers who sell to a national market. It is also a center for Negro higher education in the South. On the other hand, New Orleans, La., the largest city in the South, comprises racial stratifications similar to those of Charleston, S. C.; but in addition it has a religious complexion almost all its own.

In selecting the rural places to be studied it was thought best to take the entire county as a unit. Counties were selected on the basis of Negro population, industry or special types of farming, geographical location, and probable number of Negro churches.

The budget of the study allowed for at least fourteen months devoted to field work and the collecting of data, and ten months to the preparation of the material for publication. Within the time scheduled for the field work it was thought that twelve urban and four rural places could be studied. The twelve urban places selected were: Atlanta, Ga.;

Charleston, S. C.; Birmingham, Ala.; Memphis, Tenn.; New Orleans, La.; Houston, Texas; Chicago, Ill.; Detroit, Mich.; Cincinnati, Ohio; Philadelphia, Pa.; Baltimore, Md.; and Richmond, Va. The counties were: Peach County, Ga.; Montgomery County, Ala.; Orangeburg County, S. C.; and Fort Bend County, Texas.

The criteria for selecting churches to be studied within the units or localities was the next problem. The selection began with the denominations. The vast majority of Negroes are members of the eight denominations selected. These eight are: the Baptist, the African Methodist Episcopal, the African Methodist Episcopal Zion, the Colored Methodist Episcopal, the Methodist Episcopal, the Presbyterian, the Congregational, and the Protestant Episcopal.

In each of the twelve urban and four rural localities an attempt was made to study at least approximately fifty churches which represented these denominations. The proportion of churches of any denomination included in the study was determined largely by the number of churches the denomination had in a given place. Local churches were selected on the basis of membership (both large and small churches being included), prominence, reported program or other interesting features, denominational affiliations, and the desire to present a cross section of the Negro church life of the community.

Since the purpose of the study included an appraisal of the church today, items and features such as: leadership, organization and administration, finance, program of activities, religious instruction, preaching, membership and the influences of contemporary institutions and agencies were important and interesting. In other words, it was necessary to see the church as a whole organization in its setting to appreciate it properly.

Schedules, questionnaires, and methods were prepared to obtain these data. The schedules were prepared, one for urban and one for rural churches, for interviewing ministers, officers and secretaries of churches. These schedules dealt with the specific features of the church as an organization.

Questionnaires were prepared to query white ministers as to the attitude of their churches toward Negro churches, Negro college students, professional and business people on their attitude toward the church, and college deans and presidents concerning the religious services and practices of their schools.

With the exception of the questionnaires, which were mailed to the prospective respondents, all data were gathered directly through interviews, observations, checking of records and reports, stenographic reports, and by actual counts, by the directors of the study.

Following the preparation of the plans and instruments, the investigators made a trial study, using the church schedules especially, in Atlanta and Peach County, Georgia. The data collected were written up to test their usefulness. The criticisms, corrections, and suggestions brought out by this trial study were helpful in completing the plans and instruments of the study.

This trial study indicated that about four weeks would be required for the inquiry in each locality. The directors divided the territory between themselves, and each studied a share of the cities and rural areas. By maintaining a close contact through mail and frequent conferences, they were able to keep each other informed concerning discoveries and helpful ideas, and to maintain an alertness and interest for valuable features.

Validation of the data received was achieved in a variety of ways. The actual records of churches, juvenile delinquents, church federations, training of ministers, rural schools, county tax offices and church histories, wherever these were available, were studied. United States Census data on population, number and membership of religious bodies, and the economic status of rural Negroes were used.

APPENDIX II

Tables

TABLE 1—URBAN NEGRO CHURCHES STUDIED, BY DENOMINATIONS AND CITIES

Cities	African Methodist Episcopal	African Methodist Episcopal Zion	Baptist	Colored Methodist Episcopal	Community Churches	Congregational	Methodist Episcopal	Presbyterian	Protestant Episcopal	Total
Atlanta	14	1	22	4	0	2	4	1	1	49
Baltimore	8	0	28	1	1	0	9	3	1	50
Birmingham	8	9	25	2	0	2	6	2	1	55
Charleston	12	0	13	1	0	1	9	3	11	50
Chicago	9	4	31	6	1	2	1	2	0	56
Cincinnati	4	1	35	3	0	0	6	1	1	51
Detroit	6	4	28	2	1	1	1	1	0	44
Houston	11	0	25	1	0	1	11	1	0	50
Memphis	9	2	24	12	0	1	1	1	1	51
New Orleans	8	2	23	1	0	1	15	0	1	51
Philadelphia	8	1	21	2	1	0	8	4	5	50
Richmond	1	1	43	2	0	0	1	1	3	52
Total	98	25*	318	37*	4*	11*	72*	19*	25†	609

* In general, a disproportionately large percentage of churches in the smaller denominations was selected for study.

For example, out of fourteen Congregational churches in these cities, eleven are included in the study. See Table 32 in the Appendix.

† Includes Protestant Episcopal and Reformed Episcopal churches.]

TABLE 2—URBAN NEGRO CHURCHES RESULTING FROM RACIAL DISCRIMINATION, BY DATE OF ORGANIZATION

Year	Number of Churches
1787	1
1806	1
1831	2
1836	1
1841	1
1847	1
1865	2
1866	1
1867	1
1874	2
1891	1
1921	1
Total	15

TABLE 3—URBAN NEGRO CHURCHES RESULTING FROM INDIVIDUAL INITIATIVE, BY DATE OF ORGANIZATION

Years	Number of Churches
1792	1
1795	1
1805–1809	2

TABLE 3—URBAN NEGRO CHURCHES RESULTING FROM INDI-
VIDUAL INITIATIVE, BY DATE OF ORGANIZATION—*Continued*

Years	Number of Churches
1810–1814	1
1815–1819	1
1820–1824	0
1825–1829	2
1830–1834	0
1835–1839	1
1840–1844	2
1845–1849	2
1850–1854	0
1855–1859	2
1860–1864	2
1865–1869	18
1870–1874	16
1875–1879	10
1880–1884	34
1885–1889	15
1890–1894	30
1895–1899	18
1900–1904	25
1905–1909	30
1910–1914	29
1915–1919	33
1920–1924	29
1925–1929	31
1930	7
1931	3
Total	345

TABLE 4—URBAN NEGRO CHURCHES RESULTING FROM SPLITS,
BY DATE OF ORGANIZATION

Years	Number of Churches
1822	1
1843	1
1844	1
1845	1
1860–1864	1
1865–1869	1
1870–1874	1
1875–1879	2
1880–1884	5
1885–1889	5
1890–1894	7
1895–1899	5
1900–1904	4
1905–1909	5

TABLE 4—URBAN NEGRO CHURCHES RESULTING FROM SPLITS, BY DATE OF ORGANIZATION—*Continued*

Years	Number of Churches
1910–1914	10
1915–1919	13
1920–1924	14
1925–1929	17
1930	5
Total..............	99

TABLE 5—URBAN NEGRO CHURCHES RESULTING FROM THE MIGRATORY MOVEMENT, BY DATE OF ORGANIZATION

Years	Number of Churches
1864	1
1875	1
1893	1
1909	1
1914–1915	4
1916–1917	5
1918–1919	11
1920–1921	2
1922–1923	5
1924–1925	1
1926–1927	1
1930	1
1931	1
Total..............	35

TABLE 6—URBAN NEGRO CHURCHES RESULTING FROM MISSIONS OF OTHER CHURCHES, BY DATE OF ORGANIZATION

Years	Number of Churches
1809	1
1843–1852	3
1853–1862	4
1863–1872	8
1873–1882	9
1883–1892	2
1893–1902	4
1903–1912	4
1913–1922	6
Total..............	41

TABLE 7—ORGANIZATION OF 609 URBAN NEGRO CHURCHES, BY PERIODS

Period	Years	Number of Years	Number of Churches
Pre-Civil War	1787–1859	73	41
Civil War	1860–1865	6	16
Post Civil War	1866–1899	34	223
New Century	1900–1914	15	140
World War Migratory Movement	1915–1931	17	189
Total	1787–1931	145	609

TABLE 8—ORGANIZATION OF 169 RURAL NEGRO CHURCHES, BY PERIODS AND ORIGIN

Period	Years	Individual Initiative	Splits	Prayer Meeting	Withdrawal from White Churches	Missions	Racial Discrimination	Sunday School	Organized by Whites	Total
Pre-Civil War	1750–1859	3	0	1	0	0	0	0	1	5
Civil War	1860–1865	4	1	7	0	0	0	0	0	12
Post Civil War	1866–1899	90	13	0	4	2	1	0	0	110
New Century	1900–1914	16	7	0	1	1	0	1	0	26
World War Migratory Movement	1915–1931	10	6	0	0	0	0	0	0	16
Total	1750–1931	123	27	8	5	3	1	1	1	169

TABLE 9—ACADEMIC TRAINING OF 591 URBAN NEGRO MINISTERS

Academic Training	Number	Per Cent
A.B.* Degree	118	20.0
Some College	90	15.2
Normal	22	3.7
High School	202	34.2
Grades	159	26.9
Total	591	100.0

* Includes also B.S., B.R.E., and Ph.B.

TABLE 10—THEOLOGICAL TRAINING OF 591 URBAN NEGRO MINISTERS

Theological Equipment	Number	Per Cent
B.D.* Degree	79	13.4
B.Th. Degree	30	5.0
Without Seminary Degree	482	81.6
Total	591	100.0

* Includes also S.T.B.

TABLE 11—COLLEGIATE AND SEMINARY TRAINING OF 591 URBAN
NEGRO MINISTERS

	Number	Per Cent.	
Without Degree of Any Kind........	427	72.3	
A.B. Degree Only..................	55	9.3	
A.B. and B.D. Degrees.............	55	9.3	
B.D. Degree Only..................	24	4.1	27.7
B.Th. Degree Only.................	22	3.7	
A.B. and B.Th. Degrees............	8	1.3	
Total.......................	591	100.0	

TABLE 12—COLLEGES FROM WHICH 118 URBAN NEGRO PASTORS
RECEIVED A.B. DEGREES

College	Number Receiving Degrees
Allen	2
Arkansas Baptist	3
Barrett	1
Benedict	2
Boston	1
Brown	1
Burnett	1
Central University	1
Chicago Musical College...............	1
Claflin	3
Denver	1
Fisk	2
Foreign Universities	5
Friendship	1
Guadalupe	3
Howard	5
Iowa	1
Johnson C. Smith.....................	5
Lane	1
Leland	1
Lincoln (Pa.)	9
Livingstone	5
Miles Memorial	3
Morehouse	7
Morgan	5
Morris Brown	7
Morris College	1
New Orleans	4
New York University..................	1
Northwestern	2
Paine	1
Philander Smith	1
Roger Williams	1
Rust	1
Samuel Houston	1

TABLE 12—COLLEGES FROM WHICH 118 URBAN NEGRO PASTORS RECEIVED A.B. DEGREES—*Continued*

College	Number Receiving Degrees
Selma	1
Shaw	2
Simmons	2
Springfield Y.M.C.A.	1
Talladega	2
Tougaloo	1
University of Michigan	1
Virginia Seminary and College	5
Virginia Union	8
Wesleyan (Conn.)	1
Wilberforce	3
Wiley	1
Total	118

TABLE 13—SEMINARIES FROM WHICH 79 URBAN NEGRO PASTORS RECEIVED B.D. DEGREES

Seminaries	Number Receiving Degrees
Allen	1
Bishop Payne	4
Bluffton	1
Boston University	2
Colgate	1
Crozer	1
Drew	1
Gammon	5
Garrett	4
Harvard	1
Johnson C. Smith	5
Howard	2
Lincoln	8
Livingstone	2
Morris Brown	3
Oberlin	3
Paine	1
Paul Quinn	1
Philadelphia Divinity School	1
Rochester	2
Seabury	1
Selma	1
Shorter	2
Simmons	2
Talladega	3
Virginia Seminary	2
Virginia Union	6
Wilberforce	9
Yale	4
Total	79

TABLE 14—609 URBAN NEGRO CHURCHES BY SIZE-GROUPS, AND NUMBER WITH PASTORS HOLDING A.B. DEGREES

Membership of Churches	Number of Churches	Number Pastored by College Men	Per Cent.
Less than 200	217	27	12.4
200 to 400	141	24	17.0
400 to 600	74	21	28.4
600 to 800	47	12	25.5
800 to 1,000	34	6	17.6
1,000 to 1,200	18	8	44.4
1,200 to 1,400	13	6	46.2
1,400 to 1,600	18	4	22.2
1,600 and more	47	10	21.3
Total	609	118	

TABLE 15—PREVIOUS OCCUPATIONS OF 425 URBAN NEGRO PASTORS

Army	1	Gas Engineer	1
Baggageman	1	Government Service	4
Barber	5	Grocerman	1
Blacksmith	2	Grocery Clerk	2
Boiler Maker	4	Hotel Work	3
Brickmason Helper	2	Insurance	11
Business	7	Janitor	1
Butcher	1	Laborer	45
Butler	2	Laundry	1
Carpenter	10	Longshoreman	2
Carpenter and Teacher	1	Lumber Grader	2
Car Shop	1	Lumberman	1
Caterer	2	Machinist	1
Cement Worker	1	Mail Carrier	2
Chauffeur	2	Mail Porter	2
City Worker	1	Mechanic	6
Clerk	2	Merchant	1
Contractor	4	Messenger at Capitol	1
Cook	8	Mill Worker	1
Cooper	1	Miner	1
Denominational Secretary	1	Missionary Worker	2
Domestic	1	Newspaperman	1
Drayman	2	Oil Mill Worker	1
Dye Maker	1	Painter	3
Electrician	1	Porter	6
Elevator Boy	1	Presser	1
Engineer	1	Printer	2
Factory	3	Promotional Secretary	1
Farmer	51	Public Work	2
Fireman	3	Public Work and Farmer	1
Foreman R. R.	1	Pullman Porter	2
Foundry Worker	2	Railroad Service	7

TABLE 15—PREVIOUS OCCUPATIONS OF 425 URBAN NEGRO PASTORS—*Continued*

Recording Secretary National Baptist Convention	1	Tailor	4
Salesman	2	Tailor and Barber	1
Shipping Clerk	3	Tailor and Insurance	1
Shoe Repairer	5	Teacher	59
Shop Rigger	1	Teamster	1
Steel Mill Worker	1	Tie Maker	1
Stereotype Operator	1	Transfer Man	1
Stone Cutter	1	Truck Farming	1
Stone Quarry	1	Undertaker	2
Store Keeper	2	Waiter	5
Student	82	Y.M.C.A. Work	4
Supt. (Asst.) Coffee Co.	1	Total	425

TABLE 16—MEMBERS, CONTRIBUTORS AND AVERAGE ATTENDANCE OF 609 URBAN NEGRO CHURCHES, BY SIZE-GROUPS

No. of Members	No. of Churches	Total Membership	Contributors	Per Cent. Contributors	Average Attendance	Per Cent. Attendance
Less than 1,000	513	152,986	75,687	49.5	73,970	48.4
1,000 to 2,000	59	78,733	39,247	49.8	38,375	48.7
2,000 to 3,000	21	47,900	18,248	38.1	17,600	36.7
3,000 to 4,000	7	23,179	6,800	29.3	7,800	33.7
4,000 and above	9	54,371	16,370	30.1	14,000	25.7
Total	609	357,169	156,352	43.8	151,745	42.5

TABLE 17—DISTRIBUTION OF 2,850 ROOMS IN 609 URBAN NEGRO CHURCHES ACCORDING TO USE

Kind of Room	Number
Auditorium Only	140
Auditorium and Basement only (84 churches)	168
Auditorium and Basement with Other Rooms (385 churches)	770
Church Offices	158
Pastor's Study Rooms	331
Auxiliary Rooms	1,002
Classrooms	281
Total	2,850

TABLE 18—DISTRIBUTION OF 609 URBAN NEGRO CHURCHES, BY NUMBER OF ROOMS

Number of Rooms	Number of Churches
1– 2	224
3– 4	143
5– 6	99

TABLE 18—DISTRIBUTION OF 609 URBAN NEGRO CHURCHES, BY
NUMBER OF ROOMS—*Continued*

7– 8	61
9–10	36
11–12	17
13–14	11
15–16	9
17–18	2
19–20	2
Over 20	5
	609

TABLE 19—DISTRIBUTION OF 609 URBAN NEGRO CHURCH AUDI-
TORIUMS, ACCORDING TO SEATING CAPACITY

Capacity	Churches
200 or less	93
200 to 400	188
400 to 600	118
600 to 800	76
800 to 1,000	54
1,000 to 1,200	30
1,200 to 1,400	21
1,400 to 1,600	17
1,600 to 1,800	3
1,800 to 2,000	3
2,000 and over	6
Total	609

TABLE 20—TOTAL EXPENDITURES OF 609 URBAN NEGRO
CHURCHES COMPARED WITH SUNDAY CHURCH SCHOOL COL-
LECTIONS, BY SIZE-GROUPS

Number of Members	Number of Churches	Total Expenditures	Number of Sunday Church Schools	Collections	Per Cent. S. C. S. Collections of Total Expenditures
Less than 1,000	513	$1,662,456	512	$ 83,262	5.0
1,000–2,000	59	671,803	59	37,032	5.5
2,000–3,000	21	247,675	21	15,033	6.1
3,000–4,000	7	129,111	7	5,805	4.5
4,000 and above	9	273,920	9	13,431	4.9
Total	609	$2,984,965	608	$154,563	5.2

TABLE 21—ENROLLMENT AND AVERAGE ATTENDANCE OF SUN-
DAY CHURCH SCHOOLS IN 609 URBAN NEGRO CHURCHES,
COMPARED WITH CHURCH-MEMBERSHIP AND ATTENDANCE,
BY SIZE-GROUPS

Number of Members	CHURCHES				SUNDAY CHURCH SCHOOLS				Per Cent. S.C.S. Enrollment of Church Membership
	Number	Total Membership	Average Attendance	Per Cent. Attendance	Number	Enrollment	Average Attendance	Per Cent. Attendance	
Less than 1,000..	513	152,986	73,970	48.4	512	62,323	38,566	61.9	40.7
1,000–2,000.....	59	78,733	38,375	48.7	59	24,624	14,162	57.5	31.3
2,000–3,000.....	21	47,900	17,600	36.7	21	9,564	5,627	58.8	20.0
3,000–4,000.....	7	23,179	7,800	33.7	7	3,594	2,026	56.4	15.5
4,000 and above.	9	54,371	14,000	25.7	9	9,760	4,830	49.5	18.0
Total........	609	357,169	151,745	42.5	608	109,865	65,211	59.4	30.8

TABLE 22—DISTRIBUTION OF 608 URBAN NEGRO SUNDAY
CHURCH SCHOOLS, BY NUMBER OF WORKERS

Number of Persons	Number of Sunday Church Schools
1– 4	171
5– 8	177
9–12	102
13–16	55
17–20	38
21–24	14
25–28	17
29–32	9
33–36	7
37–40	4
41–44	0
45–48	6
49–52	1
53–56	3
57–60	2
100	1
105	1
Total	608

TABLE 23—DISTRIBUTION OF 720 WHITE CHURCHES, BY
DENOMINATIONS

Denomination	No. of Churches
Presbyterian	157
Lutheran	82
Baptist	77
Methodist Episcopal	62
Episcopal	48
Methodist Episcopal, South	43
Congregational	33

TABLE 23—DISTRIBUTION OF 720 WHITE CHURCHES, BY
DENOMINATIONS—*Continued*

Denomination	No. of Churches
Evangelical	33
Methodist	31
Reformed in United States	27
Disciples of Christ	20
United Presbyterian	12
Church of Christ	11
United Brethren	11
Christian Church	10
Protestant Episcopal	7
Methodist Protestant	5
Unitarian	4
United Lutheran	4
Friends	3
Catholic	2
Church of the Brethren	2
Reformed Episcopal	2
Universal	2
Advent Christian	1
All Saints	1
Danish Lutheran	1
Reformed in America	1
Interdenominational	1
Jewish	1
Missionary Alliance	1
Moravians	1
Pillar of Fire	1
Seventh Day Adventist	1
Swedenborgian	1
Zion	1
Denomination not given	20
Total	720

TABLE 24—DISTRIBUTION OF 602 WHITE CHURCHES, BY
SIZE-GROUPS

Members	Number
Up to 500	375
500 to 1,000	152
1,000 to 1,500	47
1,500 to 2,000	12
2,000 to 2,500	9
2,500 to 3,000	6
3,500 and over	1
Total	602

TABLE 25—DISTRIBUTION OF 594 WHITE MINISTERS, BY
AGE-GROUPS

Ages	Number
21–30	50
31–40	174
41–50	170
51–60	118
61–70	65
71–80	16
81–90	1
Total	594

TABLE 26—DISTRIBUTION OF 607 WHITE MINISTERS, URBAN AND
RURAL, ACCORDING TO YEARS OF MINISTERIAL EXPERIENCE

Years of Experience	Number of Ministers	
	Urban	Rural
1– 4	74	91
5– 9	78	66
10–14	75	40
15–19	44	19
20–24	37	11
25–29	14	5
30–34	17	3
35–39	14	0
40–44	11	1
45–49	5	1
50–54	1	0
Total	370	237

TABLE 27—NEGRO JUVENILE DELINQUENTS IN SEVEN CITIES, BY
NUMBER AND PER CENT. AND NEGRO PER CENT. OF TOTAL
POPULATION *

City	Negro Juvenile Delinquents		Negro Per Cent. of Total Population
	Number	Per Cent.	
New Orleans	566	46.3	28.3
Baltimore	929	36.5	17.7
Memphis	1,267	33.0	38.1
Cincinnati	631	29.5	10.6
Philadelphia	1,916	25.5	11.3
Chicago	657	21.0	6.9
Detroit	919	17.5	7.7

* Data for delinquents for 1930, except in Memphis (1931).

TABLE 28—PER CAPITA EXPENDITURE OF 609 URBAN NEGRO
CHURCHES, BY SIZE-GROUPS

Membership	Number of Churches	Total Membership	Expenditures	Per Capita
Less than 500.............	390	70,872	$ 869,604	$12.27
500 to 1,000...........	123	82,114	792,852	9.65
1,000 to 1,500...........	38	44,799	421,024	9.40*
1,500 to 2,000...........	21	33,934	250,779	7.39
2,000 to 2,500...........	16	35,544	182,733	5.14
2,500 to 3,000...........	6	15,356	64,942	4.23†
3,000 to 3,500...........	4	12,979	106,610	8.21
3,500 to 4,000...........	2	7,200	22,501	3.13
4,000 and above..........	9	54,371	273,920	5.04‡
Total................	609	357,169	$2,984,965	$ 8.36

* Per capita for 551 churches with a membership less than 1,500, $10.53.
† Per capita for 43 churches with a membership 1,500 to 3,000, $5.88.
‡ Per capita for 15 churches with a membership 3,000 and above, $5.41.

TABLE 29—DISTRIBUTION OF 386 URBAN NEGRO CHURCHES, BY
SIZE OF DEBT

	Number	Per Cent.
Owing $1,000 and less..........................	54	14.0
Owing between $ 1,000 and $ 5,000...............	122	31.6
Owing between $ 5,000 and $10,000...............	67	17.4
Owing between $10,000 and $15,000...............	36	9.3
Owing between $15,000 and $20,000...............	30	7.8
Owing between $20,000 and $25,000...............	19	4.9
Owing between $25,000 and $50,000...............	37	9.6
Owing $50,000 and above.......................	21	5.4
Total	386	100.0

TABLE 30—DISTRIBUTION OF 588 PASTORS, BY SIZE OF SALARY
AND NUMBER OF PARSONAGES FURNISHED

Salary	Number of Salaries		Number of Parsonages	
	Number	Per Cent.	Number	Per Cent.
Less than $1,000..............	202	34.4	66	32.7
$1,000 to $2,000	206	35.0	128	62.1
$2,000 to $3,000	125	21.3	104	83.2
$3,000 to $4,000	46	7.8	29	63.0
$4,000 to $5,000 ....:....	5	0.8	5	100.0
$5,000 to $6,000	4	0.7	2	50.0
Total....................	588	100.0	334	56.8

TABLE 31—SALARIES OF NEGRO PASTORS COMPARED WITH TWO GROUPS OF WHITE PASTORS

	Per Cent. Distribution Negro	White Group A*	Group B†
Less than $1,000	34.4	3.9	.0
$1,000–$2,000	35.0	33.2	11.0
$2,000–$3,000	21.3	24.5	20.6
$3,000–$4,000	7.8	14.7	19.9
$4,000–$5,000	0.8	8.0	13.2
$5,000–$6,000	0.7	6.6	12.5
$6,000–$7,000	.0	4.5	13.2
$7,000–$8,000	.0	2.8	6.6
$8,000 and over	.0	1.8	3.0

* 286 Pastors in Slightly Adapted Churches. Douglass, H. Paul, *1000 City Churches* (New York: Institute of Social and Religious Research, 1926), p. 335.
† 136 Pastors in Internally Adapted Churches. *Ibid.*

TABLE 32—NEGRO CHURCHES IN TWELVE CITIES, BY DENOMINATIONS

	Seven Southern Cities									Five Northern Cities							Grand Total	
	Atlanta	Birmingham	Charleston	Houston	Memphis	New Orleans	Richmond	Total No.	Per Cent	Baltimore	Chicago	Cincinnati	Detroit	Philadelphia	Total No.	Per Cent	No.	Per Cent
Baptist	116	131	17	101	89	145	62	661	61.5	85	144	56	69	112	466	45.3	1,127	53.6
Holiness	21	21	2	20	15	3	13	95	8.8	41	86	30	38	49	244	23.7	339	16.1
African Methodist Episcopal	23	28	15	11	12	12	1	102	9.5	15	20	6	10	26	77	7.5	179	8.5
Spiritualist	0	2	0	11	0	23	0	36	3.3	7	51	1	10	9	78	7.6	114	5.4
Methodist Episcopal	8	8	6	9	3	15	1	50	4.7	15	6	7	3	12	43	4.2	93	4.4
Colored Methodist Episcopal	5	10	1	2	15	2	2	37	3.4	1	9	3	3	3	19	1.8	56	2.6
African Methodist Episcopal Zion	1	4	0	1	3	3	1	13	1.2	2	6	2	5	4	19	1.8	32	1.5
Episcopal	2	1	8	1	1	0	3	16	1.5	0	3	1	0	10	14	1.3	30	1.4
Catholic	1	1	1	1	1	10	2	17	1.6	5	1	1	3	2	12	1.2	29	1.4
Presbyterian	2	3	4	1	1	0	1	12	1.1	3	4	1	2	5	15	1.4	27	1.3
Christian	0	2	1	0	1	0	2	6	0.6	5	1	3	0	0	9	0.9	15	0.7
Congregational	2	2	1	1	1	4	0	11	1.0	0	2	0	1	0	3	0.3	14	0.7
Seventh Day Adventist	1	1	1	1	1	1	0	6	0.6	2	2	0	1	1	6	0.6	12	0.6
Lutheran	1	1	0	0	0	3	0	5	0.5	1	1	1	0	1	4	0.4	9	0.4
Methodist, other than above	0	1	4	0	0	1	1	7	0.6	0	1	0	0	1	2	0.2	9	0.4
Community	0	0	0	0	0	0	0	0	0	2	4	0	1	0	7	0.7	7	0.3
Evangelical	1	0	0	0	0	0	0	1	0.1	0	0	0	0	3	3	0.3	4	0.2
Unity	0	0	0	0	0	0	0	0	0	0	1	0	0	2	3	0.3	3	0.1
Universal	0	0	0	0	0	0	0	0	0	2	0	0	0	0	2	0.2	2	⎫
African Orthodox	0	0	0	0	0	0	0	0	0	0	1	0	0	0	1	0.1	1	⎬ 0.2
Friends	0	0	0	0	0	0	0	0	0	0	1	0	0	0	1	0.1	1	⎭
Kodesh Church	0	0	0	0	0	0	0	0	0	0	0	0	0	1	1	0.1	1	
Total	184	216	61	160	143	222	89	1,075	100.0	186	344	112	146	241	1,029	100.0	2,104	100.0

TABLE 33—CHURCHES IN TWELVE CITIES—TYPES OF BUILDINGS, BY DENOMINATIONS

Denomination	Conventional Church Buildings	Store-Fronts, Houses, etc.	Total
Baptist	764	363	1,127
Holiness	99	240	339
African Methodist Episcopal	150	29	179
Spiritualist	17	97	114
Methodist Episcopal	84	9	93
Colored Methodist Episcopal	49	7	56
African Methodist Episcopal Zion	23	9	32
Episcopal	29	1	30
Catholic	28	1	29
Presbyterian	25	2	27
Christian	9	6	15
Congregational	14	0	14
Seventh Day Adventist	11	1	12
Lutheran	9	0	9
Methodist, other than above	8	1	9
Community	4	3	7
Evangelical	2	2	4
Unity	0	3	3
Universalist	0	2	2
African Orthodox	0	1	1
Kodesh	1	0	1
Friends	1	0	1
Total	1,327	777	2,104

INDEX

A

African Baptist church, first of Savannah, 4

African Methodist Episcopal church, 192, 209, 210, 214, 220, 222, 223, 234, 239; first church of, 22; number of churches of, 96

African Methodist Episcopal Zion church, 192, 210, 214, 220, 222, 234; increase in membership of, 97

Allen, Richard, 21

Announcements in church, 148 ff.

Anthems, 145

Antioch Baptist Church, Montgomery Co., 27

Assistant pastors, not in demand, 187

Atlanta, 97, 106, 107, 176, 187, 204, 205, 206, 208, 218, 226

Atlanta University, 31

B

Badger, Rev. John, 25

Baltimore, 22, 31, 36, 96, 106–7, 120, 159, 176, 180, 183, 187, 215, 218 ff.

Baptist church, 12, 28, 199, 209, 210, 214, 220, 222, 223, 227, 231, 234, 239; freedom in, 10

Baxter, Hon. Sidney S., 23

Berean Presbyterian Church, Philadelphia, 30

Bethel A. M. E. Church, Richmond, 31

Bi-racial worship, problems of, 25

Birmingham, 96, 106, 107, 176, 187, 191, 204, 205, 206, 208, 210–1, 218

Boston University, 46; School of Religion, 53; School of Theology, 52

Boy Rangers groups, 121

Boy Scout activities, 120–1

Brown University, 46

Bull Swamp Baptist Church, 31

C

Calvary M. E. Church, Cincinnati, 30

Camp Fire Girls, 121

Canaan M. E. Church, 32

Card-playing, 156

Catholic church, 210, 214, 222

Charleston, 25, 26, 96, 106, 158, 175, 176, 180, 187, 204, 205, 206, 209, 211, 218, 228

Chicago, 31, 36, 96, 106–8, 115, 120, 131, 159, 160, 176, 179, 183, 187, 215, 218, 219, 226

Choirs, 139, 141, 142; directors of, 191

Christian church, 214, 222

Christian Endeavor, 135

Church, defined, 199

Church buildings, chap. vi, 250; condition of, 115; interiors of urban, 116–7; kinds of, 115; rural, 257–8; sites, 116; use of, 122

Church federations, 159–60

Church financing, methods of, 178

Church papers and bulletins, 149

Church records, 16, 99, 127, 190, 237

Church school, 119, 122 ff.; attendance at, 127, 255; curriculum of, 131; enrollment in, 126–7, 254–5; equipment of, 125 ff., 257–8; finance, 126; housing problem of, 124 ff.; leadership of, 18, 128–9, 136, 254; lesson materials of, 131, 142, 256; membership of, 126; music in, 140; number of workers

316 *Index*

in, 255; of rural churches, 252, 254 ff.; one-department, 124; prayers used in, 140–2; pupil participation in, 132 ff., 142–3; records of, 127–8; supervision in, 129, 256; teaching in, 132, 227; use of songs in, 136–7; vacation activities of, 120, 136–7; week-day activities of, 136–7; workers available for, 196; workers' conferences, 129–30, 256; worship services of, 139 ff., 153; young people's work in, 135 ff., 257

Church splits and schisms, 13, 28, 29, 35–6

Cincinnati, 30, 96, 106, 107, 159, 160, 176, 180, 183, 187, 214, 215, 218, 222

Civil War epoch, 27 ff.

Clubs, 154 ff.

Colgate-Rochester, 53

Coliseum Baptist Church, New Orleans, 26

Colored Methodist Episcopal church, 192, 210, 214, 220, 222, 234, 239; increase in membership of, 97

Comity, 154, 228–9

Commercialized amusements, coöperation with, 157

Community Chest, 157

Congregational church, 192, 210, 214, 222, 234

Crisis, The, 49

Cultural level of the Negro, 91

D

Dancing, 156

Denominational rivalry, 12

Detroit, 34, 36, 96, 98, 106–8, 115, 131, 159, 160, 175, 176, 179, 180, 183, 187, 215, 218, 219, 222, 285

Douglass, H. Paul, 188, 229

Drew University, 53

DuBois, W. E. B., 38

E

Ebenezer Baptist Church, Orangeburg Co., 31

Educational level of the Negro, 91

Educational work of the churches, 17, 122 ff., 154

Edwards, Paul K., 206, 207

Elem Church, Montgomery Co., 27

Ellison, John M., 232

Emancipation proclamation, 5

Epworth League, 135

Evangelists, professional, 102–3, 254

F

Fayetteville, 4

Fear, appeal to, 103

Federal Census of Religious Bodies, 96, 97, 99, 106, 112, 169, 174, 202, 240, 243, 259

Fellowship activities, 17, chap. ix

First African Baptist Church, New Orleans, 26–7; Philadelphia, 27; Richmond, 24

First Baptist Church, Philadelphia, 27; Richmond, 24

First Congregational Church, Atlanta, 31

Fort Bend Co., 231, 232, 234, 236, 260, 262, 266, 274, 275

Fort Valley, 269–70

Fry, C. Luther, 40, 112, 176, 195, 239–40, 243

G

Garrett Biblical Institute, 53

General Methodist Conference, political manoeuverings at, 9

Gloucester, 4

Gloucester Mission, Philadelphia, 30

God, attitude toward, 145; concepts of, 86 ff.; dependence upon, 147

Gospel, of faith, 85; of works, 85

Governmental agencies, coöperation with, 157